Places of Privilege

Innovations and Controversies: Interrogating Educational Change

The titles published in this series are listed at *brill.com/icie*

Places of Privilege

*Interdisciplinary Perspectives on Identities,
Change and Resistance*

Edited by

Nicole Oke, Christopher C. Sonn and Alison M. Baker

BRILL

SENSE

LEIDEN | BOSTON

All chapters in this book have undergone peer review.

The Library of Congress Cataloging-in-Publication Data is available online at http://catalog.loc.gov

ISSN 2542-9302
ISBN 978-90-04-38138-4 (paperback)
ISBN 978-90-04-38139-1 (hardback)
ISBN 978-90-04-38140-7 (e-book)

This book is printed on acid-free paper and produced in a sustainable manner.

Printed by Printforce, the Netherlands

CONTENTS

Part 3: Place, Privilege and Social Settings

ACKNOWLEDGEMENTS

The editors of this volume, acknowledge, recognise and respect the Elders, families and forebears of the Boonwurrung and Wurundjeri of the Kulin who are the traditional owners of University land.

The idea for this book was developed at the Place, Politics, Privilege conference that was held in 2017 in Melbourne, Australia. That event was a partnership between the Community, Identity and Displacement Research Network (CIDRN) at Victoria University and the Identity Research Network (IRN) at Swinburne University, both located in Victoria Australia. The book was developed with the support, encouragement, and collegiality provided by the CIDRN members and Moondani Balluk, the Indigenous Academic Unit at Victoria University.

There is of course also a lot of hard work behind the scenes that goes into producing a book. We want to acknowledge Sam Keast, a project manager. Your organizational skills, critical input, and efficiency has helped produce this book in a timely manner. We also want to acknowledge the reviewers who have contributed their time and critical insights that have been essential to elevate the scholarship and quality of the chapters represented in this volume. Thank you also to Lee Miller for his outstanding contribution as a copy editor on this volume.

We would also like to acknowledge the support that we received from the College of Arts and Education, and Office for Research. A very special thank you to Professor Kitty Te Riele and Associate Professor Julie White, editors of the book series, for their support and encouragement to produce this volume.

FIGURES AND TABLES

FIGURES

NICOLE OKE, CHRISTOPHER C. SONN AND ALISON M. BAKER

1. INTRODUCTION TO *PLACES OF PRIVILEGE*

Our initial interest in developing this book stems from the place in which we find ourselves. As a group of scholars from a range of disciplines, we have in common the place in which our university is situated, Footscray. This suburb, just west of the city of Melbourne, is a place with a dynamic and rich history, shaped by economic, cultural and social change. As a network of scholars from different disciplines, but with shared interests in the process of social change, we pondered the effects of economic, social, cultural and planned forms of change around us. Our research also intersects in terms of our focus on implications for the various groups of people in Footscray – long term residents, service providers, shoppers, students, traders and more. We started with an interest in the intersection between global and local networks, curious about the ways the local was constitutive, and the various ways in which very differently positioned communities of people give meaning to Footscray. The questions we have been considering in light of these ongoing changes include: How have the histories of economic, cultural and social change shaped Footscray into the place that it is today and how are the current day contestations changing the landscape of this town? To what extent does it reflect the broader social contexts in the city and to what extent is locality important? These questions are central to the sense book series on "Innovations and Controversies: Investigating Educational Change" as it seeks to advance inclusive and transformative knowledge that can contribute to the disruption of privilege and promote social inclusion and equity.

Footscray is a place that is being transformed and is transforming. It is in many ways unique. Dynamics centred around class and migration are particularly significant in shaping the history and the current day portrait of Footscray. The waves of cultural and ethnic migrant groups that have come to Footscray have each contributed to the diverse and dynamic fabric of this place. The earlier history of migration in the suburb has been shaped by a migration hostel that was nearby. An immigration detention centre was also located nearby, but its presence has not had the same impact on the locality. Racism and racialisation have also been part of the dynamics of Footscray. Racism and racialisation appear in many forms, but a range of groups and agencies are also contesting racism by using various forms of social intervention, advocacy, and public pedagogy. The changing ethnic and economic composition of the town also points to patterns of gentrification and 'urban renewal'. Historically Footscray was populated by a sizable working class Anglo-European population and has since seen the settlement of a number of migrant communities including the Vietnamese and more recently those from the African diaspora. Yet it is

© KONINKLIJKE BRILL NV, LEIDEN, 2018 | DOI:10.1163/9789004381407_001

fair to say that gentrification is now displacing some of the existing ethnic networks. Changing patterns of ethnicity point to the differing patterns of migration. There is increased development by investors from Asian countries, while there would also appear to be an increase in workers in the suburb on temporary visas. Thus class, ethnicity and racialisation are key shaping forces in Footscray but are also key to some of the ways the suburb is changing today, and the ways it is being contested today. Some of these changes are specific to Footscray. But others, including those reflective of urbanisation and gentrification of inner-cities and the contraction of heavy manufacturing, are similar to changes in other cities.

We were interested in understanding Footscray as a global city and have been building knowledge toward this through research. In an initial study, we considered the range of ways differently positioned people give meaning to Footscray through diverse understandings of culture and difference, the effects of urban renewal, and the segmented physical geography which signals how different communities are carving out spaces of commerce and for social engagement in Footscray (Oke, Sonn, & McConville, 2016). This work raises further questions for us about migrancy, diaspora and place; urban renewal and gentrification; racialisation, whiteness, and place; and Indigenous people, place and memory. At the core of these questions were the concepts of place, privilege and power and the extent to which these are useful for developing deeper insight into the interconnections between place, privilege and the dynamics of identity and community making-in-place. These questions are central to the Sense book series on "Innovations and Controversies: Investigating Educational Change" as it seeks to advance inclusive and transformative knowledge that can contribute to the disruption of privilege and promote social inclusion and equity.

CONCEPTUALISING PLACE

In considering these questions about place, about the ways in which place was both constitutive but also constituted by different dynamics, we sought to unpack the dynamics of social contestation and privileges in Footscray. These various social change processes have generated many questions about place, politics and privilege in the context of the local. Place, as a concept, suggests a set of interactions and contestations within a locality – however broadly defined – or between localities. But these are situated within a set of social contexts and histories. As such it is not a broad sense of contested ideas per se, but the ways in which these are embodied by a group of people. Thus, it makes change. Doreen Massey in her 1994 essay *Double Articulation: A place in the world*, argues for a non essentialised understanding of place to be approached through an analysis "… of the social interactions which intersect at that particular location and of what people make of them in their interpretations and in their lives and, second, of the fact that the meeting of those social relations at that location in itself produces new effects, new social processes" (Massey, 1994, p. 117).

In arguing that a place does not have 'an essence' and should not be understood in an essentialist way, she draws on the differing meanings of place and the understanding of the histories of place in the contestations over the future of the Docklands in East London. Massey described the contestations between the working-class residents and the encroachment of yuppies into the area. While supporting the working-class residents she argues the need to unpack the ways in which ideas about place were being used as a form of defence against this encroachment. She argues that while yuppies and developers were constructing an image of themselves and their changes as 'forward looking', the local working class was often portraying an essentialised image of themselves, in terms that included manual labour, pubs and football. But this is an essentialised reading of the histories of the place, she argues. The focus on manual labour, pubs and football is, for example, a masculinist version of a place. Neither, she argues, can the place be essentialised because it has changed over time. It has changed as a result of historical dynamics, interactions and contestations within this place, as well as because of its location in a wider world; it is neither enclosed nor bounded. More broadly she uses this example to make this point in critiquing the literature which suggests globalisation as a universalising dynamic. She argues that writers such as David Harvey understand place as inward looking and static, while conceptualising space as interactive and dynamic.

Following from this is the question of how place is conceptualised within a broader social setting. If it is difficult to frame place as bound within a locality, how does place 'stretch' – to take Massey's term – beyond the locality? This is key to understanding the dynamics of power in place and how power is constituted within a locality or bound within broader social processes and discourses. These are empirical questions about the extent to which places are shaped by local histories and/or broader social change. Much of the early globalisation literature – including the work on global cities – suggested a clear delineation between places and spaces. Places, it has been argued, are somewhat powerless against the bigger generic dynamics understood as space. However, there are other ways of thinking about place in a global context. Massey (1994) suggests that place could be seen not as an insular locality but as part of a broader whole. Its histories are intertwined with the global. While unique, they are a "... subset of the interactions which constitute space, a local articulation within the wider whole" (Massey, 1994, p. 115).

In considering how a place is shaped by broader social contexts, other authors have placed a greater emphasis on the ways in which these contexts are comprised of a multiplicity of dynamics and networks. Taking a transnational approach, Michael P. Smith argues that a place is an intersection of different social networks. In the context of the urban he argues that these come together, and that both places and transnational networks are altered and transformed in their contestation:

> Transnational urbanism is thus a cultural rather than a strictly geographic metaphor. I use the term as a marker of the criss-crossing transnational circuits of communication and cross-cutting transnational circuits of communication

and cross-cutting local, translocal and transnational social practices that "come together" in particular places at particular times and enter into the contested politics of place-making, the social construction of power differentials, and the making of individual groups, national, and transnational identities, and their corresponding fields of difference. (Smith, 2001, p. 5)

Smith and Bakker (2008) offered a useful frame to look at the global and local dimensions of power in these transnational settings. In their study of transnational politics between localities in Mexico and the US they argued that there are four key dynamics. These include the political-economic context, the historical context, the sociocultural context and the institutional context (Smith & Bakker, 2008, pp. 4–5).

With the borders of place unpacked by the authors above, it is also the scale of what we call place that is being unpacked. The scale at which a place is understood is not pre-given, and it is political. While place can be understood as locality based, to focus on national scales or global scales can show up different politics, different dynamics of privilege. But at what point does the concept of place 'stretch' too far to be meaningful? Can place denote a worldwide phenomenon, such as colonialism, a set of relationships between different and specific places in the world? Within this how we denote the boundaries of a place is powerful. For example, Epeli Hau'ofa (1994) argues in *Our Sea of Islands* that colonial boundaries have denoted the Pacific Islands as small individual entities, which by this fact cannot be self-reliant in a global world. But these boundaries he argues are boundaries created out of colonialism. These do not account for on-going cultural connections and exchange communities and miss what he refers to as the "world enlargement that is carried out by tens of thousands of ordinary Pacific Islanders ..." (Hau'ofa, 1994, p. 151). Rather than using the term Pacific Islands, denoting separation, he argues that the area can be seen as a sea of islands, noting the scale and the connections instead. Amongst other matters, this conception has material implications for ways in which it is understood as a viable region in the world rather than as a set of states that are necessarily dependent on wealthy states (Hau'ofa, 1994, p. 150). There is, he argues, "... a world of difference between viewing the Pacific as 'islands in a far sea' and as 'a sea of islands'" (Hau'ofa, 1994, p. 151).

POLITICS AND PRIVILEGE

As a conceptual starting point, place opened up ways for us to consider some diverse social processes, in particular the dynamics of privilege. Twine and Gardner's (2013) conceptualisation of privilege is useful as it offers a way to examine the coloniality of power. They suggest that privilege is often a synonym for power, and is used in situations in which groups or individuals exert power over another group. Privilege is defined as unearned benefits, which include psychological, material and economic benefits, afforded by virtue of our social group memberships. The flipside of privilege is dispossession and the accumulation of disadvantage. Whiteness has been used as a metaphor for privilege in much of the literature as a means of shifting the focus from groups who are excluded because of racism and racialisation in order to unpack how dominance is maintained and reproduced through symbolic, structural and institutional means (Hage, 1998; Green, Sonn, & Matsebula, 2006). Importantly, while much work has focused on the reproduction of racialised inequalities, the notion of privilege is multifaceted and context-dependent, thus inviting analyses that are not binaries but instead are sensitive to the ways in which power is produced locally and globally, at intersections, and manifest in specific places and relations. Guided by this, we were interested in understanding how privilege can be used to examine the ways in which people were constructing relations, social identities and opportunities for belonging, and how new forms of privilege were constructed or de-constructed. Using place as a way to consider politics and privilege was useful in looking at some of the diverse social practices that were coming together locally, but within the context of broader social dynamics and cultural processes.

Colonialism and coloniality, and the attendant process of boundary making, have relevance to our interest in exploring Footscray as a global city. Specifically, the coloniality of power as theorised by Quijano (2000) names the "continuities … of social hierarchical relationships of exploitation and domination between Europeans and non-Europeans built during centuries of European colonial expansion emphasising cultural and social power relations" (p. 95). In our work, we have used place to open up new avenues for exploring dynamics of privilege and whiteness and gentrification from the vantage points of differently positioned migrants and networks (Oke et al., 2016), Indigenous people in place (Sonn, Jackson & Lyons, this volume), and class and place (McConville & Oke, this volume). Several Indigenous scholars have written about colonialism and its practices of dispossession and the implications for individuals and communities. For example, Behrendt (2009) and Fredericks (2013) write about the importance of place, home and land for Aboriginal people who have been dispossessed and who live in urban contexts away from traditional country. Both these authors highlight the complex and contested ways in which people go about making identities and subjectivities in the multiple contexts produced by colonisation and in the current postcolonising context. Like Moreton-Robinson (2003), they highlight the unique ontological relationship to land that grounds both cultural and political identities. These avenues for theoretical engagement point to place understood as intersections of differently positioned people with unequal access to economic, social and cultural resources, and of historical inheritance.

These broader dynamics and cultural processes are important and find expression in everyday contexts and social relations in terms of identity negotiation, intergroup relations, belonging, and the ways in which groups carve cultural memories into physical environments through placemaking practices. In Footscray for example, we found that there were varied meanings of diversity for members from different ethnic groups who reside or visit the suburb. For some diversity was an experience of multiculturalism and it provided a sense of safety and security. For others diversity was expressed in a segmented physical geography and shopfronts signalling that African and Vietnamese traders occupy different blocks in the area. For some experiences of racism in other 'white bread' areas shaped how they experienced Footscray, while for outsiders Footscray was stigmatised as a working class migrant town. These varied meanings all informed people's engagements and attachments to the place and responses to perceived changes. These changes are reflected in transformations in the physical environment embodied in several high-rise apartment buildings springing up at various sites in the town.

While important, these processes and practices of negotiating belonging and adapting cultures into new environments requires engagement with Indigenous writing and understandings of place, privilege and placemaking in settler colonial contexts such as Australia. Indigenous writing about place and placemaking brings to our attention the deeper politics relating to assumptions about place, and how we often erase or silence those understandings through epistemological ignorance and historical blindness. Indigenous writers have highlighted different conceptions of place and land, arguing that place, land and culture are intimately tied to identity and community. For example, Moreton-Robinson (2003) has suggested that Indigenous people's relationship to land is differently constituted to that of non-Indigenous settlers. For Moreton-Robinson, "Indigenous people's sense of belonging is derived from an ontological relationship to country derived from the Dreaming ..." and "during the dreaming ancestral beings created the land and life and they are tied in particular tracks of country" (p. 31). Moreton-Robinson stated that: "Our ontological relationship to land, the ways that country is constitutive of us, and therefore the inalienable nature of our relation to land, marks a radical, indeed incommensurable, difference between us and the non-Indigenous" (p. 31). This different conception is at the centre of decolonial writing and calls for critical place inquiry (McCoy, Tuck, & McKenzie, 2016; Tuck & McKenzie, 2015). Critical place inquiry is anchored in Indigenous ways of knowing and being. This inquiry recognises the agency of people as they navigate histories of colonialism and resistance, and its continuities in the current global context marked by new forms and relations of oppression and resistance within which people construct identities, subjectivities, belonging and community. Indigenous and settler colonial scholars bring into clear focus the political nature of place and placemaking, the continuity of various forms of dispossession and displacement, and important ontological and epistemological approaches required to address ecological and climate change justice (Birch, 2015, this volume; Bird-Rose, 2004; Tuck & McKenzie, 2015). These approaches to knowing and being provide conceptions of culture, identity and community that are vital for individual and collective wellbeing.

THIS VOLUME

These conceptual and theoretical approaches highlight various dimensions of place: local and global networks; the politics inherent in particular approaches

INTRODUCTION TO *PLACES OF PRIVILEGE*

that have displaced or ignored Indigenous knowledge in understanding place and its relevance to identity, community, and belonging in settler colonial contexts; the ways in which the dynamics of privileging are distinct in different places. From our vantage point we asked, if we understand place as neither essential or contained to locality, what does the concept add in relation to the conception of privilege and the dynamics of power that underlie these privileges. These privileges and powers relate to colonialism, whiteness, class and racialisation, to name some key dimensions. We would argue that in understanding these processes the concept of place allows us to take some of the broad understandings of privilege and consider the ways in which they were co-joined and contested. We were also interested in how prevailing privileges and power relations are challenged by new forms of resistance, solidarities and new possibilities for belonging. We invited responses in the following areas: *the politics, power and privilege* within – or between – places; *privileges and borders* at the local, national or global scales, including the digital and non-material, and the reconfiguration of political space; and *the politics of new meanings of community*, including new strategies of cultural identity and resistance, new solidarities or exclusions, and possibilities for belonging.

The contributions to this volume come from various disciplines and have focused on a range of substantive issues such as displacement, climate change justice, refugee and migrant belonging, Indigenous knowledge, culture and healing, as well as whiteness and race in research. Contributors have taken different conceptual and methodological approaches and as such unpacked a range of different dynamics of power in place. Following our review, we organised the chapters around three key themes. The first focuses on the range of ways for boundary making of place. The second theme focuses on expressions of culture and identity within a place and the dynamics of privilege in the context of decolonisation, resistance and cultural reclamation. The final set of chapters is organised around the issue of place as a social setting or settings within community contexts. These contexts are encounter spaces (see Leitner, 2013) where differently positioned people negotiate, contest, and construct new narratives for belonging in place.

PLACE, POWER AND BOUNDARY MAKING

While place may not usefully be considered as a bounded entity, boundary making is a useful concept with which to consider how privilege occurs within places and between them. Boundaries can be maintained, navigated, contested, and can be confines in which people experience social settings, belonging and identity. We start with two chapters which highlight the ways in which political borders shape people's subjective experiences of place, belonging and identity. For Alexandra Ramírez, it is about creating identity across a demarcation of boundaries of the nation-state. Sally Clark examines identity and belonging for people seeking asylum in an Indonesian transit site. Here state bordering is central to asylum seekers' identities. The social and cultural construction of borders is also examined in this section. Poala Bilbrough unpacks the exclusions of Somali men in Australia, and the ways in which the terms of belonging are bounded. Moving to an institutional setting, Lou Iaquinto considers the boundaries to participatory decision making within the social services context, focusing on the ways institutional cultures maintain boundaries to participation.

Alexandra Ramírez, in an auto-ethnographic piece, looks at the tensions within identity making for herself and other Colombian migrants, many of whom left Colombia due to political violence. This exodus, she argues, means that she and others need to keep two identities in constant tension. One is the refusal to identify with a country that has excluded them. The other is a sense of self that is anchored in *berraquera*, an important Colombian concept and identity resource. This notion denotes strength in the face of challenge, and so it is here that the inclusion into a Colombian identity is significant. This is important in facing the adversities she and other Colombian migrants experience based on culture, language, citizenship status and those structures of work which function to exclude.

Sally Clark considers how asylum seekers in the small town of Cisarua in Indonesia created belonging and solidarity. People under UNHCR refugee determination status can remain and live in the community. This is a migration 'transit site'. It is a place of 'waiting', where there is a sense of being in limbo, with 'normal life' on hold. Clark examines the ways in which a school set up and staffed by refugees, the Cisaura Learning Centre, was able to provide a place of belonging and solidarity in this limbo space. She argues that while the school was providing education it was also creating spaces for belonging, solidarity and purpose. It linked people who were living isolated in the community and gave them a common purpose. She argues, though, that it is important not to romanticise projects such as this, given the urgent need for re-settlement.

Paola Bilbrough takes on the cultural maintenance of boundaries. These are boundaries between who is included and excluded in a nation, and on what terms. Bilbrough examines screen portrayals of Sudanese men. As distinct to most portrayals which, she argues, frame these men as a threat, these all portray the Sudanese protagonists in a positive light. This media includes a celebrated advertisement for Western Sydney University which focuses on one man's journey from child soldier to successful lawyer – via the university. These, she argues, draw on an orientalist trope which might not be that of threat, but instead of fascination with the other. In these representations, 'to belong' these men need to show themselves to be 'heroic', to transcend difficulties, to show they are not a burden to the state, and as such need to be portrayed as an "… exemplary Sudanese-Australian hero".

Lou Iaquinto, drawing on interviews and focus groups with social service provider organisations and the clients of these organisations, examines why these organisations limit the participation of clients in decision making. Reasons included broad societal attitudes. But within the organisations participation was limited because management felt it was conceptually and practically difficult. Conceptually, to define participation was considered overwhelmingly difficult. Practically, they believed that to implement such an approach would be beyond the capabilities of their workforce. Service users said that what was most important in enabling them to participate was having a relationship of trust and respect with at least one person in the organisation. Iaquinto argues that barriers to participation can stem from the values within the organisations' culture, where professional staff may value their professional status over their relationships with clients.

PLACEMAKING – PRIVILEGES OF CULTURE AND IDENTITY

The set of chapters on this theme is held together by the overarching idea that they are drawing from the experiences of those who have been marginalised, excluded or silenced in hegemonic versions of placemaking. The collection of chapters draws out stories from the underside highlighting how through various cultural practices groups are able to mobilise memory and culture as resources for placemaking in the present. Sonn, Jackson, and Lyons discuss how members of the Stolen Generations are negotiating their histories and constructing places for identity and belonging. Birch points to the significance of Indigenous knowledge for climate change justice with a focus on mutual recognition and respect in decolonisation. Spaaij and Broerse offer insights from the viewpoint of Somali migrants by looking at the ways in which they make place in local settings that provide opportunities for culture sharing and learning, belonging and transnational connection. McConville and Oke call attention to the limits of the gentrification discourse and its conflation with urban renewal. For them gentrification needs to be understood within local dynamics or placemaking.

Christopher Sonn, Karen Jackson, and Rebecca Lyons examine how members of the Stolen Generations and their descendants are making places within which they can safely negotiate coloniality and its effects on their identities and subjectivities. They adopt an Indigenous methodology and argue the research process itself is an important part of placemaking. Through the method of storytelling and creative writing people shared stories about their histories of removal, its effects and how this continues to plague their efforts to decolonise their identities and subjectivities. The authors also show the ways in which people go about constructing Aboriginal identities in specific settings and how through creative arts practice people are able to progress towards self-determined identities and subjectivities. The authors argue that it is important to support Aboriginal placemaking and cultural strengthening initiatives and they describe the ways in which research can be utilised toward this goal.

Ramón Spaaij and Jora Broerse argue for community sport to be understood as a space to form belonging. Based on ethnographic fieldwork in both Australia and the Netherlands with sports teams made up of Somali migrants they examine the role sport plays in forming belonging for these two communities, and they argue against the idea common to policy makers that such mono-ethnic sports teams do not encourage 'integration'. They argue that there are several levels at which belonging is being fostered in these community sports clubs but they focus on three main dimensions. These sport clubs are a space to foster a feeling of belonging to a

Somali community, of 'being Somali', through being able to connect to homeland and diaspora. Likewise, they found that this was a way people felt more part of an international Somali diaspora. But membership of these teams also fostered a sense of belonging to the nation in which they lived, by virtue of being involved with an activity such as sport which is seen as closely connected to the national identity.

Chris McConville and Nicole Oke explore the processes and politics of gentrification in Footscray. In Footscray gentrification is understood in terms of the displacement of working class residents and migrant communities. To examine the ways in which displacement is occurring in this suburb McConville and Oke argue gentrification and urban renewal need to be disaggregated. In doing so gentrification can be understood as having different cultural implications rather being a universalising dynamic and can be placed within the broader political economy of the city. They draw on interviews from Footscray where participants had concerns about the displacements gentrification was bringing about, but also hope that the history of Footscray meant it was strong enough to withstand some of the pressures. In the current contestation of the politics of the suburb at least, newcomers do not dominate its politics and culture.

Tony Birch argues that to tackle climate change justice an acknowledgement of the destructive legacies of colonialism needs to be a priority. Climate change is linked to the dispossession and appropriation of Indigenous lands for agriculture and industrial expansion. For climate change justice, there need to be innovative relationships between Indigenous and non-Indigenous people, including restorative measures. Drawing on the example of the Adani coal mine to be built on land belonging to the Wangan and Jagalinou traditional owners, Birch argues that this can be seen as in the tradition of settler-colonialism's fixation with extraction as nation-building. He argues that there needs to be a shift to a philosophy that privileges country and respects and values Indigenous knowledge.

PLACE, PRIVILEGE AND SOCIAL SETTINGS

The final set of chapters is organised around the issue of place as a social setting or settings within community contexts. These contexts are encounter spaces where differently positioned people negotiate, contest and construct new narratives for belonging in place. The authors focus on different settings ranging from neighbourhoods, healthcare and restaurants to academia and research as sites for examining the dynamics of privilege. In these settings, the authors unpick material practices and various discourses about race, ethnicity and gender and how they shape subjectivities, identities and possibilities of belonging. The authors also point to the coloniality of power generated by the ways in which race continues to shape relationships in places. The chapters also each point to the work of border crossing and the labour its entails. Hsu highlights the negotiation of whiteness, Americanness and Chineseness in a restaurant. Cornell, Kessi and Ratele analyse the dynamics and intersectionalities of identity negotiation at a university. Along the same lines, Baker, Quayle and Ali address the dynamics of privilege in what they refer to as a contact zone. They highlight the tensions and challenges of working as insiders and outsiders as well as the impossibilities of transcending the material realities produced by histories of colonialism and the power of coloniality. Lastly, Lavis also highlights the powerful way in which colonial and biomedical paradigms can produce epistemic violence in a specific context, which results in the devaluation and dismissal of Indigenous knowledge.

Yon Hsu draws on ethnographic and documentary research undertaken on a large and long-standing Chinese restaurant in a very white suburb in Boston – 90% of the residents are white. The restaurant is constructed as an exotic space – incongruously it has, for example, a Polynesian themed cocktail bar. But it is constructed as a space 'in between' the exotic and the culture of the white suburb in which it is located. It is a 'palatable' form of the exotic; the food for example is Chinese, but cooked in a form that suits white Americans. Likewise the 'Americanness' of the restaurant owner is portrayed as in between. That he served in the US Army has been displayed prominently on the menu in more recent years. From her research Yon Hsu argues non-white Americans are made to conform to the framing of Americanness in a way which conforms to the notions of Americanness forged in these suburbs.

Josephine Cornell, Shose Kessi and Kopana Ratele analyse the ways in which inclusion and exclusion operate in a South African University. Black students are now the majority on campus but privilege and exclusion occurs on the basis of race, as well through a series of other identities such as gender, class and sexuality. Cornell et al. argue that the ways in which different identities intersect need to be understood when considering privilege in an institutional space such as this. One participant, for example, understood his experience of exclusion at the university in terms of the intersection between his class and his limited familiarity with English, the language of tuition. Another participant explained how the intersection between being black and middle class was central to his experience on campus. These intersecting identities created exclusions but also – sometimes at the same time – created resistance.

Alison M. Baker, Amy F. Quayle and Lutfiye Ali use moments of discomfort in their research to examine their personal positionalities in terms of power and privilege. They centre on the normativity of whiteness and how their different discomforts can be understood as spaces to promote reflexivity. They discuss where they are silent, what they are uncomfortable speaking about, and how this can be used to reflect on their positionalities around whiteness. While they note that self-reflexivity can be a space to re-inscribe privilege, through uncomfortable dialogue it can also be a place for connections, and one in which these privileges can be 'worked though'.

CONCLUSION

We set out in the project to develop new insights into Places of Privilege and how place has been used in different disciplines. To this end we invited responses in the following areas: *the politics, power and privilege* within – or between – places; *privileges and borders* at the local, national or global scales, including the digital and non-material, and the reconfiguration of political space; and *the politics of new meanings of community*, including new strategies of cultural identity and resistance, new solidarities or exclusions, and possibilities for belonging. We received several chapters all dealing with the issue in different ways, and these pointed to the ways in which histories of colonialism, oppression, and displacement continue to impact communities of people differentially. In the different chapters authors also highlight the varied and complex ways in which the dynamics of privilege are expressed in places, and that these places cannot be understood without the contexts of history, economy, politics and culture. Places are local and global. They are constituted by and through cultural activities, and through engagement in places people construct identities, narratives and stories. Not everyone has equal access to places and settings, and not everyone's capital is valued and mobilised in order to construct inclusive places. The various chapters point to a range of conceptual resources and in some cases to epistemological tools that can be utilised to produce critical analyses of placemaking practices in order to tackle the coloniality of power or the production of privilege. As is shown in some chapters, this task is tricky and goes beyond a self-focused reflexivity. It requires a critical lens and practice that can be brought to bear on examining and producing places that are inclusive, plural and always attuned to the dynamics of privilege.

REFERENCES

Behrendt, L. (2009). Home: The importance of place to the dispossessed. *South Atlantic Quarterly, 108*(1), 71–85. doi:10.1215/00382876-2008-023

Birch, A. (2015). 'The lifting of the sky': Life outside the Anthropocene. In J. Adamson & M. Davis (Eds.), *Humanities for the environment: Integrating knowledge, forging new constellations of practice*. London: Taylor and Francis.

Fredericks, B. (2013). 'We don't leave our identities at the city limits': Aboriginal and Torres Strait Islander people living in urban localities. *Australian Aboriginal Studies, 1*, 4–16.

Green, M. J., Sonn, C. C., & Matsebula, J. (2007). Reviewing whiteness: Theory, research and possibilities. *South African Journal of Psychology, 37*(3), 389–419.

Hau'ofa, E. (1994). Our sea of Islands. *The Contemporary Pacific, 6*(1), 147–161.

Leitner, J. (2013). Spaces of encounter: Immigration, race, class and the politics of belonging in small town America. *Annals of the Association of American Geographers, 102*(4), 828–46.

Massey, D. (1994). Double articulation: A place in the world. In A. Bammer (Ed.), *Displacements: Cultural identities in question* (pp. 110–121). Bloomington, IN: Indiana University Press.

McCoy, K., Tuck, E., & McKenzie, M. (Eds.). (2016). *Land education: Rethinking pedagogies of place from indigenous, postcolonial, and decolonizing perspectives*. New York, NY: Routledge.

Moreton-Robinson, A. (2003). I still call Australia home: Indigenous belonging and place in a White postcolonizing society. In S. Ahmed, C. Castañeda, A. Fortier, & M. Sheller (Eds.), *Uprootings/regroundings: Questions of home and migration* (pp. 23–40). Oxford: Berg.

Oke, N., Sonn, C. C., & McConville, C. (2016). Making a place in Footscray: Everyday multiculturalism, ethnic hubs and segmented geography. *Identities: Global Studies in Culture and Power*, 1–19. doi:10.1080/1070289X.2016.1233880

Quijano, A. (2000). Coloniality of power and Eurocentrism in Latin America. *International Sociology, 15*(2), 215–232.

Rose, D. (2004). *Reports from a wild country: Ethics for decolonisation.* Sydney: University of New South Wales Press.

Smith, M. P. (2001). *Transnational urbanism: Locating globalization.* Malden, MA: Blackwell Publishers.

Smith, M. P., & Bakker, M. (2008). *Citizenship across borders: The political transnationalism of El Migrante.* Cornell: Cornell University Press.

Tuck, E., & McKenzie, M. (2015). Relational validity and the "where" of inquiry: Place and land in qualitative research. *Qualitative Inquiry, 21*, 1–6. doi:10.1177/1077800414563809

Twine, F. W., & Gardener, B. (2013). Introduction. In F. W. Twine & B. Gardener (Eds.), *Geographies of Privilege*. New York, NY: Routledge.

Nicole Oke
Victoria University
Australia

Christopher C. Sonn
Victoria University
Australia

Alison M. Baker
Victoria University
Australia

PART 1

PLACE, POWER AND BOUNDARY MAKING

ALEXANDRA RAMÍREZ

2. COLOMBIAN *BERRAQUERA*

Personal and Cultural Experiences on the Journey
from Displacement to Belonging

INTRODUCTION

Violence in Colombia has the power of a hurricane in full force: enveloping all in
its wake, affecting all human relationships in the country, inflecting the nation's
language and symbols, and in the process displacing and expelling millions of
people.

Not surprisingly, of all the Latin American countries Colombia has the largest
number of its citizens living abroad. Despite the severity of their many personal
experiences, they are not considered refugees or asylum seekers when they end up as
part of the group of Colombian nationals who since last century have been seeking
a better life in foreign lands.

Once abroad, Colombians have to cope with misrepresentation and misrecognition
through stereotypes informed by messages about drug-trafficking, the over-
sexualisation of women and armed conflict. This makes it challenging, if not
impossible, to renew the processes of belonging.

Harsh conditions back home as well as in their new places of settlement have the
paradoxical effect of fostering a sense of resilience, which is called *berraquera* in
the Colombian context.

Berraquera is the concept of survival invoked in the face of difficulties. It becomes
an attitude to life which underpins new subjectivities. It encourages Colombians to
persevere against all odds. It is the glue of national identity, reconciling regional
differences.

This chapter relies on sociological, historical and biographical insights to
contextualise Colombian migration, its causes and its characteristics. It also
provides cultural analysis to show better how Colombians deal with hardships and
why. Moreover, it illustrates autoethnographically the intrinsic contradictions that
encompass and subtly connote my identity as a Colombian. On the one hand there is
my refusal to belong to a country that has expelled me and on the other my ongoing
recourse to those elements that shape my own *berraquera*.

Berraquera represents a starting point to comprehend both my physical, emotional
and social exile, and also my growing sense of settlement and belonging, first in
Italy and later in Australia.

© KONINKLIJKE BRILL NV, LEIDEN, 2018 | DOI:10.1163/9789004381407_002

A. RAMÍREZ

First Autoethnographic Moment, June 2003

My head was against the pavement, and I realised something was not right. I tried to get up while passersby screamed, "She is alive, she is alive!"

It was a warm morning in June 2003 and I was living with my father in a beautiful apartment near the centre of Itagui, a southern suburb of Medellín. Even though I had just finished my Bachelor in Social Work at the University of Antioquia, the climate of insecurity that enveloped the country and the lack of opportunities for prosperity made me feel uneasy about making my future in Colombia.

I had a dream: I wanted to undertake a doctorate in Italy. I had fallen in love with that country ever since the time my primary school geography teacher showed it to us, shaped like a boot, the country that had influenced the history of the world from the Roman Empire through to the artwork of Michelangelo and the genius of Da Vinci.

Unfortunately, Spanish was the only language I knew, so study in a country of Hispanic origin like Mexico or Spain made more sense. Quite apart from this my family's financial situation, though not as desperate as that of many others around us, did not allow me the opportunity to study abroad. To achieve my goal, I would have had to find a scholarship or apply for a loan with Icetex, a government institution that supports students who have the capacity but lack the financial means to undertake tertiary education courses.

Though my family was not poor, my parents' separation before I finished High School not only changed our family dynamic at home, it also diminished the chances of success for my sister and me in a society that is obsessed with class and where a private university education is a status symbol.

With the break-up of our family, our financial resources were considerably reduced, and at 16 it was already quite clear to me that my only option would be to enrol at the public University of Antioquia. I am certain that my situation was no different to the 20,000 or so other people who presented themselves to attempt the 1997 entrance exam. Many tried but only a few succeeded and I managed to get in on my second attempt. The experience taught me that the wealth of being poor lies in a fierce will to achieve one's goal. Mine was to study.

My parents' words during my childhood kept running through my head: "My daughter, you must study so that one day you will be independent. No-one ever knows what the future will bring but even if you end up marrying a bad man who does not respect you, as a professional you will be able to look after yourself anywhere in the world. Do not rely on anyone and do not let anyone mistreat you. Study, study, study, this is the only advice we can give you!"

Those words were imprinted in my mind. For my family, study represented the only opportunity to climb the social ladder. Their plan for my life was that I would finish university, find a good job, get married to a good man, have children, buy a nice house and live a happy and stable life. No-one, especially not me, would have imagined that the violence and bloodshed that is an everyday part of Colombian life

18

would befall me, maim my body, destroy the hopes of an entire family, and inflict on all of us a wound that would never heal.

That morning in June the bullet that passed through my skull was the result of a premeditated action by an unknown assailant. He rang my doorbell and asked for me but I had left home early and gone to run some quick errands without having breakfast, a fortunate oversight, as an empty stomach made it easier to vomit up the blood I swallowed from the bullet-hole in me.

Coming back home, I saw my father speaking with someone I had never seen before. I can still picture that boy. With his beret, checked shirt and a carry-bag slung over one shoulder, he made quite a convincing postman. As I approached I started swinging my arms in an exaggerated way to give my father a laugh as he told the presumed postal worker, "Here she comes now". The boy turned towards me. We looked at each other as he waited without saying a word. I kept walking, unaware that I was approaching something fateful.

The 'postman' remained behind me, so I did not see what was about to happen. He aimed at my head and fired. I hit the ground while an electric jolt ran through my body. Thousands of thoughts invaded my mind, "What is it? What's happening to me? I don't want to feel this electrical discharge. Did a bus hit me? No impossible, I was on the pedestrian path ..." My mind was still active – I did not lose consciousness.

I only found out what had happened when my father jumped out of our taxi in front of the nearby hospital shouting to the doctor who ran to help me, "She's been shot!"

Before that moment of violence, no more than five steps lay between my father and me. In a few months, those five steps would become 9,408 kilometres.

HISTORY OF VIOLENCE

The Republic of Colombia is the result firstly of the Spanish Crown's domination and subsequently of the struggles between two political factions (the Liberal and Conservative parties).

The goal of the Spanish conquerors was to accumulate wealth by land appropriation and exploitation. As a consequence the indigenous population was almost eliminated by forced labour and unfamiliar illnesses. Africans were then brought in as slaves to satisfy European greed. As the sociologist Hristov states, "the domination of the indigenous people, and the imposition of Spanish authority through political and economic institutions, were achieved by violence" (Hristov, 2014, p. 62).

Politics and Violence

The two major Colombian political parties emerged in the mid 19th century. The Liberal Party was founded in 1848 and the Conservative Party a year later. They established a bipartisan hegemony that lasted until the beginning of the 21st century. Slaveholders, bureaucrats, landowners, high-ranking military and clergy formed the

Conservative Party, advocating that their established political position was to be maintained at all costs. Conversely the Liberal Party consisted of merchants, the indigenous population, slaves and artisans who aimed to transform the Colombian state. The Catholic Church controlled education and represented another polarising element in the hostilities. The Conservatives' goal was to fight against any change, attempting to perpetuate the status quo, and in this they were supported by the Church which was at that time the guarantor of social order and authority, whereas the Liberals' aim was to change the state, while denouncing the Church for being a "bastion of privilege" (Pearce cited in Hristov, 2014, p. 67).

La Violencia was the name given to the 1946–1958 period, although some scholars extend this period until 1966. The assassination of the Liberal candidate, Jorge Eliecer Gaitán, in 1948 represented a critical moment, triggering warfare which resulted in a death toll of 300,000 and displaced more than two million Colombians (Rueda Bedoya, 2000). At this time uneducated peasants and armed civilians formed a partisan *sicariato* (hit squad) called *Los Pájaros*, affiliated with the Conservative Party. In response, between 1955 and 1965, the Liberal Party resisted with its own squad, the *cuadrillas liberales*, who in some regions became bandits for profit (Betancourt Echeverry, 1990; Vasquéz Piñeros, 2007). In other areas peasants with communist sympathies formed self-defence groups, out of which was born some years later the FARC (*Fuerzas Armadas Revolucionarias de Colombia* – Revolutionary Armed Forces of Colombia).

Colonial Vestiges

The unequal political system which Colombia inherited from Spanish colonisation is linked directly with this ongoing violence. That system was based on exclusion. Power was concentrated in the hands of the wealthy land-owning Catholic elite, partisans of the Conservative party, who excluded others from participation in the system. Marin Taborda (2005) emphasises this link between the modern period of La Violencia and the frequent civil wars of the 19th century.

By 1966, this political upheaval had mutated into revolutionary violence, epitomised in 1964 by the official formation of the FARC and the ELN (*Ejército Liberal de Colombia* – National Liberation Army). Founded by students, Catholic radicals and left-wing intellectuals, the ELN was inspired by the Cuban Revolution. Three years later (1967) another revolutionary group was born, the EPL (*Ejército Popular de Colombia* – National Popular Army). Broadly speaking, the initial idea of the Colombian guerrilla movements was to fight for an equitable state, where social justice would be achieved through the implementation of communist principles.

The revolutionary violence involved guerrillas fighting against the national army and the paramilitary groups which had entered the scene as illegal right-wing collectives formed by landowners and other members of the upper class to combat the left-wing revolutionaries. The war was fought in the countryside. Although it did not gain much attention from those living in big cities, the rural areas were replete with stories of death, forced disappearances and displacement.

It did not take long, however, before the conflict hit the major cities, instigated during the 1970s by the appearance of new insurgents such as the 19th April Movement, known as M-19, which constituted itself as an urban guerrilla force. Formed by a group of university intellectuals, it was inspired by the urban guerrilla movements in Uruguay (Tupamaros) and Argentina (Montoneros) and took its name from the date of an allegedly fraudulent presidential election (Federal Research Division, 1988).

Moreover, drug trafficking and the commercialisation of cocaine added to this already complex situation. The Medellín and Cali cartels emerged to lift the violence to a new level. It was within this context that the state and its most prominent figures came under threat. The conflict spread from the most remote places to reach the heart of the capital and shake its institutions.

The 1980s were years of social disruption and the rise of armed gangs of young people. The homeless, drug addicts, homosexuals and anyone outside "the norm" became targets for acts of senseless violence (Pécaut & González, 1997). The major cities started to witness the devastating force of numerous illegal organisations. A wide spectrum of groups – right-wing militias connected to paramilitary groups, left-wing militias associated with guerrilla groups, drug traffickers and hitmen – caused fear and death. Little by little, violence dragged in all Colombians.

In the meantime, in 1984, the Quintin Lame Armed Movement (*Movimiento Armado Quintin Lame, MAQL*) was officially formed in the Southern province of Cauca to fight for land rights (Peñaranda Supelano, 2010). A year later the FARC founded the Patriotic Union (UP), a political party, in the hope of achieving peaceful outcomes. Instead this new political party was ruthlessly exterminated, with some sources claiming that 3,000 members were murdered while an additional 5,000 of those who survived the massacre left the country.

The Law of the Strongest

The idea that dissent is not allowed was gradually instilled in the minds of the population with the tacit law of "either with us or against us" (Ramírez, 2016). As the scholarly group Historic Memory writes: "in Colombia ... the opposition, instead of being seen as a fundamental element of the political community, is at each moment considered a threat to the integrity of the dominant order" (my translation, Centro de Memoria Histórica, 2013, p. 15).

By the 1990s, two features were clear in Colombian society: the absence of a legitimate state and violent actions increasingly going unpunished (Pécaut & González, 1997). The 21st century opened with an unprecedented record of violent deaths.

Alvaro Uribe Vélez was elected in this climate in 2002. He was a bitter enemy of the guerrillas, whom he accused of his father's murder in 1983. His politics of "democratic security" transformed the language, the symbols and the historical framework of the conflict. "War against Terror" was the name Uribe gave to his massive military offensive. The government in labelling the guerrillas "terrorist groups", eliminated through this linguistic term references to redistribution of wealth, land reform and access to basic services. Uribe's military achievements increased his popularity, leading to congressional approval of a constitutional amendment that allowed him to be elected for a second term from 2006 to 2010 (Sojo, 2009).

Juan Manuel Santos, a former defence minister serving with Alvaro Uribe, was his successor as president in 2010 and won re-election in 2014. A new process of peace negotiation with the FARC began in 2012. The other revolutionary groups (ELN, M-19, EPL and Quintin Lame) had already demobilised. Peace negotiations were mainly held in Havana, Cuba, and produced a final agreement which aimed to end what had become the longest ever internal conflict on the American continent.

The agreement was subject to a plebiscite, held in October 2016, in which a narrow majority of voters (50.21%) rejected the treaty. The leader of the anti-treaty forces was Alvaro Uribe, who opposed the alleged concessions to the so-called terrorist group. Since then, a climate of uncertainty and confusion has reigned in the country, while the civilian population clamours for peace and justice.

FRAGMENTED STATE, FRAGMENTED SOCIETY

Although Colombia has an extensive electoral tradition going back to the 1820s, the people's will has not been unambiguously applied, making this democracy a somewhat empty ideal (Robinson, 2015). The number of politicians associated with violent groups is very high and human rights are constantly violated. During the local elections of 2015, the Fundación Paz y Reconciliación published a list of 140 candidates for Mayor and Departmental Governor who had criminal records, links with armed groups, or connections with criminal organisations (Robinson, 2015).

The unfinished political project enables normalised acts of violence to take place in numerous social contexts, where violence is produced, used and reproduced by anyone. The holistic nature and duration of violence paradoxically contributes to the particularities of those enacting it as perpetrators or enduring it as victims, while their specific logic is disregarded. Its oppressive presence has also led to the neglect of the political and social problems that underlie its origins.

In their analysis, Pécaut and González (1997) refer to two overlapping systems of violence, one organised and the other disorganised, whose intersection creates a diffuse subculture of violences. Organised violence focuses on power and control of wealth and territory. Disorganised violence is relational, unpredictable and spontaneous; it emerges as a regular way to 'solve' disputes and disagreements. It threatens everyone and its dynamics mean that the same people are sometimes victims and at other times perpetrators. Violence, then, creates new dynamics and new contexts where perceptions, meanings and interactions are regulated by it in an ongoing manner.

A lack of national unity, exemplified in Colombia's regional fragmentation and the lack of a government presence in some parts of the country, also operates as a significant element in feeding violence. The fragility of the divided state has been an ongoing challenge, as argued by Safford and Palacios (2001) in their book *Colombia: fragmented land, divided society*: "… spatial fragmentation … has found expression in economic atomisation and cultural differentiation. The country's … most populated areas have been divided by its three mountain ranges … that fostered the development of particularised local and regional cultures, regional antagonism and local rivalries …" (cited in Coatsworth, 2003).

Belonging and identity during the 20th century were ideas shaped by the two political parties existing at that time. The state was not a collective and shared project, and that resulted in two different value systems and representations being adopted (Pécaut, 1987). For years all relations in Colombia were regulated by a dualistic mutually exclusive logic which did not allow access to a third option or a new way. The totalitarianism of the political parties not only regulated the polls, it took over life itself.

A role in setting national values and public morality was played by the Church until the 1960s (Vasquéz Piñeros, 2007). The advent of drug-trafficking and the figure of Pablo Escobar represented a new symbolic order. The working class population sought a new class position by subverting the rules of the elite, while US consumer culture penetrated homes via TV series and films which portrayed an ideal life of big houses, cars, beautiful women, fashion and luxury. Young people wanted to consume both goods and life as "*la vida se gasta lo mismo que el dinero*" (life is spent like money) (Pécaut & González, 1997, p. 911).

In this divided context, *berraquera* – the sense of resilience among Colombians – emerges to act as a social glue against the political and religious ideology that amplifies the breach of relations and also as a distinctive personal trait to cope with difficulties. Exclusionary political projects, retaliation for power, inequality, corruption, poverty, distrust and social fragmentation have all contributed to the ongoing violence. *Berraquera* then became the personal and collective value to endure the violence while seeking for survival.

Slowly silence became the default position in a society dominated by terror. Terror took over our sensibilities and, at times, we denied ourselves the capacity to feel. Fear prevented social cohesion and hindered us from reacting positively against such barbarism.

The frequency and quantity of violent interactions put our nervous systems under great stress. We wanted to ignore it, to pretend we lived in a normal country instead of living in a chaotic space in which death and turmoil were part of the daily routine. Those who could left, and those who could not, dreamed every day of emigrating.

Second Autoethnographic Moment, November 2003

> *Now there is no other,*
> *Now there is not sadness,*

23

Time keeps running,
Damn time that condemns me to die,
Without hope, without illusions,
All that is left is empty space,
and despite all of this,
I do not miss that other time.
I am learning to remake myself,
Today I create for myself a stranger's soul
and I feel that I do not belong anywhere in the world.
I have lost my name,
my family,
my city
and I begin to live in absurdity.
(Translation of the original published in Italian, Ramírez, 2013)

I was still alive as the astonished doctors looked on, and I wanted to stay that way.

It would be a shame for anyone to die like this. I was 25 years old and I had no idea why I had been shot. If I had to die before my time, I would like to have sewn my funeral veil first, the same way Gabriel Garcia Marquez (1967) described his beloved grandmother preparing her own veil.

When I recovered four weeks later, I continued on with my plans to leave. The Italian Consulate in Medellin did not respond to my request for asylum. That institutional refusal, together with my fear and the concerns of my family, made me accept a marriage proposal from an Italian friend who had shown me much care and attention in the past. He knew this was the only way I could leave Colombia and reach Italy. There was no party, not even a photograph. There was nothing to celebrate. The only thing that remains from that moment is the black dress I wore to declare, "Yes, I accept that I must leave". Ours was an honest relationship – the marriage finished the same way it started.

When good news from a Spanish university arrived, I was already in Europe. The Italian autumn welcomed me coldly. What else should I have expected? I had just been violently expelled from my own city (or at least that was the way I felt) and, even if I was devastated inside, knowing that I had come to a safe place gave me the strength to rethink my outlook on life.

I began attending an Italian language school. Without command of the language there is no work and without work there is no possibility of social integration. The school gave me so much more than basic grammar. There I met other foreigners who, like me, dreamed of a better future. It was through interacting with people from other countries that I began to take notice of the particular features of my own culture and to appreciate its distinctiveness.

My days were spent studying in the morning to become a personal care attendant (despite my bachelor in social work), working as a cleaner in the afternoon, and attending Italian school in the evening. My personal care attendant course was funded by the European Social Fund and made available only to migrant women in an attempt to integrate new arrivals and to meet the needs of an ageing Italian population. They were difficult days. The winter cold in Trentino was a tremendous strain for me to endure. I had rarely worn wool and, suddenly, I found myself compelled to cover myself from head to toe in this unfamiliar fibre to defend my body from temperatures that I had never felt in my home, the city of eternal spring.

My faith in humanity was harshly tested, especially my faith in Colombia and Colombians. I tried to stay clear of them. My first friends were other Latin Americans and, even if the reasons for being in Italy were quite varied, we all shared a common experience. We were immigrants, "immigrati extra-communitari" *(non EU migrants), as the Italians say, with some disdain. I always found this attitude appalling.*

Over time my whole life – the food I ate, the clothing I wore, the customs I followed, the music I listened to, the language I spoke – changed radically. My interactions with the Italian world increased greatly thanks to the university and to work. My professional degree was recognised by the University of Trento and I began a Masters course in Social Work there. Little by little, I reached a balancing point, even though it was rather delicate. I began to assimilate into the society into which I had inserted myself. I adopted the aperitivo tradition after work: a spritz, prosecco or white wine served with olives and other finger food. But I struggled to eat a whole pizza by myself. I learned to use the polite form of Italian language whenever my interlocutor was unknown or of high status. I even became a little quieter to avoid agitating the peace of mind of the Trentini (people from Trento) with my Colombian moodiness. I reluctantly covered my body with yet more clothes to respect an implicit code of decency, in a city historically governed by a bishop.

From my past experiences, it normally takes three or four years for any effort of mine to bear fruit. 2003 was the worst year for me, while 2007 was a year of great personal satisfaction. I was finally granted Italian citizenship and with it I could fulfil my desire to travel around the world. The first thing I did was request a passport. Goodbye queues! Goodbye suspicious security guards and immigration officers and goodbye airport checks and controls! Goodbye bureaucracy and visa requests! Goodbye immigration police, goodbye "permesso di soggiorno" (residency permit)! You will not be missed.

Citizenship divides people into those who are privileged and those who are not. I was happy to have that privilege. From that moment, I was able to work in the public sector, an essential requirement for my career as a social worker. Yet, the more familiar I became with Italian society, the more I realised the shortcomings of the system that governed it, a system that does not help a country paralysed under the weight of its own history. It seemed to me that change was problematic for Italians, as they preferred to look back to the past than ahead to the future.

Slowly I began to see that ethics and aesthetics do not go together well in the "Bel Paese". I sought in every way possible to make a solid position for myself and, even

though I managed to achieve many goals, after ten years of overcoming obstacles I understood that Italy demands much and offers little.
Between 2008 and 2013 more than 500,000 Italians left Italy, including me.

GETTING AWAY: MIGRATION TO AND FROM COLOMBIA

Colombia is the Latin American country with the highest number of people living abroad. In 2016, the Ministerio de Relaciones Exteriores (Ministry of Foreign Affairs) estimated that roughly 4.7 million Colombians, 10% of the total population, live overseas. Since the formation of the Republic, Colombians have been on the move. Initially internal movements were from rural to urban spaces with floods of people following the wave of industrialisation of the country in the 20th century.

According to Restrepo Vélez (2006), the movement of Colombians to foreign lands started to be relevant at the end of the 1950s.

The first international migratory movements were towards the neighbouring countries of Panama, Venezuela and Ecuador. Economic reasons combined with the desire to escape political violence were the main incentives. These earliest emigrants came from lower-middle and working-class backgrounds.

The second wave of emigrants moved further away, landing in the US during the 1970s, when the "American Dream" was an appealing narrative.

During the 1990s and 2000s, the growing armed civil conflict and the imposition of neo-liberal politics generated a third wave of emigration to the US and Spain as small businesses and farmers were expelled from the national production system (Sassen, 2014).

Successive restrictions on visa requirements in Spain and the US made it almost impossible for lower- and middle-income workers to migrate at the beginning of the 21st century. In addition, the prolonged economic crisis in both countries reoriented the flow of migration.

Influxes of migration respond to connections that have been historically formed as part of colonialism in the case of Spain, or from new colonialism in the case of the US (see Plan Colombia[1]). In this regard, research has found that international migration follows patterns created by the dynamic of colonisation/dependency between sending and receiving countries (Rumbaut, Portes cited in Upegui Hernández, 2014). However, in newer migration flows, other factors intervene in redefining these movements. Market opportunities and recruitment promoted by migration channels, such as skilled visas or facilitated access to universities, redirects people towards emerging places.

According to Ochoa (2012), Ecuador, Venezuela and Panamá have been relevant to Colombian emigration because of two factors. Firstly, shared historical roots compel these countries to recognise the ideal of *unidad bolivariana*.[2] Secondly, there are shared frontiers which are crossed on a daily basis by displaced inhabitants from the departments of Putumayo, Nariño, Norte de Santander and Chocó. These migrants find themselves located between poverty and war, fleeing from the conflict by crossing the border to save the only value they have, their lives.

There is general clarity in the legal definitions and treatment to be given to those who are called internally displaced persons, refugees or asylum seekers. However such definitions do not take into account the number of people forced to leave as a result of exposure to violence, drug trafficking or the economic situation.

Unfortunately an indeterminate number of Colombians have had to leave Colombia and they do not meet the requirements for refugee status, despite their human rights having been violated (Ramírez & Mendoza, 2013).

Third Autoethnographic Moment, April 2016

Here I am, sitting among unknown people.
All of them are foreigners to me;
even though, I am the only foreigner tonight.
They talk in a strange way about things that I hardly understand.
They are now and I am with them.
They do not know my name, what my story is.
I do not say anything and they do not ask.
It is not important.
I am here and they are as well.
We do not look at each other,
it would be embarrassing.
I am the only woman between them.
While they chat,
I think of Henry Miller and his adventure in Paris.
This is not Paris and I am not Henry Miller;
but, as usual,
the only thing that really matters
is to feel without words.
So, let's be silent,
Let's follow the night Down Under.

Southbank, Melbourne, 6 April 2016

The island-continent never featured in my plans. I only knew that it was enormous and very far away, but meeting a cousin of my future husband changed my perspective. I had fallen in love with an Italian musician, a master of the art of drumming who was able to speak to me without words. He became my other half in 2013. The civil ceremony was followed this time with a party for many friends, food, a white dress and lots of photos. He plays and I dance, a perfect combination!

His cousin, a young engineer, left Milan two years ago to come to Australia. With a working holiday visa, he took the chance to visit the country and see if there was a possibility of finding work. For him, Perth was the gateway to opportunity. He found dreams, work, friends, and then obtained citizenship and was able to buy himself a house, all within the span of five years.

His enthusiasm for Australia provoked our curiosity so when we were deciding on the ideal destination for our upcoming honeymoon, we naturally thought of this country.

The honeymoon changed into a permanent unplanned stay. The initial idea was to spend six weeks visiting the country, but after two weeks in Perth I looked at il mio amore and discussed with him my desire to stay here longer. He was in shock. Italy was the only place he knew and the prospect of being an immigrant did not suit him. Everything was back home, and apart from his cousin we had neither family nor friends to help us in the endeavour I was proposing. He knew though that I was tired of Italy, tired of living in a place that does not recognise meritocracy. I had my bachelor's degree plus two masters, experience in different areas, I was bilingual (Spanish and Italian) but I had to compromise and work more for less alongside people who did not even have a bachelor's degree. My salary was just enough to survive and when I tried to hold more than one job it did not pay off because of the high amount of tax. The worst element was that there was no indication of change. Instead I had to be grateful just to have a job in a period where the level of unemployment started to increase dramatically. At that time it seemed that the only option was to stay there until I died, gradually losing my soul. That was until we arrived in Australia and I began to dream about a new life in a place where 'the fair go' was an appealing narrative.

Despite his reticence, my husband eventually acquiesced. We reached a compromise. He told me, "OK, let's try to stay for one year but not in Perth. My condition is that we have to go to Melbourne, where there is more going on in the artistic scene". I was over the moon. Any city was fine for me!

Of course, new challenges presented themselves and there would be much to do and re-do, starting with the language. At that time I did not know English, not even one word. It is funny to write that now in English getting ready for my first conference in English too – my hands start sweating, panic!

The story, at least for me, would repeat itself again: school (this time in English), the search for work, a place to stay and a network of people on whom we could rely. To my advantage, this time I was not alone.

BERRAQUERA: RESILIENCE, STRENGTH AND FLEXIBILITY IN COLOMBIA

Colombian migration predominantly has a feminine face. It is mostly well-educated, middle-class and in the receiving countries Colombians work in the areas of care, hospitality and cleaning as a starting point (Hernández Pulgarín, 2016; Murillo Muñoz & Molero Alonso, 2016; Restrepo Vélez, 2006).

The feminisation of migration is the result of different elements (Wichterich, 2000): their level of employability, as women are generally paid less than men for the same role; the high demand for care services in Western societies which has produced what has been called "the care drain"[3] (Dumitru, 2014); and the high prevalence of single mothers who are obliged to go abroad in order to provide sustenance for their children and extended families in Colombia, leaving their offspring with the other women of the family (Mahler, 1998).

Although research about Colombians is not extensive, from some of the scholarly work that has been undertaken it is possible to discern how Colombians negotiate their social and personal identities.

Overall, the Colombian identity has been widely and extensively associated with the clichés of drug trafficking, criminality and violence. The media's glamorisation of drug dealers, beautiful 'easy' women and the armed conflict has created a powerful stigma. The popularisation of the image of Pablo Escobar, presented as the most notorious drug-dealer in the world, has exacerbated this bad reputation. Furthermore, the massive commercial success of TV series depicting violence, prostitution, drugs and war in Colombia have reinforced pejorative stereotypes over time.

"One bad apple spoils the barrel" and in the Colombian case this popular expression becomes disturbingly real. Acquiring a visa to visit the vast majority of the countries in the world[4] remains a complex undertaking for Colombian citizens. Many of them have to go through tedious bureaucratic procedures to obtain a visa, sometimes being humiliated during the application phase, and stigmatised in airports. Colombians are subjected to meticulous controls once they land abroad.

Under these conditions, bearing another nation's passport is liberating; the world becomes barrier free. It is not a surprise then that many Colombians, despite the hurdles in foreign lands, persist in order to secure a second citizenship and a second passport.

The Ambivalent Colombian Identity

Colombian migrants tend to have an ambivalent attitude toward their national identity. On the one hand, they hesitate to identify as Colombians because they do not want to be associated with the negative image with which their nation has been portrayed (Semana, 2011) yet there is also something intrinsic in their culture and upbringing that is pivotal to their ability to overcome new and confronting challenges, especially in their migratory experience.

Amézquita Quintana (2013) studied the experiences of stigmatisation of Colombians migrants in the United States from 1990–2010 and refers to their "identity wounds". In a context as highly racialised as that of the U.S, the word 'Latino' is an ethnic label recalling a multiplicity of narratives which undoubtedly have an impact on immigrant self-perceptions. Disjuncture between what people think of themselves and the social judgment based on stereotypes leads to the idea of "not me" (McCall, 2003) in that "no, I am not a drug-dealer, I am not a delinquent, I am not a prostitute".

Moral sufferance then becomes part of the migratory experience which involves a process of differentiation. Colombian migrants are compelled to demonstrate that they are not as the media has portrayed them. They have to expend energy and effort not only to adapt to their new context, but also to challenge misrepresentation.

Something similar occurs in Spain, where one may hear the derogatory term '*sudaca*' denoting South Americans. Many Colombians there engage in "identity work" (Snow & Anderson, 1987) seeking to present themselves in a different way to counterbalance the pejorative Colombian '*sudaca*'.

Taylor (1994) claims that human identity is dialogical: identity is the result of interacting with others. As a human, one creates oneself and others intersubjectively. Identity is thus a product of ongoing relationships within the social context in which they occur. Therefore "non recognition or misinterpretation can inflict harm, can be a form of oppression, imprisoning someone in a false, distorted and reduced mode of being" (Taylor, 1994, p. 25).

One's social relationships occur partly as expressions of and partly as responses to an experiential and conceptual space between 'objective' living conditions and 'subjective' experiences of living in such conditions. Hence it is imperative to analyse this 'space' to grasp its outcomes.

The stigmatisation of drugs and violence has paradoxically fomented a great division between Colombian immigrants as well, profoundly affecting their own interrelationships, as confirmed by Upegui Hernández (2014, p. 44) who says "research on the transnational political participation of Colombians has identified mistrust and social fragmentation among Colombian immigrant communities in Canada, United States, Britain and Spain".

Suspicion and distrust inhibit social cohesion among Colombians, so their individual and social identities are reconstructed abroad based on status, social class, networks and affinities with other people and groups, rather than based on their place of birth (Upegui Hernández, 2014).

In his article about Colombian immigrants in France (Bordeaux) and Spain (Seville) (some of whom had returned to Colombia) Hernández Pulgarín (2016), however, argues that Colombian immigrants' adaptation to their host country is interwoven with discourses of national identity that lead to positive performative outcomes. These discourses represent a symbolic practice of activating psychological resources, thereby inducing resilience.

In particular, Hernández describes how Colombian immigrants resist and overcome hardships such as exploitation at work, professional disregard (specifically when being employed in areas considered unworthy despite their professional titles), discrimination and so on. These difficulties lead Colombians to recall their national identity to engender *berraquera*.

Berraquera alludes to an individual's strength and capacity to endure adversity, overcome difficulty and bear suffering. It becomes a personal ideology used to tackle challenges and achieve goals. Being *berraco* (for men) or *berraca* (for women) leads to success in Colombian culture. Within this framework, difficulties, barriers and discriminations are faced by adopting personal strategies to obtain positive and favourable results. *Berraquera* can be understood with reference to those moments in sport where we want to quit but we carry on, where we search deep inside ourselves for something that seems to almost transcend our own humanity so as to overcome adversity. *Berraquera* is thus the propulsive, discursive and symbolic force sustaining Colombian immigrants in their search for wellbeing.

Finally, a Colombian's ambivalent identity is characterised as oscillating, just like a pendulum. On one extreme, in social contexts, Colombians distance themselves from negative images related to their country while at the other extreme, being Colombian is individually embodied as a propulsive force to achieve goals and develop resourcefulness towards being successful in "the era of migration" (Castles & Miller, 2009).

Fourth Autoethnographic Moment, January 2017

My long stay in Italy and the few chances I had to visit my family in Colombia had weakened my Colombian soul. Gradually I learned to be someone else and belong somewhere else by nurturing positive emotions. They make me feel safe and part of a greater community, where people take care of me and I take care of them. It is an implicit agreement to spread acceptance, recognition and empowerment.

However, I never lost the strength of character with which I had been raised. I still remember the phrase that marked my entrance to adulthood, to becoming a woman and choosing to be a migrant: "pa' trás ni pa' coger impulso" (never take a step back, not even to gain momentum). There was certainly no shortage of occasions to repeat it as a mantra.

Tenacity and a devil-may-care attitude brought me to dream the impossible and seek to reach it. How else could you explain my decision to journey on this path to obtain my doctorate in Melbourne? It is the Colombian in me who says this. It is my berraquera that pushes me ahead.

My doctorate is a tool for answers. As a result of my own story and experiences, I am interested in knowing what kind of interactional spaces there are between immigrants and local residents in Melbourne and Trento; how cultural and ethnic difference is created and perceived in both places; how belonging is expressed; what process of otherness is displayed and how people subvert or resist it.

I would like to hear other voices and position myself as a bridge that connects diversity in a globalised context. No more "them and us". Stories must be told and I am sharing mine.

In Australia, my past, present and future identities meet each other. The multi-cultural environment of this place opens spaces in which my different identities can be reconciled and it pushes me to search for something else that is yet to come.

NOTES

¹ Plan Colombia is a US aid program to fight drug cartels and left-wing insurgent groups operating on Colombian territory.

A. RAMÍREZ

[2] Simon Bolivar, the liberator of Colombia, Ecuador and Venezuela from Spanish domination had the dream of creating a united South America.
[3] Dumitru (2014) problematises this concept by alluding to its sexist ground.
[4] Some progress has been made in bilateral agreements. Recently, Peruvians and Colombians have been exempted from visa requirements to enter the Schengen area for tourist purposes. In the Index Passport (2017), Colombian passport holders have access visa free to 104 countries. Currently, the German passport is in first position, providing access to 157 countries, while Afghanistan comes at the other end with 23 countries visa free.

REFERENCES

Achebe, C. (1977). *Dove batte la pioggia*. Milano: Jaca Book.
Amézquita Quintana, C. (2013). Heridas identitarias y búsqueda de reconocimiento en los migrantes colombianos en Nueva York y Nueva Jersey 1990–2010. *Análisis Politico, 26*(79), 73–92.
Arton Capital's Passport Index. (2017). *Index passport 2017*. Retrieved from http://www.passportindex.org/
Betancourt Echeverry, D. (1990, July/December). Las cuadrillas bandoleras del norte del Valle, en la violencia de los años cincuentas. *Revista Historia Crítica, 4,* 57–68.
Castles, S., & Miller, M. J. (2009). *The age of migration: International population movements in the modern world* (4th ed.). Basingstoke & New York, NY: Palgrave Macmillan. (Revised and updated)
Centro de Memoria Histórica. (2013).*¡Basta ya!: Colombia memorias de guerra y dignidad*. Retrieved from http://www.centrodememoriahistorica.gov.co/micrositios/informeGeneral/descargas.html
Coatsworth, H. J. (2003). Roots of violence in Colombia: Armed actors and beyond. *Harvard Review of Latin America*. Retrieved from http://revista.drclas.harvard.edu/book/roots-violence-colombia
Dumitru, S. (2014). From "brain drain" to "care drain": Women's labor migration and methodological sexism. *Women's Studies International Forum, 47,* 203–212. doi:10.1016/j.wsif.2014.06.006
Ellis, C. (2004). *The ethnographic I: A methodological novel about autoethnography*. Walnut Creek, CA: Rowman Altamira.
Federal Research Division. (1988). *Colombia: The 19th of April movement*. Retrieved from http://www.country-data.com/cgi-bin/query/r-3127.html
García Márquez, G. (1967). *Cien años de soledad*. Bogotá: Editorial Sudamericana.
Hernández Pulgarín, G. (2016). Discursos sobre la identidad como recurso adaptativo entre inmigrantes colombianos en Europa. *Migraciones Internacionales, 8*(3), 191–219.
Hristov, J. (2014). *Paramilitarism and neoliberalism: Violent systems of capital accumulation in Colombia and beyond*. London: Pluto Books.
Mahler, S. J. (1998). Theoretical and empirical contributions toward a research agenda for transnationalism. *Transnationalism from Below, 6,* 64–100.
Marin Taborda, J. I. (2005). Historia y violencia en la Colombia contempóranea. In C. Castro Lee (Ed.), *En torno a la violencia en Colombia: una propuesta interdisciplinaria*. Cali: Universidad del Valle.
McCall, G. J. (2003). The me and the not-me: Positive and negative poles of identity. In P. J. Burke, T. J. Owens, R. T. Serpe, & P. A. Thoits (Eds.), *Advances in identity theory and research* (pp. 11–25). New York, NY: Springer.
Ochoa, W. M. (2012). Colombia y las migraciones internacionales. Evolución reciente y panorama actual a partir de las cifras. *Revista Interdisciplinar da Mobilidade Humana, 20*(39), 185–210.
Pécaut, D. (1987). *Orden y violencia: Colombia 1930–1953* (Vol. 1). Bogotá: Siglo Veintiuno Editores.
Pécaut, D., & González, L. (1997). Presente, pasado y futuro de la violencia en Colombia. *Desarrollo Económico, 36*(144), 891–930.
Peñaranda Supelano, D. R. (2010). *El Movimiento Armado Quintín Lame (MAQL): una guerra dentro de otra*. Bogotá: Organización Internacional para las Migraciones (OIM-Misión Colombia).
Ramírez, A. (2016). *Referéndum en Colombia*. Retrieved from https://badwordsofme.wordpress.com/
Ramírez, C., & Mendoza, L. (2013). *Perfil migratorio de Colombia 2012: OIM Colombia*. Bogotá: Organización Internacional para las Migraciones.
Restrepo Vélez, M. O. (2006). *Mujeres colombianas en España: historias, inmigración y refugio*. Bogotá: Pontificia Universidad Javeriana, Instituto Pensar, Editorial Pontificia Universidad Javeriana.

Robinson, J. A. (2015). The misery in Colombia. *Desarrollo y Sociedad, 76,* 9–90.

Rubenstein, R. (2001). *Home matters: Longing and belonging, nostalgia and mourning in women's fiction.* Berlin: Springer.

Rueda Bedoya, R. F. (2000). El desplazamiento forzado y la pacificación del país. *Programa FORHUM.* Medellín: Universidad Nacional de Colombia.

Safford, F., & Palacios, M. (2001). *Colombia: fragmented land, divided society.* Oxford: Oxford University Press.

Sassen, S. (2014). *Expulsions: Brutality and complexity in the global economy.* Cambridge, MA: Harvard University Press.

Semana. (2011). *El fenómeno del anticolombianismo.* Bogotá: Revista Semana.

Snow, D. A., & Anderson, L. (1987). Identity work among the homeless: The verbal construction and avowal of personal identities. *American journal of Sociology, 92*(6), 1336–1371.

Sojo, J. (2009). *Colombia president comes to Washington: Uribe's problematic reelection bid.* Retrieved from http://www.coha.org/colombia-president-comes-to-washington-uribes-problematic-reelection-bid/

Taylor, C. (1994). *Multiculturalism: Examining the politics of recognition* (A. Gutmann, Ed.). Princeton, NJ: Princeton University Press.

Upegui Hernández, D. (2014). *Growing up transnational: Colombian and Dominican children of immigrants in New York City.* El Paso, TX: LFB Scholarly Publishing.

Vasquéz Piñeros, M. d. R. (2007). La iglesia y la violencia bipartidista en Colombia (1946–1953): análisis historiográfico. *Anuario de Historia de la Iglesia, 16,* 309–334.

Wichterich, C. (2000). *The globalized woman: Reports from a future of inequality.* Melbourne: Spinifex Press.

Alexandra Ramírez
Victoria University
Australia

SALLY CLARK

3. RECONSTRUCTING THE TRANSIT EXPERIENCE

A Case Study of Community Development from Cisarua

INTRODUCTION

To live my life that's why I fled my home country. I wish and love to have a peaceful country where I can live my life and use my creative abilities for my society but it has always remained for me a dream. (excerpt from an interview with a young asylum seeker living in transit in Indonesia, 2012)

While philosophers have debated what constitutes 'the good life' for centuries, this metaphysical exercise has found new resonance in current scholarship on refugee movements. As global governance mechanisms continue to falter under the growing humanitarian crisis and states pursue increasingly restrictive border security policies, asylum seekers and refugees are spending longer than ever caught in the intermediate space between displacement and resettlement. Often referred to as transit sites, these spaces become places of passive waiting where all thoughts of meaningful existence are suspended. Asylum seekers are expected to wait out the crisis and be thankful for the forbearance shown by their host state. Expectations on the state to provide services beyond the mere protection of biological life are deemed excessive in a political climate where states are unwilling to expend limited resources or capital on irregular populations in their territory. As a result asylum seekers not only experience physical immobility during this time but are also denied any sense of purpose in their daily lives. In transit, forced migrants enter a type of stasis, a psychic limbo that only ends with third country resettlement. In short, they are not only denied the basic rights afforded to citizens but denied any sense of what Ghassan Hage (2009) terms *existential mobility*, which can be understood as an imagined or felt sense that one's life is going somewhere. This sense of existential mobility is diametrically opposed to what Hage labels 'stuckedness', the state of inertia one experiences when one is lacking in agency. Stuckedness is:

> by definition a situation where a person suffers from both the absence of choices or alternatives to the situation they are in and an inability to grab such alternatives even if they present themselves. (2009, p. 100)

This quality of mind and body is one easily analogous to the conditions forced migrants embody in transit as they are stripped of almost all autonomy and freedoms. Drawing on Hage's notions of 'stuckedness' and 'existential mobility' the

© KONINKLIJKE BRILL NV, LEIDEN, 2018 | DOI:10.1163/9789004381407_003

following chapter explores the lived experiences of a small group of asylum seekers 'waiting out the crisis' in Cisarua, Indonesia as they undertake the UNHCR refugee status determination (RSD) process in one of South East Asia's most prominent transit sites. As ethnographic field research and qualitative interviews conducted over a five year period show, this remarkable group subverts much of the accepted dogma regarding what life in transit can be. Through everyday actions that promote strategies for resistance and survival, these asylum seekers have forged a new community (in their host state) built on solidarity, belonging and a sense of agency. By reconfiguring this typically liminal space into a site of growth, this community has demonstrated that the transit experience can be more than something one must simply survive. As a result, Cisarua serves as a powerful case study for government and policy makers alike as it demonstrates the efficacy of a humanitarian approach to managing displaced populations within a transit/host society. Through positive investments in community programmes that actively support social engagement, governments, NGOs and refugee populations can work together to create safe and inclusive environments for people caught in transit, fostering a sense of purpose and hope that, evidence shows, acts as one of the stronger bulwarks against the temptation of secondary, irregular migration.

The following chapter will explore this further, starting with an exposition of transit migration as a modern phenomenon. It will then review the growing body of research that has explored conditions in transit including a focused look at Indonesia before turning attention towards Cisarua and the strengths and limitations of this community model.

BACKGROUND

Transit (or step) migration has emerged as a significant phenomenon in the 21st century. This is largely in response to the rapid growth in border security and non-arrival regimes implemented by the powerful states of the Global North (Koser, 1997). The targeted closure of borders surrounding traditional refugee receiving states is resulting in the creation of new migration routes, funnelling forced migrants into new regions that lack the appropriate framework for their protection (Gammeltoft-Hansen, 2012; Gerard & Pickering, 2012; Betts, 2006; Garlick, 2006; Papadopoulou, 2004; Koser, 2000).

These spaces become 'transit sites', a type of borderland between refugee creating regions and areas where the Refugee Convention is recognised (Del Sarto, 2009; Gibney, 2005; Papadopoulou, 2004). From the vantage point of the forced migrant these spaces are a legal no-mans-land where they become 'stuck'. These transit sites are most often developing countries, with insufficient reception policies, porous borders and limited resources (Hamood, 2008; Chatelard, 2008; Gil-Bazo, 2006; Garlick, 2006; Legomsky, 2003). They are also defined by the lack of permanent resettlement opportunities for forced migrants due to their lack of acquiescence to the Refugee Convention and other relevant human rights legislation. The lack of permanent resettlement opportunities in these spaces means that, for forced migrants, their time there can only ever be considered temporary. Upon entering these spaces, forced migrants are cognisant of the fact that sooner or later they will either be forced backwards or have to move forward, regardless of whether migration laws in that country allow for that movement to occur (Clark, in press).

Indonesia can be considered an archetypical transit country. Its position between a refugee creating region and a country of significant political and economic gravity (Australia) places it on a well-established migration route for forced migrants. At the time of this research there were an estimated 20,000 forced migrants living in Indonesia, with roughly 13,000 formally registered with UNHCR. This disparate group comprised more than 50 different nationalities, with Afghanis accounting for almost 50 per cent of the total number, but with considerable populations from Pakistan, Iran, Somalia, Myanmar and Sri Lanka present as well.

Porous borders, a lack of resources and corruption facilitates the irregular movement eastward as does the prolific number of people smuggling agents working across the region (Hugo, Tan, & Napitupulu, 2014; Missbach & Sinanu, 2011). Furthermore Indonesia is not party to the Refugee Convention (1951) or the Protocol (1967) which limits its legal obligations to forced migrants in its jurisdiction. The lack of appropriate international human rights legislation eliminates any rights that these forced migrants might have to permanently settle in the country through local integration programs. Yet despite the lack of durable solutions available for forced migrants in Indonesia it is here that their limited mobility, already relegated largely to irregular channels, often comes to an end. This is due in large part to Australia's border security policies that extend far beyond the bounds of the sovereign state into extra-territorial areas (Clark, in press). The totality of Australia's border security apparatus severely limits the possibility of any legal onward migration out of Indonesia. This has the dual effect of immobilising forced migrants before the Australian border and minimising Australia's own obligations under the Refugee Convention, while effectively transforming Indonesia into a migrant processing centre or 'buffer zone' where forced migrants become contained (Clark, in press; Netherly, Rafferty-Brown, & Taylor, 2012; Taylor, 2010). Thus forced migrants transiting through Indonesia find themselves in the precarious position of not being able to return home safely, not being able to move forward legally, yet not being able to stay where they are permanently.

For its part Indonesia does not completely abandon forced migrants in its jurisdiction. Like many other transit sites around the world, Indonesia adopts what can be considered a 'semi-protectionist' position towards forced migrants in its territory, allowing them to remain temporarily while denying them any formal legal status or recognition (Taylor, 2009, 2010; Taylor & Rafferty-Brown, 2010a). Under a Memorandum of Understanding (MoU) with the UNHCR, Indonesia allows the UNHCR to fill the space vacated by the state in terms of the processing of refugee claims. In accordance with regulations outlined by the Indonesian Director General of Immigration, those migrants who indicate their desire to lodge a refugee application are referred by the International Organisation for Migration (IOM) to UNHCR who 'assesses these claims pursuant to its own international mandate' (Taylor & Rafferty-Brown, 2010b, p. 138).

Under these arrangements individuals who register with UNHCR can reside temporarily in Indonesia while their claims are assessed and durable solutions are found (UNHCR Indonesian, 2014). During this time individuals are free to live in the broader community and are not confined to specific refugee camps, unlike the situation in other prominent transit countries. However Indonesia does maintain a network of immigration detention centres (IDC) across the archipelago that forced migrants can find themselves detained in for a variety of arbitrary reasons that, in practice, are both lawful and unlawful.[1] Customary international law protects individuals against 'refoulement' during this period[2] but otherwise registered asylum seekers and Convention Refugees have no formal legal status in Indonesia and are denied almost all basic civil and political rights during this time.

While the capacity to lodge a protection application in a transit site and have one's refugee status assessed goes some way to bridging the gaps in the current international protection framework, these ad hoc arrangements are not without serious limitations. Simply providing an avenue for claim recognition appears futile if this is not matched with durable solutions such as local integration or third country resettlement. With local integration rejected as an option in most transit sites, third country resettlement becomes the primary vehicle for delivering lasting outcomes for displaced people. However UNHCR statistics illustrate that the reliance on resettling people out of transit sites through voluntary third country humanitarian programmes is failing. Less than one per cent of the world's 60 million+ refugee population is resettled through these programmes each year (Phillips, 2011) meaning that for most people undertaking the RSD in transit sites, the wait can span many years, with no guaranteed outcome at the end. All the while people are expected to navigate this time despite the fact that they have little hope of resolving their situation and even fewer rights or protections, making this prolonged period in their lives extremely difficult to sustain (Dowd, 2008).

CONDITIONS IN TRANSIT

Before discussing how asylum seekers in Indonesia have radically reconstructed the transit experience, it is first necessary to elucidate the stereotypical conditions people confront during this time. Drawing on qualitative data from interviews conducted over a five year period from 2011–2016 in Indonesia alongside the broader literature on forced migration and transit sites around the global, the conditions and challenges people face will be outlined before their response to the transit experience is discussed.[3]

For developing states suddenly thrust to the forefront of refugee protection due to their location at the periphery of traditional destination countries, the presence of 'semi-permanent' populations in these jurisdictions can create a number of political and social issues (Gerard & Pickering, 2012; Lutterbeck, 2009; Baldwin-Edwards, 2006; Zhyznomirska, 2006; Papadopoulou, 2005; 2004; Kirisci, 2004). According to the former Assistant High Commissioner for the Protection of Refugees, Erika Feller, 'large scale arrivals are seen as a threat to political, economic or social stability and tend increasingly to provoke hostility and violence' (Feller, 2006, p. 514). Papadopoulou has argued:

> The presence of [an] irregular or semi-legal population can reinforce intolerance and xenophobic trends towards migrants in the country in general, and impede the process of integration of the resident migrant populations. (2005, p. 15)

As developing states grapple with the challenges associated with becoming a transit site on the road to asylum, it is the migrant communities themselves that tend to suffer disproportionately due to these 'burden shifting' arrangements. Beyond the protracted waiting period and the lack of resettlement positions outlined above, research conducted in prominent transit sites around the world including Spain (Johnson, 2013), Greece (Papadopoulou, 2004) Morocco (Baldwin-Edwards, 2006; Collyer, 2007), Jordan (Chatelard, 2008), Malta (Gerard & Pickering, 2012; Lutterbeck, 2009; Luhmann, Bouhenia, & Giraux, 2007), Turkey (Kirisci, 2004; Icduygu, 2000) and Libya (Hamood, 2008; Baubakri, 2004) demonstrate a number of reoccurring themes. These include major discrepancies in recognition rates of asylum applications across transit sites, ad hoc processing systems, lack of legal protections and human rights standards, and severe social isolation whilst in transit, all of which contribute to extreme levels of vulnerability during this stage of migration. This insecurity is further exacerbated by governments classifying asylum seekers in their territory as 'non-citizens', a positioning that places forced migrants outside of the usual judicial order and the protection it affords citizens under the common law. This makes them exceptionally susceptible to many forms of mistreatment, such as exploitation in the informal labour market, as victims of crime, state corruption, extrajudicial detainment or sexual exploitation and abuse, even refoulement.

The situation for asylum seekers in Indonesia reflects these broader themes. Studies that have explored the conditions asylum seekers confront while in transit in Indonesia point to the length and ad hoc nature of the RSD process, the lack of transparency and consistency in the outcomes, the arbitrary use of immigration detention, the fear of refoulement, often presented as 'voluntary returns', financial exploitation, police corruption and the repeated violation of their basic human rights both inside and outside of immigration detention (Dodd & Horn, 2013; Missbach, 2012; HRW, 2013; Taylor, 2009, 2010a, 2010b; Taylor & Rafferty-Brown, 2010a). Beyond the judicial neglect of the state and the failure to implement appropriate reception policies, many asylum seekers in Indonesia also suffer as a result of material deprivation (Dodd & Horn, 2013; Missbach, 2012; HRW, 2013; Taylor, 2009, 2010a; Taylor & Rafferty-Brown, 2010a, 2010b). The lack of work rights, for example, creates endless challenges for asylum seekers expected to reside in Indonesia for many years without any way to financially support themselves. This material deprivation manifests in many ways with participants in this study making frequent references to challenges including the inability to attain affordable housing, to access suitable health care and to feed and clothe their families, all of which forces individuals into a state of economic dependency while depriving them of their sense of autonomy and dignity during this time. While participants in this research navigated these challenges (along with a myriad of others) with varying degrees of success and resilience, the one issue that appeared to really push people past their point of endurance was the psychological and emotional deterioration this state of abjection induced. As one informant put it:

> People are aware that they have no future in Indonesia but also that they have no short term prospects either. People there are like smoke in the air, a gust of wind could take them anywhere. (Australian NGO worker, 2013)

One asylum seeker, who had been in Indonesia for fifteen months at the time of his interview, stated poignantly, 'I feel like my humanity has died here' (Male participant, age 28, 2012). Statements such as these illuminate the most fundamental challenge asylum seekers must overcome – the incremental destruction of self through the specific targeting and denial of all rights and personhood in the transit space, manifesting the state of 'stuckedness' described by Hage. With no meaningful activities to pass their day and no distractions from the untenable conditions, asylum seekers had nothing to do but obsess over their refugee applications and worry. In short they were reduced to a state of mere biological existence without purpose or meaning. These findings are congruent with previous research that has been conducted in this area with Taylor and Rafferty-Brown (2010, p. 573), who label this phenomenon 'dying by degrees', while Missbach (2016) summarises the situation for forced migrants in Indonesia as feeling like their life has been put on hold. She states:

> The time of waiting can be prolonged and uncertain, and often accompanied by constant anxiety. Lack of protection, uncertainty, ambiguity and contingency shape life in transit and make people vulnerable to many risks and threats. The emotions that arise from the experience of being trapped in limbo can be as influential on people's lives as legal restrictions and policy frameworks ... In short, poverty, insufficient protection, unemployment and social exclusion are the main characteristics of a life in transit. (Missbach, 2016, p. 18)

The language of participants and other scholars is not only reminiscent of Hage's (2009) notion of 'stuckedness' but of the existential philosophy it is inspired by. Central to this perspective is the normative premise that full personhood can only be achieved through the act of doing something, and that without this one cannot exist. To existential philosopher Simone de Beauvoir, for example, "there is no justification for present existence other than its expansion into an indefinitely open future" (1997, pp. 28–29). Yet it is this sense of purpose so central to human existence that the transit experience so thoroughly destroys. Upon entering this space forced migrants are expected to abandon any and all desires for the attainment of full personhood and be content with the repetition of biological life without meaning, a state criticised by Beauvoir:

> Along with the ethical urge of each individual to affirm his subjective existence, there is also the temptation to forgo liberty and become a thing. This is an inauspicious road, for he who takes it – passive, lost, ruined – becomes henceforth the creature of another's will, frustrated by his transcendence and deprived of every value. (Beauvoir, 1997, p. 21)

It is understandable, in light of the extreme physical and material deprivation people are exposed to in transit, that attention to the more ephemeral aspects of life are often sidelined by governments, NGO's and individuals alike. However, it is increasingly evident that the relegation of the psychological needs of forced migrants contributes significantly to poor outcomes for all.[4] The lack of purpose in everyday life arrests any belief that individuals may have that their life is 'going somewhere' and therefore has meaning. Evidence suggests that it is this abandonment of hope and meaning that has, in the past, led forced migrants away from the RSD process, choosing instead to embark on irregular migration despite the clear risks associated with this course of action. As one asylum seeker stated bluntly:

> It's a very big decision to take, it's about fifty-fifty whether you make it or you die under the water. (Male participant, age 37, 2013)

Despite the known dangers associated with irregular migration, participants in this research repeatedly stated that they would prefer to risk dying 'doing something', than continue to endure the slow death they perceived was happening to them in Indonesia. In this regard the participant's sentiments echoed a number of findings from other studies around the world, where irregular migration has been identified as a common strategy used by desperate people to transcend the conditions in transit sites and reach territories where the Refugee Convention is ratified and refugees' rights are protected (Koser, 2000, 1997). In short, irregular migration becomes viewed as a way for individuals to overcome their stuckedness and attain a sense of existential mobility through the act of 'reaching towards greater liberties'.

In Australia the effects of this pattern were evident with the increased frequency of irregular maritime arrivals from 2008–2013. For example in 2013 a record 20,587 asylum seekers arrived in Australia irregularly, most of whom had departed from Indonesia with the assistance of people smugglers (Phillips, 2014). Given the increased frequency of irregular migration and the highly politicised nature of 'boat arrivals' in Australia's domestic politics (Mckay, Thomas, & Kneebone, 2011; Saxon, 2003), by 2013 efforts to stem this movement had reached a crescendo with increasingly punitive policies being implemented (Grewcock, 2014, 2013). The election of the new federal Coalition government in September 2013 saw the introduction of 'Operation Sovereign Borders', a paramilitary unit tasked with physically intercepting and turning back boats to Indonesian territory. This was in conjunction with a raft of other policy changes designed to deny all legal rights to asylum for people who had arrived in Australia irregularly by sea (Grewcock, 2014).

With the intensification of border controls and the removal of permanent resettlement rights, the Australian government effectively shut down the unregulated migration channel between the two states by removing any incentive asylum seekers might have to make the crossing. This redoubling of Australia's containment efforts had the desired effect of reducing the number of onshore arrivals with whom it must deal, while simultaneously exacerbating Indonesia's protection responsibilities. For the estimated 11,000 asylum seekers caught in transit in Indonesia at the time of these changes (Missbach & Brown, 2016) the new reality was stark: they could return to their country of origin (which participants viewed as a certain death sentence) or prepare for an indefinite future in Indonesia as an unwanted stranger in a foreign land.

TRANSIT TRANSFORMED

While the intractability of this situation could reasonably be expected to amplify the desperation and despair that already engulfed people in transit, in the small town of Cisarua (about 50km south-west of Jakarta) the community responded in a manner that defied all expectations. Rather than submit themselves to their given conditions, they banded together to reshape their existence and create a community capable of nourishing its members, both physically and emotionally.

As noted above, one of the major hurdles for people to overcome was the overwhelming sense that their lives were meaningless and simply passing them by due to the harsh conditions imposed upon them in the transit space. While this caused individuals a great deal of distress, this feeling was clearly amplified for those with children. Participants in this study reported feeling like it was 'too late' for them but that they needed to do something to change the situation for their children to ensure they did not suffer the same fate; growing up stateless, without an education and with no hope for a better life. It was this overwhelming desire to create a meaningful future for their children that led a small group of adults to come together to create an environment where their children could be educated, providing them with structure and a sense of normalcy (Clark & Copolov, 2016). While it is not technically illegal for refugee children to attend an Indonesian school, a range of social and economic reasons made it almost inevitable that they did not. As for many of the adults at the time, parents often noted that the lack of meaningful activities for the children meant they were sleeping for large parts of the day and were showing clear signs of depression resulting from their stuckedness.

Determined to counteract this, the group was able to secure a small premises in town to set up a classroom, and began teaching children in their immediate vicinity after gaining the support of the local Indonesian administrator in 2014. With limited resources available to them people began to volunteer their time in any way they could, by taking up the role of educators, by helping to maintain the premises or simply by ensuring children were able to get to the school and had food to eat. This quickly attracted the attention of many other refugees and asylum seekers living in the surrounding regions and drew people to the area. As one mother stated:

> When we were in Jakarta, my children were doing nothing, sleeping all of the day not doing anything. Then I heard from a friend of mine that there was a meeting and they were thinking of opening a school so I rushed there and moved, because their education is important to me. (Female participant, age 31, 2015)

As the initiative began to grow the leadership group capitalised on their social media skills, promoting the benefits of their school to international audiences. Though they receive no formal government funding, the group garnered the support of civil society and were able to secure philanthropic support from a number of groups outside of Indonesia, including Australian teachers who worked closely with the group to develop a suitable curriculum for the children to follow. The use of social media to raise much needed funds also helped the group upgrade their facility to larger premises that could house more classrooms and access much needed supplies like textbooks and other learning materials for the children.

From these humble beginning the Cisarua Refugee Learning Centre (CRLC) was born. Starting with only a handful of students in August 2014, the school now supports 120 students per semester. It boasts 12 permanent teachers and 6 administrators comprised entirely of refugees from the community and has a revolving army of volunteers from around the world. The children undertake a classic curriculum including Maths, English, Art and Science. The school also promotes a model of good citizenship through its emphasis on the social values of healthy living, mutual respect and equality. One of the founding members of the CRLC, a former asylum seeker and UN worker from Afghanistan (who has since been resettled in a third country) reflects on his motivation for establishing the school:

> I got involved in the school first because I thought refugees will start working together around educational purposes and that is the most realistic goal we could achieve with limited resources. (Male participant, age 36, 2016)

Through these efforts this small group was able to fundamentally transform their immediate environment into a place of significant social belonging with the school at the centre of this project. While this may seem trifling, to make the conscious decision to enter the public sphere in this manner should be understood in its context as nothing other than radical and a total reversal of the conventional wisdom on how best to survive the transit experience in Indonesia. This was a place that asylum seekers and refugees had traditionally understood to be dangerous and hostile to their presence – a belief supported by numerous accounts of abuse, torture and even death (HRW, 2013; Ahang, 2012; Amnesty International, 2012). As a result forced migrants had traditionally done everything in their power to avoid drawing attention to themselves and eschewed public interaction as best they could.

> We would not leave the house, we were too scared. We would stay indoors all the time. We thought we would be caught by police and they would send us home or put us in detention. It got so bad that when we ran out of food we would argue – whose turn is it to go buy the food; we were all that scared of going out. (Male participant, age 21, 2012)

To move into the public sphere in such a pronounced fashion was therefore a risky endeavour. A number of key actors in this project confided that they were cognisant of the risks in the beginning, noting that they were worried that they might provoke a negative response from the Indonesian authorities or that their involvement in the school might negatively impact upon their chances of being successfully resettled through the UNHCR process. However the school leaders were able to develop a strong relationship with local officials and eventually even gained the tacit support of the UNHCR.

The impact the centre has had on its students is astronomical. The structure and focus it provides offers them a semblance of normal life and re-establishes basic rites of passage central to childhood, inoculating against the dehumanising conditions otherwise experienced in transit, as the comments by one of their nine year old students demonstrates:

> I do remember the day when I first heard about the school. My home was close to the school and my mother told me I will also go to school soon. On the first day I made two friends. Now I have many friends and some of them are my best friends. Since I came to the school I feel really good. After school hours sometimes I go to my friends' houses and play with them. It was something I was missing since we fled from our country. (Female participant, age 9, 2015)

While the school has clearly helped its students, the positive benefits stretch far beyond this. Adults who have become involved in the everyday running of the CRLC have also benefited from the structure it provides and the social interaction it facilitates. One of the younger teachers working at the school articulated the impact that this has had on her after she tearfully recounted the excitement she felt after first being invited to be a teacher at the school:

> When I am teaching the kids, I forget that we are living a difficult life as refugees. Being a refugee, I never thought that I will ever be able to be a teacher, to meet different people and gain invaluable experience. (Female participant, age 19, 2015)

Not only does the school distract people from the banality of life in transit but actually gives people the opportunity to expand and grow as individuals, as one of the senior leader of the school states:

> Yes of course, we are more than happy and satisfied, I mean I am a teacher here, when I see my kids come, it helps, it's … helped a lot of refugees, it's brought out the refugees from detention, their time will not be wasted here, at

least for three or four years, if they have to wait here, at least they will still have the opportunity to get an education and to learn something. It's one of the releases for the people. (Female participant, 31, 2015)

For every educational benefit the school provided there were numerous social dividends, as the educational centre quickly transformed a number of disparate and isolated individuals into a community with shared life experiences, challenges, aspirations and hopes. The CRLC became the centre of the community, and became a source of pride that reflected the determination, resourcefulness and resilience of refugees. Acting as a beacon of hope it drew more refugees to the area and established a connection to place in an area that had once been perceived as inhospitable and the antithesis of belonging. Whereas once Cisarua could best be described as a space asylum seekers gravitated towards due to its promise of rural anonymity it now boasts an international reputation as a thriving example of what refugee communities can achieve with appropriate support.

Inspired by the success of the CRLC and attuned to the demand, numerous other refugee-led learning centres opened in Cisarua and the surrounding regions, further entrenching 'access to education' as a central organising principle moving forward for refugees in Indonesia. With this new epicentre flourishing, numerous other community initiatives followed in quick succession. These included the establishment of a number of sporting teams, from a dojo to men's, women's and mixed football teams, who play regularly and even hold friendly matches against local Indonesian clubs; a women's social network that provides a meeting space for refugee women to come together to discuss particular challenges they face, ranging from reproductive health to family issues; an interpreter training programme that draws on the talent of bilingual community members to create a network of translators who can accompany people to medical appointments or UNHCR interviews; and a handicrafts group that provides a creative outlet while also giving people the opportunity to make a small amount of money by selling their products at the local bazaars, just to name a few. While diverse in nature all these initiatives reflect the basic tenets of a ground up approach to community development from which a greater sense of purpose and belonging can emerge organically, counteracting the dehumanising conditions that were previously imposed on people caught in transit.

Many of the schools, including the CRLC, also rapidly expanded their mission, teaching children in the morning and teenagers in the afternoon, while hosting adult beginner, intermediate and advanced English classes in the evening. They have also been successful in forging close ties with the local Indonesian community; beyond the sporting field this includes the schools hosting local Indonesian students of all ages as part of cultural exchanges and often doing joint excursions and events with the local Indonesian children. Refugees are now also taking it upon themselves to learn Bahasa Indonesian, a sure indicator that refugees are moving from the fringes of society and engaging more readily with those around them.

While these acts may seem trivial, this is a far cry from the hostility that existed only years earlier, with local Indonesians being suspicious of these 'outsiders' in their community and refugees remaining hidden as best they could out of fear of violence or exploitation. For example, following a number of physical attacks on asylum seekers in the Cisarua area a number of NGOs who were housing asylum seekers in the region were forced to relocate those in their care back to Jakarta due to security concerns (Indonesian NGO representative, 2013). In the wake of this a report published by the Australian Immigration department claimed that 'Indonesia faces worsening public-order problems unless steps are taken to isolate asylum seekers from the general community' (Alford & Nathala, 2013). These growing tensions even led one Indonesian minister to propose the creation of a separate island where forced migrants could be interred 'to avoid social jealousy from local communities and to reduce potential negative impacts from the presence of irregular migrants and their social interactions'(Alford & Nathala, 2013).

It is examples like these that make the progress of this community so remarkable. They have not only succeeded in transforming their own daily lives but they have also challenged and reshaped attitudes toward refugees in the broader Indonesian community, creating new solidarities and connections where once there was only fear and hostility. It is this group's reconfiguration of the material world and the social relations around them that has drastically transformed the transit space. These engagements with the broader Indonesian society have challenged the socio-cultural boundaries that traditionally separated forced migrants from the broader community, allowing forced migrants to transcend their stuckedness and enter the public realm more fully.

Despite these positive developments, under the surface many of the structural challenges continue to plague individuals; anxiety regarding their application, the desperation for family reunion and monetary pressures chief among them. These burgeoning community initiatives cannot combat these realities and life as an irregular migrant in a foreign land will continue to pose serious challenges for those who must endure it. However, as this community demonstrates, small changes can go a long way to improving the lives of those effected insofar as it can alleviate the feelings associated with stuckedness and restore in people a sense of purpose or belief that their lives have meaning. This has profound implications for the health and well-being of individuals but also, I argue, can contribute to achieving policy outcomes in terms of reducing the allure of irregular migration by providing support structures for people attempting to navigate the RSD in Indonesia. Participants in this study clearly indicated that they did not want to turn to irregular migration and that they were committed to the official UNHCR pathway but that they needed support in this endeavour.

Furthermore, this model of community empowerment sits at the rare nexus between being ethically palatable and economically rational. With relatively small government investment, asylum seekers in Indonesia could be given access to affordable and stable housing, run educational programs for children and continue to promote support services and initiatives that foster social engagement and personal development. All of this has the dual effect of supporting vulnerable people through a difficult time whilst also helping to prepare people for life post-resettlement. This approach deeply contrasts with the current method favoured by governments like Australia which prioritises expensive paramilitary operations that use physical force and coercion to deter irregular migration from Indonesia (Grewcock, 2014). As one asylum seeker stated:

> I think that the Australian Government has been spending not millions but billions of dollars now on putting people into offshore detention centres, if rather they directed that money to UNHCR to care for and shelter asylum seekers ... If they provided, not very good, but reasonable accommodation and other recreational things they would obviously wait – they don't want to take this perilous ride if they know the wait is certain. (Male participant, age 35, 2013)

The effectiveness of community based initiatives in providing a bulwark against the lure of people smugglers should not be underestimated. Whether it is improving themselves or helping others, the sense of purpose that these activities restore in people provides mental resilience and is capable of transforming a protracted wait into a meaningful life in the present and combatting the slow social death that previously defined the transit experience.

LIMITS TO THE SELF-SUFFICIENCY NARRATIVE

It is clear that supporting forced migrants in a manner that allows people to be socially engaged and maintain a sense of autonomy while in transit has many benefits. However it is imperative to not romanticise these narratives lest a misleading account of the transit experience is replicated that reinforces the current lack of urgency for resettlement from the destination countries. Once more Hage's (2009) conception of existential mobility and stuckedness are useful analytical frames for understanding the limitations of an approach that values this self-organisation to the detriment of focusing on broader structural change.

Hage argues that the state of stuckedness, rather than being deplored and deplorable, has instead been scripted as a litmus test for heroism. It is viewed culturally as a sign of resilience owing to ones 'capacity to stick it out' (2009, p. 100). This 'celebration of the human spirit to endure' hardship (2009, p. 102) functions as a regulatory tool for governments as it 'encourages a mode of restraint, self-control and self-government in times of crisis' (2009, p. 102). This impulse is visible in the Cisarua case study whereby the resilience and self-sufficiency of this community is celebrated thereby deflecting attention away from the tremendous suffering they are expected to endure in the face of cruel policies and state neglect.

The creation of a more tolerable transit space through the hard fought efforts of asylum seekers is a positive development. However it should not be used as an excuse for governments to remain disengaged or to further disengage from their responsibilities to protect displaced people. Nor should they use these advances as justification for restricting much needed economic support or limiting avenues to permanent resettlement due to modest improvements in the everyday lives of forced migrants.

This normative expectation that forced migrants should 'weather the crisis' that is the transit experience is by no means unique to Cisarua and it is a position reflected in the popular discourse on refugee movements globally. In Australia there is an established political history of valorising refugees who 'wait out the crisis' – oft constructed as the 'good and deserving' refugees patiently waiting to be selected for resettlement in camps around the world contrasted against the 'bad or undeserving' asylum seeker who is unwilling to endure the crucible and instead takes it upon themselves to arrive irregularly (and uninvited) (Mckay, Thomas, & Kneebone, 2011). The narrative of endurance and 'weathering the crisis' can ironically be seen to distort the usual neoliberal order of rewarding those who seek to transcend themselves and their current conditions by equating the passivity of waiting with a nobleness of the human spirit and autonomous action with a deficiency of willpower.

The irony in this is that these forms of community organisation that enable asylum seekers to transcend their sense of stuckedness and regain a sense of existential mobility while in transit actually draw on, and potentially reinforce, the narrative trope of heroism in 'weathering the crisis' that governments have instrumentalised to justify their withdrawal from this space. It is therefore important to temper the celebration of the self-sufficiency demonstrated by refugees in Cisarua with a degree of scepticism. It is incumbent that governments (those of host nations and resettlement destinations alike) do not withdraw further from this space. To truly address this issue, host states must play an active role in ensuring the rights of all people in their territory are protected, while destination countries must play a bigger role in financially supporting over-burdened transit countries to ensure asylum seekers and refugees who are navigating official resettlement pathways have access to basic needs during this time and that resettlement positions are made available to people undertaking this process. This case study demonstrates that with small monetary investment the lives of asylum seekers and refugees can be positively transformed and transit spaces can be radically reconfigured into places of belonging and sites of significant meaning where once there was only suffering and despair. Furthermore programs that support vulnerable people during this time have the power to inoculate against the exploitation of people smugglers, as numerous members of the community noted. However it is imperative that these gains do not justify government inaction.

CONCLUSION

It seems unlikely that restrictive migration barriers will recede or access to asylum become more tangible in a world retreating to nationalism and protectionism. With this paradigm it is reasonable to assume that transit migration will continue to play a major role in the forced migration journey. As the global refugee crisis increases in severity and more people are displaced from their homes, it is likely that the time spent in transit will also increase and transit sites will continue to be stretched in terms of their capacity to host large groups of irregular migrants. The example from Indonesia demonstrates that the transit experience can be one plagued by state neglect, social isolation, hopelessness and decline. But it also shows that this is malleable; people undertaking RSD processing do not have to enter a form of purgatory, waiting years for their 'normal' lives to begin. By investing in people and community the transit experience can actually be one of personal growth, a place where new skills are developed and harnessed for the good of all. It can be a place of healing and preparation for life after resettlement. While there will always be limitations to this impact due to the nature of displacement stemming from war, trauma and family separation, the Cisarua case study demonstrates that if people are able to pursue meaningful activities throughout their time in transit and achieve a sense of belonging then one of the most damaging aspects of forced displacement, the dehumanising stuckedness of biological life without meaning, can be counteracted.

NOTES

[1] See Taylor (2009) for a detailed account of conditions inside Indonesia's detention centres.

[2] Article 33 of the 1951 Refugee Convention states that no contracting state shall expel or return (refouler) a refugee in any manner whatsoever to the frontiers of territories where his life or freedom would be threatened on account of his race, religion, nationality, membership of a particular social group or political opinion. This principle has now entered into customary international law, making it binding on signatory and non-signatory states alike.

[3] This data was collected as part of a larger study that was investigating factors driving registered asylum seekers and Convention refugees to abandon UNHCR Indonesia and the official RSD pathway in favour of irregular migration to Australia.

[4] Alarmingly, participants' narratives regarding the psychological impact that conditions in transit were having upon them tended to echo much of the psychological literature concerned with the emotional wellbeing and deterioration of people in immigration detention (for example see Silove, Austin, & Steel, 2007; Steel, Silove, Brooks, Momartin, Alzuhairi, & Susljik, 2006; Silove, Steel, & Watters, 2000).

REFERENCES

Ahang, B. (2012, February 29). *Indonesia: An Afghani refugee died due to police torture*. Retrieved September 13, 2013, from http://www.basirahang.com/?P=78

Amnesty International. (2012). *Indonesia: Asylum seeker tortured to death in detention*. Retrieved September 18, 2013, from http://www.amnesty.org.au/news/comments/28033/

Baldwin-Edwards, M. (2006). Between a rock and a hard place: North Africa as a region of emigration, immigration and transit migration. *Review of African Political Economy, 108*, 311–324.

Beauvoir, S. (1997). *The second sex* (M. M. Parshley, Trans.). London: Vintage Publishing.

Betts, A. (2006). Towards a mediterranean solution? Implication for the region of origin. *International Journal of Refugee Law, 18*(3–4), 652–676.

Boubakri, H. (2004, October). *Transit migration between Tunisia, Libya and Sub-Saharan Africa: Study based on greater Tunis*. Paper presented at Council of Europe Regional Conference on Migrants in Transit Countries: Sharing Responsibility for Management and Protection, Istanbul.

Chatelard, G. (2008). Iraqi asylum migrants in Jordan: Conditions, religious networks and the smuggling process. In G. Borjas & J. Crisp (Eds.), *Poverty, international migration and asylum, studies in development economics and policy* (pp. 341–370). Basingstoke: Palgrave Macmillan.

Clark, S. (in press). Non-arrival regimes & the making of transit sites: Australia's efforts to exclude asylum seekers. In M. Karakoulaki, L. Southgate, & J. Steiner (Eds.), *Climbing walls – Crossing lines: Critical perspectives on migration in the 21st century.* Bristol: E-International Relations. Retrieved from http://www.e-ir.info

Clark, S., & Copolov, C. (2016, March 8). Refugee-run school in Indonesia a model for governments to emulate. *The Conversation.* Retrieved from https://theconversation.com/refugee-run-school-in-indonesia-a-model-for-governments-to-emulate-55378

Collyer, M. (2007). In-between places: Tran-Saharan transit migrants in Morocco and the fragmented journey to Europe. *Antipode, 39*(4), 668–690.

Del Sarto, R. (2009). Borderlands: The Middle East and North Africa as the EU's Southern Buffer Zone. In D. Bechev & K. Nicolaidis (Eds.), *Mediterranean Frontiers: Borders, conflicts and memory in a transnational world.* London: Oxford University Press.

Dodd, A., & Horn, C. (2013, October 13). Australia's waiting room: Why they board boats in Indonesia. *Crikey.* Retrieved from http://www.crikey.com.au/2013/02/13/inside-australias-waiting-room-why-they-board-boats-in-indonesia/

Dowd, R. (2008). *Trapped in transit: The plight and human rights of stranded migrants* (New Issues in Refugee Research, Research Paper No. 156). Retrieved August 24, 2017, from http://www.unhcr.org/en-au/research/working/486c92d12/trapped-transit-plight-human-rights-stranded-migrants-rebecca-dowd.html?query=transit

Feller, E. (2006). Asylum, migration and refugee protection: Realities, myths and the promise of things to come. *International Journal of Refugee Law, 18*(3–4), 509–536.

Gammeltoft-Hansen, T. (2012). Outsourcing asylum: The advent of protection lite. In L. Bialasiewicz (Ed.), *Europe in the world: EU geopolitics and the making of European space.* Surrey: Ashgate Publishing.

Garlick, M. (2006). The EU discussion on extraterritorial processing: Solution or conundrum? *International Journal of Refugee Law, 18*(3–4), 601–629.

Gerard, A., & Pickering, S. (2012). The crime and punishment of Somali Women's extra-legal arrival in Malta. *British Journal of Criminology, 52,* 514–533.

Gibney, M. (2005). *Beyond the bounds of responsibility: Western states and measures to prevent the arrival of refugees* (Global Migration Perspectives, No. 22). Geneva: Global Commission on International Migration.

Gil-Bazo, M. (2006). The practice of the mediterranean states in the context of the European Union's justice and home affairs external dimension: The safe third country concept revisited. *International Journal of Refugee Law, 18*(3), 571–600.

Grewcock, M. (2013). Australia's ongoing border wars. *Race & Class, 54*(3), 10–31.

Grewcock, M. (2014). Australian border policing: Regional 'solutions' and neocolonialism. *Race & Class, 55*(3), 71–78.

Hage, G. (2009). Waiting out the crisis: On stuckedness and governmentality. In G. Hage (Ed.), *Waiting* (pp. 97–106). Carlton: Melbourne University Press.

Hamood, S. (2008). EU-Libya cooperation on migration: A raw deal for refugees and migrants? *Journal of Refugee Studies, 21*(1), 19–42.

Hugo, G., Tan, G., & Napitupulu, J. (2014). *Indonesia as a transit country in irregular migration to Australia* (Irregular Migration Research Programme Occasional Paper Series). Retrieved January 23, 2015, from http://www.immi.gov.au/pub-res/Documents/research/indonesia-transit-country.pdf

Human Rights Watch. (2013). *Barely surviving: Detention, abuse, and neglect of migrant children in Indonesia.* Retrieved September 13, 2013, from http://www.hrw.org

Icduygu, A. (2000). The politics of international migratory regimes: Transit migration flows in Turkey. *International Social Science Journal, 52*(165), 357–367.

Johnson, H. (2013). The other side of the fence: Reconceptualising the "camp" and migration zones at the border of Spain. *International Political Sociology, 7,* 75–91.

Kirisci, K. (2004). *Reconciling refugee protection with efforts to combat irregular migration: The case of Turkey and the European Union* (Global Migration Perspectives No. 11). Geneva: Global Commission on International Migration.

Koser, K. (1997). Negotiating entry into fortress Europe: The migration strategies of "spontaneous" asylum seekers. In P. Muun (Ed.), *Exclusion and inclusion of refugees in contemporary Europe* (pp. 157–70). Utrecht: ERCOMER.

Koser, K. (2000). Asylum policies, trafficking and vulnerability. *International Migration, 38*(3), 91–111.

Legomsky, S. (2003). Secondary refugee movements and the return of asylum seekers to third countries: The meaning of effective protection. *International Journal of Refugee Law, 15*(4), 567–677.

Luhmann, N., Bouhenia, M., & Giraux, F. (2007). *Everybody tries to get rid of us: Access to health care and human rights of asylum seekers in Malta: Experiences, results and recommendations.* Paris: Medecins Du Monde.

Lutterbeck, D. (2009). Small Frontier Island: Malta and the challenge of irregular immigration. *Mediterrianean Quarterly, 20*(1), 119–144.

McKay, F., Thomas, S., & Kneebone, S. (2011) 'It would be okay if they came through the proper channels': Community perceptions and attitudes towards asylum seekers in Australia. *Journal of Refugee Studies, 25*(1), 113–133.

Missbach, A. (2012). Easy pickings: The plight of asylum seekers in Indonesia. *Asian Currents.* Retrieved from http://www.asaa.asn.au/publications/ac/2012/asian-currents-12-06.pd

Missbach, A. (2016). *Troubled transit: Asylum seekers stuck in Indonesia.* Singapore: ISEAS Publishers.

Missbach, A., & Brown, T. (2016). The boats may have "stopped" but more refugees are stuck in limbo in Indonesia. *The Conversation.* Retrieved August 24, 2016, from https://theconversation.com/the-boats-may-have-stopped-but-more-refugees-are-stuck-in-limbo-in-indonesia-56152

Missbach, A., & Sinanu, F. (2011). "The scum of the earth?" Foreign people smugglers and their local counterparts in Indonesia. *Journal of Current Southeast Asian Affairs, 30*(4), 57–87.

Missbach, A., & Sinanu, F. (2013, July–September). Life and death in immigration detention. *Inside Indonesia,* p. 113. Retrieved April 20, 2015, from http://www.insideindonesia.org/life-and-death-in-immigration-detention

Netherly, A., Rafferty-Brown, B., & Taylor, S. (2012). Exporting detention: Australia funded immigration detention in Indonesia. *Journal of Refugee Studies, 26*(1), 88–109.

Papadopoulou, A. (2004). Smuggling into Europe: Transit migrants in Greece. *Journal of Refugee Studies, 17*(2), 167–184.

Papadopoulou, A. (2005). *Exploring the asylum-migration nexus: A case study of transit migration in Europe* (Global Migration Perspectives No. 23). Geneva: Global Commission on International Migration.

Phillips, J. (2011). *Asylum seekers: What are the facts?* Canberra: Parliament of Australia. Retrieved February 17, 2015, from http://www.aph.gov.au/binaries/library/pubs/bn/sp/asylumfacts.pdf

Phillips, J. (2014). *Boat arrivals in Australia: A quick guide to the statistics.* Canberra: Parliament of Australia. Retrieved February 17, 2015, from http://www.aph.gov.au/About_Parliament/Parliamentary_Departments/Parliamentary_Library/pubs/rp/rp1314/QG/BoatArrivals

Saxon, A. (2003). "I certainly don't want people like that here": The discursive construction of asylum seekers. *Media International Australia, 109,* 109–120.

Silove, D., Austin, P., & Steel, Z. (2007). No refuge from terror: The impact of detention on the mental health of trauma-affected refugees seeking asylum in Australia. *Transcult Psychiatry, 44*(3), 359–393.

Silove, D., Steel, Z., & Watters, C. (2000). Policies of deterrence and mental health of asylum seekers. *Journal of American Medical Association, 322*(5), 604–611.

Steel, Z., Silove, D., Brooks, R., Momartin, S., Alzuhairi, B., & Susljik, I. (2006). Impact of immigration detention and temporary protection on the mental health of refugees. *British Journal of Psychiatry, 188,* 58–64.

Taylor, J. (2009). *Behind Australian doors: Examining the conditions of detention of asylum seekers in Indonesia.* Retrieved November 3, 2010, from http://www.behindaustraliandoors.worldpress.com

Taylor, S. (2010). Australian funded care and maintenance of asylum seekers in Indonesia and Papua New Guinea: All care but no responsibility. *UNSW Law Journal, 33*(2), 337–359.

Taylor, S., & Rafferty-Brown, B. (2010a). Difficult journeys: Accessing refugee protection in Indonesia. *Monash University Law Review, 36*(3), 138–161.

Taylor, S., & Rafferty-Brown, B. (2010b). Waiting for life to begin: The plight of asylum seekers caught by Australia's Indonesian solution. *International Journal of Refugee Law, 22*(4), 558–592.

UNHCR. (2014). *Indonesian fact sheet*. Retrieved September 22, 2015, from http://www.unhcr.org/50001bda9.pdf

Zhyznomirska, L. (2006). Externalities of the EU immigration and asylum policy: The case of Ukraine. *Review of European and Russian Affairs, 2*(2), 30–55.

Sally Clark
Swinburne University
Australia

PAOLA BILBROUGH

4. THE UNLIMITED REFUGEE

The Politics of Race and Refugee-ness in Two Screen
Representations of Sudanese Australians

INTRODUCTION

Over the last decade Sudanese Australians have been routinely represented by the Australian media as threatening cultural others who are incompatible with a normative white Australian identity. This orientalising trope, which has largely portrayed young men as gang members, has been widely evidenced in a body of research (Due, 2008; Windle, 2008; Nolan & Farquharson et al., 2011; Nunn, 2012). However, in mid 2015 a television advertisement for Western Sydney University, *Deng Thiak Adut Unlimited,* went viral on Youtube, and eponymous star, Sudanese-born Deng Adut, received extensive media attention. The focus of the advertisement and subsequent media coverage (see Thomsen, 2015; Mottram, 2015; Dapin, 2016) was Adut's trajectory from child soldier and refugee to successful Sydney lawyer. Screen, print and social media responded to the affective power of *Unlimited* with one journalist claiming, "This extraordinary and moving ad for an Australian university is like nothing you've ever seen before" (Thomsen, 2015). To date *Deng Thiak Adut Unlimited*, which evokes a Hollywood tearjerker in both narrative structure and production values, has garnered over 2.5 million views.

From one perspective, *Unlimited* is simply a universal story of loss, courage and redemption delivered in less than one and a half minutes. An interpretation of *Unlimited*, that might be considered the "preferred" or "dominant" reading (Hall, 1980), frames Australia as a welcoming place of racial equality. Yet this narrative is marred by the way that belonging is ultimately withheld from the protagonist. Despite Adut arriving in Australia at least fifteen years ago, the advertisement privileges his refugee-ness, framing him as a hero-other who has triumphed over adversity through exemplary resilience and the benevolent intervention of the West. Such a representation echoes the portrayal of Sudanese-born slam poet Abraham Nouk in the Reality Television show *Living with the Enemy: Episode 3 Immigration* (SBS, 2014), which demonstrates Nouk's heroism through pitching him against a white self-described "race realist" who is opposed to African immigration to Australia. These portrayals of Adut and Nouk would have been unthinkable a decade ago. In 2007 when the murder of student Liep Gony by two white Australians was initially blamed on Sudanese-Australian gang violence, the trope of the young

© KONINKLIJKE BRILL NV, LEIDEN, 2018 | DOI:10.1163/9789004381407_004

Sudanese-Australian man as a gang member irrevocably entered the Australian media zeitgeist.

In this chapter, I propose that the framing of both Adut and Nouk enacts another aspect of the same orientalising trope, evidencing a "deep and ambivalent fascination with difference" (Hall, 2003, p. 124), and a variety of "modern racism". I utilise van Djik'S (1993) conceptualisation of "modern racism" to refer to multiple subtle discourses in society that serve to disadvantage people from marginalised cultural/ ethnic groups on an everyday, often invisible basis. Regarding the media's role in this discourse, van Djik (1993, p. 9) has argued that "a few positive representations of successful individuals" are used to "counterbalance" the media's "negative portrayals of marginalised communities". This demonstrates "the non-racism of the ruling group while ensuring the marginal group remains in its place". More recently Nolan and Burgin et al. (2016, p. 61) have cautioned against positioning the media as unified in reproducing hegemonic politics, pointing out that such an approach "produces a heuristic through which inconsistencies and contradictions in media representations are downplayed". I argue that *Immigration* and *Unlimited* are rich sites for a discussion of these inconsistencies and contradictions in terms of discourses about Sudanese-Australians, racism and belonging as both texts simultaneously include *and* exclude Sudanese-Australians from a normative Australian identity in their privileging of particular narratives and voices. While each text celebrates the success of their respective protagonist, each also enables "breathing space" (Hage, 1998, p. 247) for racism through production practices. I use the term "production practices" here to refer to the selection of specific footage, editing choices and the use of voice-over to construct particular narratives. Discussing bourgeoning scholarship around representations of race and racism on American RTV, Orbe (2008, p. 351) observes that one of the fears of critical media scholars is that RTV viewers will have their prejudices validated through watching with those who have similar beliefs. Orbe expresses the hope that scholarship on RTV will encourage viewers to "watch and discuss" the RTV shows they love and hate with "diverse sets of individuals" in order to engage in reflective questioning of "the symbolic power" of representations of race. It is in this respect that screen texts such as *Immigration* and *Unlimited* offer social justice possibilities in the context of teaching, as they can utilised to initiate dialogue on discourses around race and belonging in Australia. This dialogue encompasses the *intended* educational aims of each text, as well as the ideologies underpinning each. While pedagogy is not the focus of this chapter, I briefly make reference to my own teaching in two different educational contexts.

In my discussion of production practices, I use the notion of "framing" to discuss the construction of representations which serve a particular ideological discourse. Entman (1993, p. 51) has defined framing as 'a way to describe the power of a communicating text'. According to Entman (1993), framing involves highlighting a particular issue or piece of information, firstly via selection of the issue, then by attributing importance to the issue via the way it is communicated. Frames typically "define problems, diagnose causes, make moral judgments" and "suggest remedies"

(p. 51). A frame may include all or some of these functions (Entman, 1993, p. 52). Additionally, I draw on Trinh's (2007) notion of "giver" and "framer" in the context of documentary practice, which emphasises the potential for paternalism, even in representations which may have advocacy aims:

> In affirming righteously that one opens a space for those who do not have a voice, one often forgets that the gaining of a voice happens within a framed context, and one tends to turn a blind eye to one's privileged position as a "giver" and a "framer". (Trinh quoted in Hohenberger, 2007, p. 115)

Extending Trinh's point, I suggest that intrinsic to "giving" is an equal element of taking, and I examine the representational contradictions in *Unlimited* regarding Sudanese-Australian identity and racism through attention to "voice" and "framing". I contextualise my discussion of *Immigration* and *Unlimited* through a brief review of the visibility of people of colour on Australian television and in advertising, an analysis of Reality Television (RTV) as a genre and reflection on the relevance of the Special Broadcast Service (SBS) RTV show *Go Back to Where You Come From* (2011).

THE SIGNIFICANCE OF VISIBILITY

Any screen representation of Sudanese-Australians arguably attracts a high level of interest due to both the history of demonisation of that cultural community in the media and the pervasive whiteness of the Australian screen. It has been widely acknowledged that Australian television programming does not reflect the increasingly diverse ethnic make-up of the population (Screen Australia, 2016; Terzis, 2016; Hamad, 2016; Hamad, 2014; Nunn, 2012; Hage, 1998). A recent report reveals that of the 199 dramas that aired between 2011 and 2015 on Australian television only 18% of the main characters were from non-Anglo Celtic backgrounds as compared to 32% of the population (Screen Australia, 2016). As Terzis (2016, p. 53) has observed, "Australian television is a hermetic ecosystem, oddly resistant to real life trends". Until very recently people of colour have also been largely absent from Australian television advertising (Hamad, 2015; Blight, 2011; Higgs & Milner, 2005). Generally, when non-Anglo Saxon looking people have appeared in major brand advertising (about 5% of the time) they have been in the background (Blight, 2011). However, *Deng Thiak Adut Unlimited* is part of a wave of advertising by major Australian businesses in the last couple of years featuring Australians from diverse ethnic backgrounds. Other examples include Officeworks (*Let Their Amazing Out*, 2015), Australia Post (*Change Our Tune*, 2016), the Meat and Livestock Corporation (*You Never Lamb Alone*, 2016) and Australian Super (*It Matters*, 2016).

Increased visibility and inclusion is undeniably of positive significance in its impact on both the cultural/ethnic communities of those being represented and on the broader community. Hamad (2015) has noted, "When we see ourselves occupying space in the culture around us, it reinforces our own humanity, our very existence". In an American televisual context Hopson (2008, p. 442) has commented that growing up he was 'content' to see representations simply pertaining to him, "My brothers and I would gather around the television to view Black images of any kind. In some ways, these pictures symbolised who we were and what we could become" (Hopson, p. 442). These comments highlight the need for critical scrutiny of available representations of ethnic/ cultural groups who have been marginalised. Due to limited portrayals of people of colour on screen, those that are available can gain a heightened power, an "allegorical" significance where individuals are believed to sum up "a vast and presumably homogenous community" (Shohat, 1995, p. 169). This can result in "the burden of representation" (Cottle, 1997) where individuals feel a heightened responsibility around potentially contributing to negative perceptions of their particular community.

SOCIAL JUSTICE CACHET AND PEDAGOGICAL OPPORTUNITIES

Given the Australian government's inhumane and punitive treatment of asylum seekers (see Australian Centre for Human Rights, 2016; Butler, 2017; Foster, 2016; SBS, 2017) and previous media narratives about Sudanese-Australians (as evidenced in Due, 2008; Windle, 2008; Nolan & Farquharson et al., 2011; Nunn, 2012), Adut's ethnicity and refugee background conceivably contribute to the advertisement's apparent social justice cachet. As Holder (2017) has commented, activism rather than sex is now being used in marketing campaigns, allowing viewers to "fuel" their social conscience without disrupting their comfortable lifestyle. Critiquing *Unlimited* from this paradigm, it is evident that the advertisement aims to confer an aura of social justice on Western Sydney University – here is a university that champions and celebrates the success of people from refugee backgrounds. As a RTV show, *Immigration* harnesses social justice discourses, not for promotion of a product per se, but for promotion of acceptable attitudes towards people seeking asylum. In this regard, it is a clear thematic successor to *Go Back to Where You Came From* (SBS, 2011), an earlier RTV show which enables six 'ordinary Australians' (SBS) to go on a physical and emotional journey to gain insight into the experiences of people seeking refuge in Australia (SBS, 2011). The six participants are Caucasian, apart from one man with Afghani heritage, and are largely unsympathetic to refugees and asylum seekers. It is apparent that the show aims to encourage participants (and viewers) to develop empathy towards those who they consider to be outsiders or 'queue jumpers'. Although challenging people's xenophobic preconceptions is undoubtedly a worthy civic education aim, it has been widely argued that a polarisation of viewpoints on social and political issues, which is fundamental to many RTV shows, enables viewers to voyeuristically project the evils of society onto individual participants. Through focusing on the offensive, sometimes extremist beliefs and attitudes of individuals, viewers are reassured of their own open-mindedness, and the systemic nature of issues such as homophobia and racism are obscured (Jangodozinki, 2003; Schroeder, 2006; Kraszewski, 2008). Schroeder (2006, p. 181) has argued that particular characters in MTV's *The Real World* are framed as "objects of ridicule" and perpetrators of discrimination, to "create a politically and ideologically scripted viewer response".

Similarly, Kraszewski (2008, p. 208) proposes that production practices in *The Real World* construct a reality where racism is a "phenomenon that is located within rural conservatives". As a result, MTV's politically progressive audience are freed from "any implications in racism". According to van Djik (1993) proportioning of blame to a few bigoted or ignorant individuals is one of modern racism's strategies of denial. *Go Back to Where You Came From* (SBS, 2011) appears to be a prime example of this and Fernandez (2015) has critiqued the show as encouraging:

> latte sipping lefties to feel good about themselves by watching rednecks on a leaky boat with paramedics trying to 'recreate' the 'refugee experience' without the reality of being locked away indefinitely in offshore Australian detention centres. (Fernandez, 2015)

Fernandez (2015) has also pointed out that the refugee-background participants in *Go Back to Where You Came From* are not the main protagonists – rather they are "realistic extras" in the white Australians' "emotional journey". As such, whilst having an explicitly anti-racist agenda, *Go Back* enacts the unconscious and unreflected upon discourse of white privilege. Despite agreeing with Fernandez, I argue that to simply dismiss the show because of this is a wasted social justice opportunity. RTV has been identified by Ouellette and Murray (2004, p. 8) as a genre which "opens up new possibilities and limitations for representational politics". Arguably an area of rich possibility is, to draw upon Orbe (2008), the ways in which RTV can stimulate discussion and reflection about complex societal issues. This is particularly pertinent for teachers who are concerned with media and government discourses, representation and race.

My pedagogical experience has demonstrated that *Go Back* actually fulfils some of its intended educational outcomes as well as others that one can assume were unintended. For example, in 2011, when I screened it to a class of young men in a Juvenile Justice facility, the class was split between support of refugees and keeping them out of Australia. One can surmise that this split was compatible with the producer's intention for the RTV show as the content immediately sparked discussion about the origin of particular attitudes, who actually belongs in Australia and what constitutes human rights. A couple of Pasifika students were vocal in reminding the class that apart from Aboriginal Australians "everyone here is a migrant". However, one student, Isiah (not his real name) who was Sudanese-Australian, commented that it was "interesting to see what refugees experienced", as he had immigrated from Cairo where he had had "a nice life" with his aunt and uncle. Reunited with his parents and siblings in Melbourne as an adolescent, he didn't consider himself a refugee or feel particularly lucky to be in Australia as many of his friends had been victims of racial violence. This was a way into a discussion about reductive characterisations of people from refugee backgrounds and their role as "extras in the white Australians' emotional journey" (Fernandez, 2015), something that the other students had not previously considered. It also disrupted the notion of the refugee who is grateful for the benevolent intervention of the West (c.f Hage, 1998; Cole, 2012).

"REFUGEE": DARKNESS, DIFFERENCE, VALORISATION OF SUFFERING

Both *Immigration* and *Unlimited* move a step beyond *Go Back* as they feature Sudanese-Australians as protagonists. Yet while *Immigration* 'gives' a voice to Abraham Nouk and *Unlimited* voices Deng Adut's story, it is worth considering what is 'taken' in the process and what narratives are prioritised. Discussing the Australian media, Hamad (2016) has made the point that one of "society's unspoken but firmly entrenched notions" is that "white people are authorities who can objectively speak about all manner of topics, whereas the rest of us are subjective and can only speak from direct experience". While RTV as a genre focuses on participants' personal experience, and similarly biographical detail is intrinsic to all Western Sydney University's alumni advertisements, both Nouk and Adut are undeniably confined to their identities as refugee-others. I argue that *Immigration* also forces Nouk into the role of educator/facilitator in the emotional journey of his white counterpart, Nick Folke. In my following discussion, for the sake of simplicity, I use the first names of Deng Adut and Abraham Nouk, as this is how each man is referred to as a "character" in the respective screen text they appear in.

Before moving into a discussion of production practices in *Immigration* and *Unlimited* I want to briefly interrogate the complex associations attached to the word "refugee" in Australia as well as touch on popular portrayals of Southern Sudanese masculinity in the west, beyond the demonisation in the Australian media. A number of scholars have connected the treatment of refugees and the othering of people who visibly differ from a white homogeneity with the treatment of Aboriginals (see McCallum, 2008; Windle, 2007; Allen, 2011; Due, 2008). The myth of *terra nullius* and the "imagining of Australia as normatively home to white people" has been cited by Due (2008, p. 2) as being deeply entrenched in the white Australian psyche. Arguably, the term 'Sudanese refugee' is associated with war and loss and notions of Africa as a "place of negatives, of difference, of darkness" (Aidichie, 2009). As such to refer to someone as a "refugee" is a variety of "orientalism" (Said, 1978) and a way of stating (either consciously or unconsciously) that they do not fully belong. While 'refugee' has these pejorative underpinnings, I suggest that in some contexts there is also a romanticisation of an assumed refugee narrative. In this narrative hardship and loss are valorised, and the 'successful' refugee is one who is able to overcome extreme adversity to adapt to life in a western country. As Harris (2012, p. 36) has observed filmic portrayals of 'Lost Boys of Sudan' are characterised by the "sufferings and resilience" of the protagonists.

CONSTRUCTING THE HERO-OTHER

The representations of Abraham Nouk and Deng Adut as hero-others encompass both pejorative and romanticised notions of refugee, and each text frames its subject with more than an echo of an orientalist discourse that has traditionally portrayed non-Europeans as "childlike" and "different" (Said, 1978, p. 40). The beginnings of *Unlimited* and *Immigration* are remarkably similar, serving to frame Sudan, and more broadly Africa, as a place of "catastrophe" (Aidichie, 2009), and signaling each of the protagonist-hero's war-torn backgrounds. *Immigration* provides context for the narrative with footage of tanks and soldiers in Sudan and civilians in a displaced persons camp: a familiar news representation of a distant humanitarian crisis. A voice over provides bare facts: "Sudan: home of Africa's longest civil war". *Unlimited* offers a reconstruction of scenes from Deng's childhood as tanks and soldiers storm a village, choreographed to a catchy sentimental pop song which trivialises and romanticises the events depicted. Such production choices highlight the advertisement's utilisation of civil war in Sudan as depoliticised entertainment for western viewers as does the fact that Deng is voiceless – rather than telling the story he *is* the story. Titles succinctly communicate the transformation of a helpless child at the mercy of a civil war to a humanitarian lawyer:

> At six Deng was taken from his mother. Marched 33 days to Ethiopia. Forced to fight the rebels. At twelve he was shot in the back. Smuggled out of Sudan. The UN got him out. Western Sydney took him in. At fifteen he taught himself to read. A free man he chose to live in his car. A law degree enables him to protect others. Deng continues to fight. (Morrison, dir. 2014)

Visual shorthand ensures Deng's work as a lawyer is equated with his childhood experience and his status as refugee. A shot of Deng standing in court (after defending a man who presumably is also Sudanese-Australian), his face suffused with emotion fades to a flashback of his mother's face. *Unlimited* finishes with the title 'Deng Thiak Adut Refugee' with 'Lawyer' fading in to leave the viewer with 'Refugee Lawyer'.

A direct comparison with the representation of Deng in *Unlimited* can be made to the way Abraham is represented in *Immigration*. SBS promotion describes him in the following way (some of this information is also repeated in a voice-over at the start of the program):

> When Abraham arrived in Australia he knew two words of English, 'yes' and 'no', and he consistently confused the two of them. He is now the Slam Poet champion of Victoria and recently came third in the national titles. He is also about to have his second book published and perform at the Glastonbury festival. However, he still can't get a job, is subjected to daily racism and won't travel on the train after dark. (SBS, 2014)

English language literacy – an integral part of belonging to a normative white Australia – and the speed at which both men excel are highlighted in both representations. However, Abraham's literary achievements are prefaced by details of a childlike confusion over "yes" and "no" and in *Unlimited* the selection of particular details to communicate Deng's story serve a paternalistic discourse that hinges on notions of western charity and benevolence to those from 'developing' countries (c.f Hague, 1998; Cole, 2012). The statement "Western Sydney took him in" is matched with an image of a young Deng cycling past picturesque suburban houses, a stark contrast to the shots of tanks and soldiers thirty seconds earlier. This is clearly a reference to the western suburbs (and by extension, Western Sydney University) as a place of opportunity, generosity and safety.

While there's a cathartic sense of relief that the protagonist is over the worst, the detail of the car has the ring of "poverty porn" (Collin, 2009) – evidence of Deng's ongoing "sufferings and resilience" as an ex-child soldier and refugee. It seems unlikely that anyone would *choose* to live in a car while studying, which ironically serves to contradict notions of Western Sydney as generous. Trinh's (2007, p. 115) paradigm of the "giver" and "framer" provides a way to make critical sense of *Unlimited*. While the dominant narrative is one of giving, a celebration of Deng's success, the underpinning discourse is one of taking. *Unlimited*, a reconstruction of Deng Adut's story and a commodification of his refugee experience, sits at the uneasy juncture of entertainment, education and commerce.

Yet because of this commodification and the ideological discourses that underpin the narrative I have found the advertisement to be an ideal introduction to a foundation subject I teach in an International and Community Development course. *Unlimited* provides a dynamic, provocative way into discussions about the dominant model of development, the role that colonisation and cultural imperialism has played in the 'help' the Global North 'gives' to the Global South, representations of Africa, and the way that people of colour are othered in the western public discourse. Each semester, students are riveted by the production values of *Unlimited* and the drama of the hero-narrative. Some tears are shed. People of diverse backgrounds (including Southern Sudanese) agree that this is an important story and that it is good to see African-Australians on screen. Others label it 'cheesy' and express some indignation that a university is claiming a student's success. Some question the ethics of reconstructing the scene where soldiers storm Deng's childhood village. They query the detail of Deng living in his car. This starts a range of reflections and discussions that continue all semester around power, privilege, positionality and othering.

In direct contrast to *Unlimited*, Abraham's voice is central to *Immigration* and provides a wry, reflective commentary on Nick's explicitly racist views. This is a RTV show that apparently directly tackles issues of power and othering inherent in Australian society. After Abraham has visited Nick's political party, who are united in their perspective on the dangers of African immigration, Abraham declares to a camera 'diary': "Well Australia, this man is a product of your negligence". However, despite the prioritisation of Abraham's voice, *Immigration* presents conflicting discourses about racism and Sudanese-Australian identity. The program itself perpetrates a form of oppression via the heroic role Abraham is forced to play. In the first few minutes the viewer is presented with a range of voices (all white Australian) describing or expressing racism towards Sudanese-Australians, a production choice which frames Abraham as an outsider and a representative of a social issue. The viewer is told via voice-over that, "for many Sudanese adjusting to life in Australia has been hard; as the community has grown so has the discrimination". News footage from 2007 follows this statement with part of a report on the murder of Liep Gony, which includes a quote from one of his killers: "these blacks are turning this town into the Bronx. I'm looking to kill the blacks". This foregrounds the viewer's introduction to Nick who informs the camera, "Bringing in people from vastly different cultures, especially these African cultures that have come out of war zones, you're only asking for trouble". According to Nick, "African immigration to Australia has been a total disaster; higher welfare dependency, criminal behaviour, rape, anti-social behavior, like gangs and that sort of thing ...".

Expressed in the language of modern racism Nick's beliefs focus on the incompatibility of "African" culture with the "Australian" way of life. A "redneck" (Fernandez, 2015), Nick represents an exaggerated version of what has historically been the Australian media's representation of Sudanese-Australians. The sequencing of footage also implies a connection between Nick's views and the violence of the men who murdered Liep Gony. While this framing is an acknowledgment that racism exists on a spectrum, a complex series of blame shifting is also evident. While Nick targets Sudanese immigrants as the source of violence rather than the *victims* of violent discrimination, *Immigration* deflects attention from systemic racism, constructing individuals such as Nick and Gony's killers as the problem.

Immigration and *Unlimited* have similar narrative symmetry, demonstrating a "drive to conform to journalistic notions of what constitutes a good story" (Grindstaff, 2002, p. 260). Yet this symmetry also operates as a framing device that confines the protagonists to the category of refugee (albeit a heroic refugee who gives back to society). Deng's refugee past is explicitly linked to his success as a lawyer for people from refugee backgrounds, while Abraham's past finds expression in his slam poetry and mentoring young people in hip-hop emceeing for Creative Rebellion Youth, an organisation he leads. Abraham's first words to camera explicitly address the issue of society's negative assumptions about Sudanese Australians: "I've experienced racism all my life. It's always refugees, troubled background, war-mentality. We've been judged on our past".

This statement acts as a reflexive commentary on the footage of Sudan at the start of *Immigration*, and sums up Nick's perspective. It is also echoed in the final scene of *Immigration* where Abraham performs in a Slam Poetry event. During an argument leading up to the event Nick tells Abraham, "Your people have no regard for human life, because you're always fighting each other". On stage Abraham gives an impassioned response via a poem, which begins: "You will never understand that I'm the product of a society that used its children as child soldiers ...". While Abraham's voice is in stark contrast to the voice-less Sudanese in the news footage at the start of *Immigration*, the selection of the performance as a finale ensures that Abraham's refugee background remains his salient characteristic.

Arguably, systemic racism beyond the RTV production forces Abraham into the position of hero-exemplar. Appearing on *Immigration* would be a particularly heavy burden of representation (Cottle, 1997) for any Sudanese-Australian, and if Abraham were to display any of the aggression freely expressed by Nick he would be at risk of letting down the entire African-Australian community. Abraham's role in *Immigration* might be understood as that of a social worker or teacher patiently trying to understand a difficult client/student – in this case two hate-filled white men who, in an exaggerated example of the use of "reverse racism" (van Dijk, 1993), insist on their own victimhood. Typically, Abraham prefaces questions to Nick with a diplomatic, "How do you feel …". Seven minutes in to the episode, after a racist tirade from Nick, he asks, "Do you feel a lot of Aussies feel the same way you feel but just don't want to be frank about it?"

An outburst of emotion from Nick, which in its hyprocrisy and hyperbole frames him as "an object of ridicule" (Schroeder, 2006, p. 181), provides Abraham with an opportunity to empathise. While resolutely unsympathetic to African refugees, Nick presents Abraham with a tiny "mamushka" doll on the journey from Sydney to Melbourne and, holding back sobs, reveals that his mother was a Russian refugee. Abraham states to the camera: "to see Nick the way he was just shows how much alike we are. His fears are real and just the same as mine". When Abraham and Nick visit Nick's 'political mentor' Drew Fraser (an American-born professor who was sacked by Macquarie University for his racist views), Drew makes it clear that he believes that Africans are violent and of lower intelligence than whites, who are an "endangered species". Despite these neo-Nazi articulations Abraham points out calmly that Drew is as much of 'an outsider' as himself. Later he confides to the camera: "that was very comical that a man of his age with his academic prestige would say such things".

Nick's beliefs are framed as marginal throughout *Immigration* via a conspicuous lack of supporters in each scene. While Abraham's family, friends, and members of Creative Rebellion Youth appear on the program, Nick's family is absent. At an Australia Day barbeque his handful of 'friends' (who may be neighbours or SBS ring-ins) disagree with Nick's views and are vocal in support of Abraham as a fellow Australian. When Nick makes a speech for the political party he leads, his audience of supporters is tiny. Similarly, when Nick's party stages a protest with placards linking asylum seekers with sexual predators, there are only a few protestors. These production choices further perpetuate a discourse that "attributes racism to the white lower class" and "ideologies of the extreme Right" (van Dijk, 1993, p. 5).

BREATHING SPACE FOR RACISM

Despite this framing of Nick and Drew as ignorant, extremist individuals, *Immigration* gives Nick a public platform for racist rhetoric and exemplifies Hamad's (2016) point that white people are able to speak about whatever they wish in the media. Nick and Drew are violent in speech and the uninhibited expression of their views on television serves to validate their inherent belief in white supremacy. As Hage (1998, p. 247) has observed, "Violent racists are always a minority. However, their breathing space is determined by the degree of ordinary 'non-violent' racism a government and culture will allow". Breathing space is also given to racist discourse via the way *Immigration* seeks to answer Nick's discriminatory statements. After visiting Abraham's home in an inner-city block of housing commission flats, Nick is even more certain of his victimhood as a white Australian. He refers to the residents of the flats (whom he assumes are all African) as "colonisers" and accuses Abraham of being "on welfare".

The voice-over on *Immigration* is quick to correct this idea, stating "Abraham isn't on welfare: he earns his living performing at events like the one tonight". This perpetuates a discourse of the deserving, hard-working refugee/immigrant who must validate their presence in Australia by proving that they are not a burden to the state. It seems unlikely that Abraham would consistently earn a living from poetry performances, just as it seems unlikely that studying law while living in a car would be a life-style choice. In any case, although Nick concedes that Abe could be "an agent of good" for the Sudanese-Australian community, at the end of *Immigration* Nick's perspective on African immigration remains unchanged.

Ultimately, Abraham's role in *Immigration* is reminiscent of Lorde's seminal comment that "Black and Third World people are expected to educate white people as to our humanity ... The oppressors maintain their position and evade responsibility for their own actions" (Lorde, 1984, p. 115).

I have not used *Immigration* in a classroom context. On an emotional level, I can hardly bear to watch the interactions between Abraham and Nick, and I inwardly flinch when I think of inflicting them on Sudanese-Australian students. Yet as a teaching resource the program combines the issues raised by the text of *Go Back* with those raised by *Unlimited*. It provides a rich case-study of systemic racism in Australia by gratuitously enabling the voices of right-wing extremists and demonstrating through its production choices a discourse of left-wing paternalism towards Sudanese-Australians.

CONCLUSION

In this chapter I have argued that *Unlimited* and *Immigration* herald what appears to be a new media trope, that of the exemplary Sudanese-Australian hero. An indisputably positive departure from earlier media representations of young Sudanese-Australians as gang members, this trope is also of significance in a media realm that persists in perpetuating an "imagining of Australia as normatively home to white people" (Due, 2008, p. 2). However, the respective framing of Deng Adut in *Unlimited* and Abraham Nouk in *Immigration* still evidences a variety of Orientalism that serves to over-determine both men in terms of their ethnicity and refugee-ness. The necessity for Sudanese-Australians to possess exemplary, heroic levels of resilience and transcend hardship in order to demonstrate that they are not a burden to the state is an underpinning discourse in both texts. Colonialist oppression is also enacted via production practices in each text. *Unlimited* emphasises Australian generosity and benevolence while commodifying Deng's refugee experience for promotional purposes, and *Immigration* inadvertently validates white privilege through giving breathing space to the expression of racial hatred.

I have also briefly touched on the social justice possibilities offered by such screen representations in classroom contexts in terms of the critical dialogues around power and privilege that they can be used to initiate. In concluding I suggest that it may be productive to see *Immigration* and *Unlimited* as part of a step towards a greater diversity of representations of Sudanese-Australians on screen where eventually ethnic background and refugee-ness is no longer the explicit or implicit focus of the story. In March 2017 it was announced that a forthcoming drama from SBS, *Sunshine* starring Anthony La Paglia and Melanie Lynskey, would also include "an outstanding South Sudanese Australian cast being seen for the very first time on Australian TV" (SBS Guide, 2017). Although none of this cast are named, *Sunshine* has been "written and developed with close community consultation" (SBS Guide, 2017). Given this is the first time an Australian drama has featured Sudanese-Australian characters, it is likely that this will initiate a great deal of discussion around representational politics. Will the cast be over-determined by their ethnicity and refugee backgrounds? Will they be extras in the white characters' emotional journeys or will they be well-rounded, complex protagonists in their own right?

REFERENCES

Aidichie, C. (2009). *The danger of the single story*. Retrieved from https://www.ted.com/talks/chimamanda_adichie_the_danger_of_a_single_story/transcript?language=en

Allen, M. (2011). Family stories and "race" in Australian history. *Critical Race and Whiteness Studies, 7*(2), 1–12.

Australian Human Rights Centre. (2016, February 29). *Embarrassing truths: Australia's treatment of asylum seekers*. Sydney: University of New South Wales. Retrieved from http://www.ahrcentre.org/news/2016/02/29/779

Blight, D. (2011, November 4). Australian advertising fails to recognise ethnic diversity. *AdNews*. Retrieved from http://www.adnews.com.au/adnews/australian-advertising-fails-to-recognise-ethnic-diversity

Butler, J. (2017, July 25). All the times the UN has slammed Australia's asylum seeker policy. *The Huffington Post*. Retrieved from http://www.huffingtonpost.com.au/2017/07/25/all-the-times-the-un-has-slammed-australias-asylum-seeker-polic_a_23046469/

Collin, M. (2009). What is "poverty porn" and why does it matter for development? *Aid Thoughts*. Retrieved from http://aidthoughts.org/?p=69

Cottle, S. (1997). *Television and ethnic minorities: Producers' perspectives: A study of BBC in-house, independent and cable TV producers*. London: Ashgate Publishing Limited.

Dapin, M. (2016, January 29). *Child soldier turned Blacktown lawyer: Lunch with Deng Thiak Adut*. Retrieved from http://www.smh.com.au/nsw/lunch-with-deng-thiak-adut-20160128-gmfy49.html

Due, C. (2008). Who are strangers? "Absorbing" Sudanese refugees into a White Australia. *ACRAWSA E-Journal, 4*(1), 1–13. Retrieved from http://citeseerx.ist.psu.edu/viewdoc/download?doi=10.1.1.472.8264&rep=rep1&type=pdf

Entman, R. M. (1993). Framing: Towards clarification of a fractured paradigm. *Journal of Communication, 43*(4). 51–58.

Fernandez, R. (2015). *'Go back to where you came from': The coloniser's story*. Retrieved from http://riserefugee.org/go-back-to-where-you-came-from-the-colonisers-story/

Foster, M. (2016, November 4). Turnbull's asylum seeker ban violates Australia's Human Rights obligations. *The Conversation*. Retrieved from https://theconversation.com/turnbulls-asylum-seeker-ban-violates-australias-human-rights-obligations-68475

Gatt, K. (2011). Sudanese refugees in Victoria: An analysis of their treatment by the Australian government. *International Journal of Comparative and Applied Criminal Justice, 35*(3), 207–19.

Grindstaff, L. (2002). *The money shot: Trash, class and the making of TV talk shows.* Chicago, IL: The University of Chicago Press.

Hage, G. (1998). *White nation.* Annandale: Pluto Press.

Hall, S. (1980). Encoding/decoding. In S. Hall, D. Hobson, A. Lowe, & P. Willis (Eds.), *Culture, media, language: Working papers in cultural studies 1972–1979* (pp. 78–87). London: Hutchison.

Hall, S. (2003). What is this Black in popular culture? In V. Smith (Ed.), *Representing blackness: Issues in film and video* (pp. 123–133). New Brunswick, NJ: Rutgers University Press.

Hamad, R. (2014, November 23). 'Why is Australian TV still so White? *Sydney Morning Herald.* Retrieved from http://www.dailylife.com.au/news-and-views/dl-opinion/why-is-australian-tv-still-so-white-20141123-11s9j0.html

Hamad, R. (2015, March 26). Why Are Australian ads so white? *Sydney Morning Herald.* Retrieved from http://www.dailylife.com.au/news-and-views/dl-opinion/why-are-australian-ads-so-white-20150325-1m7bi3.html

Hamad, R. (2016, August 2). *Why whitewashing in the Australian media must end.* Retrieved from http://www.sbs.com.au/topics/life/culture/article/2016/08/01/why-whitewashing-australian-media-must-end?cid=inbody:does-australian-advertising-reflect-our-changing-multicultural-nation

Harris, A. M. (2012). *Ethnocinema: Intercultural arts education.* Dordrecht: Springer.

Higgs, C., & Milner, L. (2005). *Portrayals of cultural diversity in Australian television commercials: A benchmark study.* Conference paper, ANZMAC Conference, Advertising/Marketing Communication Issues, VU Research Repository. Retrieved from http://vuir.vu.edu.au/877/1/1-Higgs.pdf

Holder, A. (2017, February 3). Sex doesn't sell any more, activism does: And don't the big brands know it. *The Guardian.* Retrieved from https://www.theguardian.com/commentisfree/2017/feb/03/activism-sells-brands-social-conscience-advertising?CMP=share_btn_link

Hopson, M. C. (2008). "Now watch me dance": Responding to critical observations, constructions and performances of race on reality television. *Critical Studies in Media Communication, 25*(4), 441–446.

Lattouf, A. (2016, August 26). Changing the whitewash channel on Australian television. *ABC News.* Retrieved from http://www.abc.net.au/news/2016-08-25/whitewash-channel-australian-tv-diversity/7783428

McCallum, K. (2007). *Indigenous violence as a 'mediated public crisis'.* Paper presented at the Australian and New Zealand Communication Association Conference. Retrieved from http://6024120857.static.tpgi.com.au/anzca_x/images/stories/past_conferences/ANZCA07/mccallum.pdf

Ndhlovu, F. (2013). "Too tall, too dark" to be Australian: Racial perceptions of post-refugee Africans. *Critical Race and Whiteness Studies, 9*(2), 1–17.

Nolan, D., Burgin, A., Farquharson, K., & Marjoribanks, T. (2016). Media and the politics of belonging: Sudanese Australians, letters to the editor and the new integrationism. *Patterns of Prejudice, 50*(3), 253–275.

Nolan, D., Farquharson, K., Politoff, V., & Marjoribanks, T. (2011). Mediated multiculturalism: Newspaper representation of Sudanese migrants in Australia. *Journal of Intercultural Studies, 32*(6) 655–671.

Nunn, C. (2010). Spaces to speak: Challenging representations of Sudanese-Australians. *Journal of Intercultural Studies, 31*(2), 183–198.

Orbe, M. P. (2008). Representations of race in reality TV: Watch and discuss. *Critical Studies in Media Communication, 25*(4), 345–352.

Ouellette, L., & Murray, S. (2004). *Reality TV: Remaking television culture.* New York, NY: NYU Press.

Said, E. (1978). *Orientalism.* New York, NY: Pantheon.

SBS. (2014). *Living with the enemy episode 3.* Retrieved from http://www.sbs.com.au/programs/article/2014/08/20/episode-3-immigration

SBS. (n. d.). *About us.* Retrieved from http://www.sbs.com.au/aboutus/faqs

SBS Guide. (2017, March 27). *Melanie Lynskey and Anthony LaPaglia to star in new SBS crime drama Sunshine.* Retrieved from http://www.sbs.com.au/guide/article/2017/03/27/melanie-lynskey-and-anthony-lapaglia-star-new-sbs-crime-drama-sunshine

SBS News. (2017, August 27). 'Shocking cruelty': Government launches welfare crackdown on asylum seekers in Australia. *AAP – SBS Wires*. Retrieved from http://www.sbs.com.au/news/article/2017/08/27/shocking-cruelty-government-launches-welfare-crackdown-asylum-seekers-australia

Schroeder, E. R. (2006). "Sexual racism" and reality television: Privileging the White male prerogative on MTV's "the real world". In D. S. Escoffery (Ed.), *How real is reality TV? Essays on representation and truth*. Jefferson, NC: McFarland & Company.

Screen Australia. (2016). *Milestone study of diversity on television released*. Retrieved from https://www.screenaustralia.gov.au/sa/newsroom/news/2016/mr-160824-study-of-diversity-on-tv-released

Shohat, E. (1995). The struggle over representation: Casting, coalitions and the politics of identification. In R. de la Campa, E. A. Kaplan, & M. Sprinker (Eds.), *Late imperial culture* (pp. 166–178). London: Verso Books.

Terzis, G. (2016). Comedy is kin, the family law and diverse television. *Metro Magazine: Media & Education Magazine, 189*, 52–57.

Thomsen, S. (2015, September 7). This extraordinary ad for an Australian university is like nothing you've ever seen before. *Business Insider Australia*. Retrieved from http://www.businessinsider.com.au

van Dijk, T. A. (1993). *Elite discourse and the reproduction of racism*. Retrieved from http://www.discourses.org/OldArticles/Elite%20discourse%20and%20the%20reproduction%20of%20racism.pdf

Windle, J. (2008). Racialisation of African youth in Australia. *Social Identities, 14*(5), 553–566.

AUDIOVISUAL REFERENCES

Australia Post (Producer). (2016). *Change our tune* (Video file). Retrieved from https://www.youtube.com/watch?v=5BGgHdp_iYo

Australian Super. (2016). *It matters* (Video file). Retrieved from https://www.youtube.com/watch?v=T6t7DrkMq1A

Batalibasi, A. (dir.). (2016). *Lit: A video projection with Nyawuda Chuol* (Video projection). Melbourne. West Projection Festival.

Centre for Multicultural Youth (Producer) & Bilbrough, P. (Writer/Director). (2015). *This is me: Agot Dell* (Video file). Retrieved from https://vimeo.com/147534094

Finch (Producer) & Morrison, J. (Director). (2015). *Deng Thiak adut unlimited* (Video file). Retrieved from https://www.youtube.com/watch?v=buA3tsGnp2s

New Hope Foundation (Producer), & Bilbrough, P. (Writer/Director). (2010). *No one eats alone: From Sudan to Melbourne* (DVD). Melbourne: New Hope Foundation.

SBS & Shine Australia (Producer). (2014). Episode 3: Immigration. In *Living with the enemy*. Sydney, Australia.

The Meat and Livestock Corporation (Producer). (2016). *You'll never lamb alone* (Video file). Retrieved from https://www.youtube.com/watch?v=-9Ka3a7cdYw

Paola Bilbrough
Victoria University
Australia

LOU IAQUINTO

5. A CONVERSATION BETWEEN NORMAL & ABNORMAL

INTRODUCTION

This chapter examines the matters of privilege and identity that surface in the context of the provision of social services. Its purpose is, first, to illuminate the professional and societal attitudes, values and beliefs that combine to perpetuate the further stigmatisation of the clients of these services and, second, to offer examples of how this behaviour can be fashioned to confront the important individual aspects of clients' self-esteem. The aim of this chapter is to contribute to the knowledge and understanding of the practice of client participation in social services. The chapter makes use of the enablers of participation determined by a review of the academic literature and the qualitative data from an original study. The study's results offer understandings of how services within divergent organisational cultures propagate professional and personal values, attitudes and beliefs that may prolong or put an end to the further stigmatisation of their clients.

The analysis of the data shows that significant barriers to participation may exist in the culture, structure and practice of social services and that these barriers appear to be caused by professional relationships with and attitudes toward clients. Not unexpectedly the data also indicates that professional relationships, built on mutual respect, that value the knowledge and experiences clients have to offer, are an essential enabler of participation.

A number of popular models of participation have offered insight into the complexity service providers face in meeting the needs of vulnerable clients (Arnstein, 1969; Checkoway, 1998; Hart, 1992; Lardner, 2001; Shier, 2001; Treseder, 1997). Such models, however, left me with two principal questions. First, do practitioners understand participation in ways compatible with academic discussions of this concept? Second, how can practitioners operationalise a commitment to participation in their own practice settings?

All professional social service organisations maintain some form of commitment to service user participation and yet the goal of maximising service user participation remains elusive. This research has explored both the reasons for this situation and the potential for achieving higher and more meaningful levels of service user participation in the social service sector in Victoria, Australia.

In seeking answers for the apparent limited success in implementing participatory processes in social services, this study has investigated the current representation

© KONINKLIJKE BRILL NV, LEIDEN, 2018 | DOI:10.1163/9789004381407_005

of the problem of participation from three distinct theoretical categories. These categories relate to three key perspectives: the perceptions and attitudes of the wider society toward people "on welfare"; the social constructs that cause the marginalisation of these people; and the recurring examples of professional practice that often diminish, rather than enhance, the self-esteem of service users. By focusing on these three perspectives the study confronted questions as to why participation is important, why social services require it, what constitutes participation in the practice of social services, and why it is difficult to achieve.

THEORETICAL FRAMEWORK

This research mobilises concepts from several different theoretical approaches, particularly those developed by Donald Schön, Carol Bacchi and Erving Goffman. In this section I briefly survey the key concepts drawn from each author to outline the theoretical framework that inspired the research design.

Schön (2013, p. 42) suggests professional practice has "high ground" where practitioners make decisions based on research and technique and "swampy lowland" where situations are confusing messes, incapable of technical solutions. For Schön, the problems of the high ground are often unimportant to others and to society in general: the swamp is where the "problems of greatest human concern" are found.

Schön (p. 45) notes the work of Simon (1972, 1996) and others who have identified gaps between professional knowledge and the difficulties of real world practice. Simon (1996, p. 150) describes the traditional definition, that the professional's role has clear-cut and limited goals and this is compatible with what Simon refers to as "bounded rationality". Put simply, bounded rationality states it is impossible for people to consider all existing choices and possible outcomes of decisions. Therefore rational behavior is bounded by "people's minds – memory content – and their processes", as well as by the real world in which they act and "which acts on them" (Simon, 2000, p. 25). Simon points out that, as knowledge grows, the role of the professional becomes more complicated and he suggests this complication is a by-product of the growth of knowledge. He offers the example of advances in medical technology that have given the physician "some degree of control over life and death" (1996, p. 152). In Schön's (p. 46) view, it was Simon who linked this evolving predicament of professional knowledge to the "historical origins of the Positivist epistemology of practice". Schön's idea of "problem setting" (p. 18), which he describes as making sense of a real world problem that initially makes no sense, is an important activity of professional practice.

The results of my study suggest that the potential risks for clients of social services relate to the way some professionals prefer to take the "high ground" of labels and to adopt preconceived views of service users that have no connection to the service user as a person or to the causes that led them to become a service user. Gupta (2015, p. 134) speaks to the experience of shame by service users and how the simple fact of using a service is humiliating. Often such feelings of shame and worthlessness are compounded by the impact of dehumanising treatment from professionals. This point brings us to the influence of the wider community's attitudes toward people 'on welfare', and the community's capacity to accept difference and reject stigmatisation.

Bacchi (2009) describes the ways that problem representations can create social relationships within discourses that create inequality and turn people against one another. Bacchi (p. 16) notes Foucault's (1982, p. 208) use of the term *dividing practices*. An example would be the way an elderly man or woman with a cognitive impairment or mental illness is looked upon, in contrast to an elderly man or woman attending the local senior citizens club. Bacchi (2009, p. 17) refers to such contrasts as examples of the "lived effects" of dividing practices. One central aim of Bacchi's work is to reveal the state's part in contributing to stigmatisation, prejudice, inequality and misinformation in all aspects of policy development.

Goffman's (1986, p. 3) concept of stigma is also salient here. Goffman defines stigma as the product of relationships that occur as a result of the interaction of an individual and their society. Stigma is a shared experience among clients of social services in general. In this sense the exclusion of a single mother receiving welfare payments from participation in her local community is no different from the experience of the lifetime member of the local bowling club who is banned from the club because of their occasionally erratic behavior as the result of mental health issues. As Stoecklin (2012, p. 6) observes, a person's actual status in the community is determined by a diversity of factors. The factor that seems to stand out, however, involves the attitudes of others toward those of us who are perceived as different.

By contrast, Schön (2013) presents his notion of reflective practice as built upon the "quality of the collaboration" between all actors, which is underpinned by mutual accountability (p. 295). Collaboration forms relationships that challenge the power imbalance between the service user and the service provider, creating a partnership – specifically, a partnership where the focus is on empowering the service user to share their lived experiences and to frame problems (Beadle, Needham & Dearing, 2012, p. 353).

In completing this discussion of the theoretical categories that underpin this research I return to Schön (2013) and what he describes as one of the most important functions of a manager, which is the education of their staff. Schön is concerned specifically with a manager's role in educating staff on the "phenomena of organisational life", which include the cumulative knowledge attitudes, experiences and identity of the organisation (p. 242). For Schön the characteristics of interpersonal relationships within the organisation represent its "behavioural world". This behavioural world, combined with the organisational structure, creates what he calls the "learning system" of the organisation. Schön suggests that an organisation's learning system can limit or strongly support a manager's practice with clients and staff. Challenging the learning system of an organisation requires a professional to have a strong commitment to their personal values (Argyris & Schön, 1974, p. 162). Argyris and Schön particularly emphasise the importance of the professional's personal values, which guide their decision making, while Schön (p. 295) also highlights the relationship between the client and professional, underpinned by values and mutual accountability. These concepts are also thematised in Bacchi's (2009) notion of the need to search for the intrinsic values that underpin problem representations and in Ife's (1997) conviction that social service organisations cannot operate in a value-neutral fashion. Each of these theoretical constructs highlights important factors in the foundation of the knowledge and necessities of client participation, which I then explored in this study in the context of applied professional practice. This research therefore contributes to translating these theoretical concepts into practical examples of the power that professional values exert over service user experiences of participation in social services.

METHOD

This chapter draws on the results of a study conducted in two stages, with stage one taking place from September 2011 to April 2012, and stage two from February 2012 to April 2016. In stage one of the study I invited a range of stakeholders – including service users with varying needs and staff and board members from a range of social service organisations – to comment on the participation models and on the barriers and enablers to participation drawn from the academic literature on participation. Stakeholders were invited, first, to discuss whether they found such models and concepts useful, meaningful and valid. Second, they were asked whether they would find such models a useful means to help them articulate their own experiences as well as their attitudes and approaches to client participation. The data collected in this study was then used alongside insights from the academic literature to design and construct a simple, practical discussion rubric intended to guide a structured, reflective professional conversation about client participation in social service organisations.

The second stage of the research process asked focus group participants to reflect on their experiences of the barriers and enablers to participation and on the approach to participation taken within their own and other organisations, and to give their feedback on the content and usefulness of the discussion rubric. Below I highlight some of the key methodological considerations of the study.

METHODOLOGICAL CONSIDERATIONS AND RESEARCH DESIGN

I adopted a participatory approach to conducting this research, which ensured that all participants were included as active collaborators (Creswell, 2007, p. 22). This perspective strengthened the way that the study would assist in identifying examples of the barriers and enablers of participation. It also enabled me to collect examples of good practice that could serve as models for services to consider in improving their practice and that promoted the right of service users to participate fully and have a voice in the development of their services. Finally a collaborative approach would lessen the risk of further marginalising individual client participants by allowing their voices to be heard throughout the research process.

The study collected data from participants who managed, delivered and received social services. Their combined views and experiences created a picture of the practice of participation found within and/or absent from these services. This data also enabled an analysis of whether participants perceived that any factors that influenced participation, whether in positive or negative ways, were more significant than others.

Participants

Stage one included 29 participants from three social services. Participants included 16 clients, some with complex communication needs, 7 staff at team leader level and 6 board of management members. Two of these services operated in the Melbourne metropolitan area and the third was located in a large regional center in Victoria. Stage two included 35 professional practitioners from seven community sector social services located in the Melbourne metropolitan area. None of the services that participated in stage one participated in stage two. The programs of these ten organisations included disability services and accommodation, family services (including case management and emergency accommodation), drug and alcohol treatment, youth counselling services, youth refuges and family violence programs.

Ethical Considerations

The stage one study was approved by the RMIT University Human Ethics Advisory Network of the Science, Engineering and Health College, and stage two was approved by the Design and Social Context College Human Ethics Advisory Network, both sub-committees of the RMIT University Human Research Ethics Committee, and both studies were classified as low risk in accordance with the National Statement on Ethical Conduct of Human Research. All participants provided written consent prior to the collection of data and consented to the interviews and focus groups being recorded. Participants were made aware that their participation was voluntary and that they could withdraw from the session at any time.

In stage one participants with cognitive impairment were assessed on their ability to give consent utilising a method developed by Arscott, Dagnan, and Kroese (1998, 1999), which they adapted from an *Ability to Consent to Treatment Questionnaire* developed by Morris, Neiderbuhl, and Mahr (1993).

DATA COLLECTION

Stage one data was collected through 22 semi-structured individual face-to-face interviews and two group interviews with a total of seven participants. The interview questions were grouped under five themes, which were reflective of the enablers and inhibitors of participation found in the academic literature on participation and are listed in Table 5.1.

Stage two was prompted by the results of stage one and concentrated on examining what appeared to be a disconnect between service providers' clear understanding of client participation and their difficulty in embedding it in their practice with clients. Given the apparent influence of personal and professional values on organisational culture in the stage one results, I investigated the current perceptions of values in social services from a number of different perspectives. Guided by the work of Agbényiga (2011, p. 1776), I sought data in regard to the ways in which an organisational culture, in acting out its values, influences the day-to-day work with clients. Stage two was therefore designed to consider the current understanding of client participation in Victorian social services, and in what manner does participation merge with the three main aspects of an organisation – namely culture, structure and practice – to form an "integrated model of participation" that departs from the customary ladder metaphor used by Arnstein (1969), Hart (1992) and other popular models of participation (Hernandez, Robson, & Sampson, 2010, pp. 716–717).

Data Analysis

I conducted a thematic analysis of the de-identified interview and focus group transcripts, which I had transcribed from each interview and focus group recording. Pseudonyms were used to maintain confidentiality. The procedures used to construct the codes are reflective of what Boyatzis (1998, p. 31) describes as the "structure of a useful, meaningful code". I adopted a systematic approach to my analysis, reading each transcript and listening to each recording repeatedly, searching for categories and sub-themes. Table 5.1 provides an overview of the five major themes and their

Table 5.1. Stage one themes and descriptors

Themes	Descriptor
Values	Personal and organisational values influence an individual's approach to their work and how an entity conducts its business.
Processes	Processes that support client choice by providing opportunities to influence available choices and exercise the right to make decisions and/ or to practice and learn decision-making.
Management	Management decisions are based on the principles of equity, fairness and the acknowledgement of client needs.
Relationships	Relationships between all actors are built on dignity, respect, honesty and trust.
Leadership	Role models organisational values and behaviours and provides the vision for continuous improvement.

descriptors utilised in stage one. The process used for analysing the transcribed focus group data was the *classic analysis strategy* (Krueger & Casey, 2009, p. 118). The analysis is presented as two broad themes and three sub-themes.

RESULTS

The results are presented according to the themes that emerged from the academic literature and the thematic analysis of the data. The results offer insights into why the social services that participated in the study appear to have difficulty embedding client participation in their practice. There was also agreement among participants as to which components of practice, what I call the *enablers of participation*, are important contributors to good practice in their day-to-day work with clients. In particular their comments highlighted the themes of *Values* and *Relationships*, which have been consistently noted in the academic literature, and these appeared in both stages of the study as critical enablers of participation. There was consensus among participants regarding the potential for a discussion rubric as a useful prompt for discussion as well as for a back of the envelope self-assessment of their client participation practice.

Experience of Client Participation

The stage one study found a reasonable conformity between the academic literature on participation and the views of participants. Surprisingly, although participants agreed on the importance of the enablers as contributors to good practice, they articulated a lack of capacity to fully operationalise a process to realise participation in their service delivery. None of the services participating in stage one had a formal process in place for obtaining feedback from clients on the services they received. The following board member quotes are examples of responses to a question that asked: *What information do you collect during the course of your work to help you judge the quality of your work?*

> As a board, we don't have a way of measuring the quality of our service. We have no real mechanism to gather and see client-based feedback. So as a board we don't see anything.

> No, there is no mechanism (for client feedback) that I am aware of other than there is a suggestion box that sits in the foyer of the building.

A board member from another service noted a similar situation but suggested service user feedback was dependent upon the relationship staff have with the service user:

> I think we primarily rely on the relationships between our staff and clients to get that feedback.

One group articulated a clear approach to engaging with clients, while another suggested social services were not good at learning from one another.

We identify three factors for engagement: motivation, readiness and confidence. The belief that, 'I can do this'. If these three factors are in play; then, it's a pretty good chance the client will stay here and do a good program.

There are practical living examples of organisations that exist with high levels of consumer participation. What we don't do in community services is to look for these living, breathing examples. What they did and how they did it and what didn't work and what did and why.

The first quote above, which indirectly refers to a method that will likely contribute to client participation, is actually grounded in good practice through establishing relationships with clients, and then supporting clients in building their confidence to succeed. Ignoring the knowledge and experiences of service users restricts opportunities for clients and improving services.

Values and Relationships

Service user participants reinforced the importance of values in various ways. For example, an adolescent in a residential program said, "staff treat us with respect", when asked how he got along with staff. Another said their team leader "had been a good support to me, especially last year when I lost my parents". Other clients made negative statements regarding staff not taking their complaints seriously.

I tried to make complaints but I got told off by the team leader: 'We don't want to know any of that. We just want you to get better'.

What appeared to be important for service users was their need for a relationship with at least one person in the service – a person they felt they could trust and depend on to be responsive to their needs and concerns. The following quote is typical of responses when a board member participant was asked to describe how they thought staff formed relationships with service users:

Are they (clients) going to somebody for support and if they are who do they trust? Once that's happened, there will be choices about their life situation. Choices evolve from relationships that are built on trust.

Further analysis portrayed personal and professional values as the foundation of organisational culture. The prominence of such values as an enabler of participation stood out in the stage one results. The emphatic views expressed by participants on the significance of the 'appropriate' intrinsic values that people carry with them to the workplace precipitated the need to investigate this aspect of the stage one results in a more pointed manner in stage two. The following quotes reinforce the necessity of collaborative relationships in the form of engaging with clients as individuals:

The development of relationships is the key to participation and holding people.

When people (clients) leave here they say, 'These friendships are what helped me and kept me here'. 'I've never had a friend in my life and now I've got a friendship group'. That's what the program is based on, relationships.

It takes a bit of giving of yourself and opening up. Relationship building is probably around how much they (clients) are willing to trust and how trustworthy are they?

Bacchi (2009) points out that policies give shape to problems and that these problem representations can sometimes develop relationships that create stigmatisation and inequality. The nature of the relationships that professionals establish with clients is a matter of choice for the professional. How professionals frame their role, as well as their capacity to take action in difficult circumstances, is guided by their values (Argyris & Schön, 1974, p. 162). When the practitioner states that relationships are the key to 'holding people', they are offering an example from their practice of what they value in their work, which, in the case above, is the importance of establishing balanced relationships with their clients. Schön (2013) takes this further when he suggests a commitment to take action by a practitioner should be "intrinsically satisfying" and not for external rewards (p. 231).

For one organisation in stage one, the values of the board members differed greatly from the staff participants. When asked about their personal values, board member participants from this service responded in a manner that suggested they did not appreciate the difference between personal values and experience:

For me it's the 36 years of experience of working with people with disabilities. The empathy I have for people with disabilities.

A second board member from the same service made a similar comment: "I suppose my greatest attributes are my years of experience, knowledge and participation", and then went on to say:

No family makes a choice to have a child with a disability. So these clients that we work with have never been the great joy and celebration in life that our children have been.

This disturbing comment captured a sense of moral superiority over service users rather than a concern for their dignity and human rights, and this conflicted with the views of staff at this service. Further reflections from these board members reinforced this impression. In particular, when asked to describe their relationship with service users, the response was, "We have a very high respect for them" and a comment from another board member regarding their motivation to be on the board because "I have a genuine commitment to people that are less fortunate".

The comments by board members from other services, by contrast, were more concerned with respect as a necessary component of establishing relationships with service users:

> It (service) certainly has the view that relationships are important and the staff should be working to establish relationships that are respectful and have dignity with (service users).

> It depends on the quality of the relationship you establish with them (service user), but you also need to have a degree of respect.

These comments may represent an organisational culture that first empowers their workforce, which in turn facilitates building positive relationships with service users (Spence Laschinger et al., 2009, p. 303).

Operationalising Participation

The quotes to follow reflect a common assumption expressed in all but one focus group regarding the difficulty in operationalising participation. I believe this view is the result of two main influences. The first influence is the complexity of constructing a definition for participation itself. An inability to arrive at a universally acceptable definition has been a feature of the academic literature on participation for the past fifty years. Secondly, when service providers confront the task of operationalising client participation in the context of their practice so that it both meets the needs of their clients and is within the skills of their workforce the level of difficulty appears insurmountable. The quote below is an example of this view.

> I think we don't do it very well at all. I don't think it has been an active part of our program, but it has become more so in terms of the kind of environment we want to create but there is no real consistent format for including clients in all sort of stages of that.

> Another thing that stands out for me is that a lot of organisations don't understand what consumer participation is. Some are also scared of it because if you share power with consumers it will harm the business.

The quote above touches on aspects of the second influence, which are the attitudes of workers toward clients in the first instance and also their understanding of the significance of involving service users in the services they receive.

Fear and Client Capacity

Beginning with Arnstein (1969), the literature on participation offers numerous examples of the resistance that professionals and powerholders display toward sharing power or changing professional attitudes that sometimes damage clients' self-esteem (Gupta & Royal, 2015; Bennetts et al., 2011; Happell & Roper, 2008). Schön's (2013, p. 42) features of professional practice that inhabit his "swampy lowland" include the aspects of fear and doubts about client capacity presented here.

The fear is that sharing power with clients will damage the business and, as the following quote suggests, for some services this fear is a major driver of resistance to implementing client participation.

When we talk to organisations about auditing their consumer participation we really need to talk with them about their fears. We learned that with one organisation where we hadn't done that initial work and had this huge resistance and when I unpacked it we found that it was fear.

The data suggest that a common reaction to this fear is that the leadership and management of an organisation become risk averse in their approach to service delivery:

Management needs to understand and be honest about risk. It really does play a role because if you're engaging with consumers who are technically in a more fragile space at that particular time than are the providers of the service there is a risk element that needs to be considered.

The essence of the discussion in one focus group centered on the view that service providers are operating in a risk controlled, litigious environment where client participation requires a paradigm shift that, in the managers' minds, increases risk.

The quotes below suggest how workers underestimate the capacity of clients to participate – a finding which also features in the broader literature on participation. For example, Tritter and McCullum (2006) suggest that Arnstein's (1969) work has outlived its usefulness precisely because in their opinion Arnstein neglected to include capacity building to enable clients to participate effectively. Nevertheless, Arnstein did provide examples of a professional culture that assumed clients had nothing to contribute.

I think for a lot of it is also that they (organisations) feel they (clients) don't have the capacity to contribute and that is a personal judgment. I think that's a failure of a lot of the community health sector is they feel consumers can't offer expertise but often they can.

We involve our consumers in our strategic planning day as an organisation. I think that is a fear of some organisations that consumers will turn up and speak up and things will go in the wrong direction.

In trying to develop capacity for consumer participation is that people's good will is that we want to involve our consumers (sic) but it actually becomes disempowering to collect data and shelve it. You create a disheartened consumer base that feel they wasted their time doing this and they never see any fruit of their input.

The three quotes presented here are also examples of the further stigmatisation of clients by making judgments on their capacity to contribute, fearing what might happen if clients are given an opportunity to participate and failing to listen and act on their feedback if they do participate. This type of treatment from professionals perpetuates the feelings of uselessness and isolation that some clients experience, which continues to damage them and their self-esteem.

Content, Structure and Use of the Rubric

In each focus group more than one participant's initial reaction to the example of the discussion rubric (Table 5.2) was both enthusiastic and positive, with agreement from the rest of the group.

> I think it's a good document, I think it really makes you think about where you're at by looking at this document.

> It was overwhelming when I first looked at it but I thought oh yeah, that's a tool. It is very easy to read and it's clear. I found it, just by reading it for a while, it didn't take me long to work out how to use it.

> My instant thought when I first looked at it is gee we really have a hell of a lot of work to do.

My assessment of this feedback is that, first, organisations appreciated the value of the rubric as a method to stimulate discussion on the process of client participation and, second, participants valued being able to refer to concrete definitions and practical examples of what was necessary for them to have in place when reflecting on their practice with clients.

DISCUSSION

The results of the stage one study suggest that the most influential enabler of participation is *Values*. Personal values are what we use to measure what is important to us. The decisions we make in this regard determine how we behave and form relationships. Staff participants described the process of building relationships with clients through strategies which include listening, being respectful of their views and opinions, having a sense of curiosity for each individual and being responsive to their needs. These points are examples from practice of the influence of the participants' personal values.

Examples of how *Values* influence *Relationships* can be found in the staff participant descriptions of the effort they make to first consider the practical needs of the client in how they might deliver services. Simple considerations like this demonstrate to the client that staff value and care about them as individuals and are interested in helping them to achieve their goals.

Participants articulated three important factors in establishing *Relationships* that contribute to client participation. The first is trust, which applies to all participants and is part of any positive relationship. The second is the need to concentrate on providing opportunities to give feedback and discuss their needs and experiences, which is in turn dependent on the third element, which requires service providers to take note of and manage the professional attitudes and culture within the organisation.

In answering the question of whether any of the enablers of participation were of greater significance to service users, the results clearly indicate that in the minds of service users *Relationships* is the most important.

From *Values* and *Relationships* comes an approach to *Management* and the subsequent *Processes* that pays attention to the principles of fairness, equity and the human rights of clients. Although the responses from participants did not envisage a significant number of choices for their clients, the flexible service delivery style of some service providers did generate choices for clients. This was primarily the result of an individual staff member's level of confidence in management to back staff decisions, combined with staff knowledge of the client's needs. This exemplified the personal values of participants and the organisational values that underpinned the client focused culture of the service provider.

Ife (1997, p. 16) notes the trend (which continues today) in social services towards "managerialism", which is the belief that management is a generic skill that can be applied to any organisation without regard to the nature of its business. What is significant for Ife in this trend is the change in perspective of senior managers from a personal and professional identity based on the values of a human service professional to a view of themselves as managers. The findings of the stage one study imply that in some social services a management focus on efficiency without effectiveness ignores the appropriate personal and professional values that enable respectful relationships to be formed with clients.

The data suggested four barriers to participation, which included *fear, client capacity, knowhow* and *resources.* Combining these four barriers would produce an environment that: perceives client participation as a complicated addition to the day to day work with clients (Hernandez et al., 2010); fails to take into account the vulnerability and feelings of stigmatisation that clients experience (Gupta & Blewett, 2008; Hickey & Kipping, 1998); lacks an understanding of the importance of culture in developing a commitment to participation (Wright, Turner, Clay, & Mills, 2006; Happell & Roper, 2008); and ignores the elements of influence, stigma, tokenism and resistance to change which come from fear of losing power and control (Bennetts, Cross, & Bloomer, 2011, p. 156).

What became clear from the participants' responses is that the practice of client participation in social services continues to be perceived as something inherently complex, unconnected to good practice, difficult to do well and often too hard to try. As Stoecklin (2012) put it, participation remains a "concept in need of an explicit theory of action" (p. 13).

Participants were consistent in their view of client participation as engaging clients in a collaborative relationship aimed at improving the quality of a client's life in some way, and as a process that involved, in part, obtaining evidence from clients regarding the effectiveness of the services they received and then feeding that information back through the management structure to the board of management. Participants did not offer specific detail on how this flow of client-specific evidence would be obtained, what processes would be required to encourage it, what training and support clients would require to accomplish this and what actions, if any, would be taken.

A consistent view was that overcoming the barriers of *fear* and *client capacity* begins with being honest with clients about what the service has to offer them and explanations about how and why decisions are made. The power imbalance between staff and clients never disappears, but it can be balanced through the actions of honesty and explanation, which assist in building trust.

The barrier of *knowhow* seems to surface when the apparent goodwill and motivation in social services to improve participative processes appear to be overwhelmed by not knowing where to start. To begin embedding client participation in their service an organisation needs to be clear on what client participation means in the context of their practice so that it meets the needs of their clients and is compatible with the skills of their staff.

Again Wright et al. (2006), while acknowledging the plethora of definitions of participation, offer at least two causes for the difficulty social services have in implementing participation in their practice. The first is the failure of services to establish an agreed understanding of what participation means at the organisational level, so that it can be understood, shared, marketed and embedded in practices across the organisation. The second is the risk that participation may become the latest buzzword for policy and practice so that it becomes simply a "tick box" exercise, a requirement that leaves organisations with little time to fully understand how to properly operationalise it (Wright et al., 2006, p. 6).

The findings of this study, if merged together as the natural attributes of a hypothetical ideal social service, would give birth to an organisation that contained a core group of committed professional staff that believed in and understood the necessity of building a culture of participation. Their tasks would be: first, to engage with clients to ensure they gain an understanding of what participation means for them; second, to educate management on participation to establish an organisation-wide understanding of participation; third, to assist management and some professionals to overcome their fear of losing power and control; fourth, to define participation in the context of their service as inclusive of everyday practice with clients, not as an additional activity; fifth, to work with all segments of the organisation to develop processes that enable and sustain the active participation of clients; and sixth, to review progress using a discussion rubric that summarises the participation literature and offers examples of participation in practice (Table 5.2).

CONCLUSION

In conclusion I return to Stoecklin's (2012) statement that participation is a "concept in need of an explicit theory of action" (p. 12). The academic literature offers fifty years of a diverse range of approaches to and perceptions of participation that, in the

Table 5.2. Discussion rubric

Indicator	Insignificant	Limited	Fair	Good	Very Good
			Levels		
Values: Take actions that are intrinsically satisfying, not for external rewards	Staff provide no or very little opportunity for choices/decisions	Staff provide information only	Some acknowledgement of the importance of asking clients what they think, want, need	Clients are listened to and their views valued and put into action when appropriate	No limit on what level a client is able to participate, e.g. co-design of services
Relationships: Evenness in relationships with others, both internal and external	One-sided. Staff maintain control of day to day living	Some acknowledgement of importance of good relationships between clients and staff	Clients are actively encouraged to participate and made aware of their choices	Client/staff interactions are collaborative and representative of views and needs of clients	Clients and staff relationships are formed as a partnership for the benefit of clients
Processes: Both formal and informal do not inhibit or exclude participation for clients and staff	Non-existent	Documented participative processes exist but are imposed by external funding provider	Participation occurs but is ad hoc and dependent on individual staff/client relationships	Views and needs of clients are the primary focus of service planning processes	Processes for user participation embedded in organisational culture, processes and policies
Management: Problem solving and decision making enable and support client participation	Not inclined to consider client participation as a meaningful component of practice	Some participation encouraged to meet imposed objectives	Participation is short term and passive	What is in it for clients, is first consideration of decision making processes	Acts to ensure client participation incorporated into all systems and everyday practice
Leadership: Role models values, drives continuous improvement	Maintain status quo	Some personnel changes in management positions	Makes some effort to obtain client and staff views on need for change	Actively seeks input from clients and staff on service improvements	Champions and leads best practice in client participation

eyes of professional practitioners, appear as fragments of practice. This study has attempted to name the critical dimensions of the barriers and enablers of participation in the academic literature and in the practice of social services in order to form a coherent and practical body of knowledge that assists social services to advance their practice of participation.

The notion of fear, discussed earlier, appears to originate from, and is sustained by, the internal beliefs and values of the leadership and management that set and maintain the environment of the organisation. Such beliefs stem from a lack of respect for clients in the practice employed by some professionals. Their lack of respect for clients is illustrated in their disinterest in the knowledge and life experience that clients hold, and in their limited understanding of what this experience has to offer them as professionals. Social services wanting to improve their practice must first, acknowledge that barriers to participation may exist within their culture, structure and practice. Second, they must undertake an appraisal of all staff relationships with, and attitudes toward clients, with a particular focus on how they balance the "double-blind" relationship of authority over, and care for, their clients; and third, reflect on whether staff value their "professional status" over their relationships with clients (Stoecklin, 2012, p. 9).

REFERENCES

Agbényiga, D. L. (2011). Organisational culture influence on service delivery: A mixed methods design in a child welfare setting. *Children and Youth Services Review, 33*(10), 1767–1778.

Argyris, C., & Schön, D. A. (1974). *Theory in practice: Increasing professional effectiveness.* San Francisco, CA: Jossey-Bass.

Arnstein, S. R. (1969). Eight rungs on the ladder of citizen participation. *Journal of the American Institute of Planners, 35*(4), 216–224.

Arscott, K., Dagnan, D., & Kroese, B. S. (1998). Consent to psychological research by people with an intellectual disability. *Journal of Applied Research in Intellectual Disabilities, 11*(1), 77–83.

Barnes, D., Carpenter, J., & Bailey, D. (2000). Partnerships with service users in interprofessional education for community mental health: A case study. *Journal of Interprofessional Care, 14*(2), 189–200.

Beadle, M., Needham, Y., & Dearing, M. (2012). Collaboration with service users to develop reusable learning objects: The ROOT to success. *Nurse Education in Practice, 12*(6), 352–355.

Bennetts, W., Cross, W., & Bloomer, M. (2011). Understanding consumer participation in mental health: Issues of power and change. *International Journal of Mental Health Nursing, 20*(3), 155–164.

Bersani, H. (1996). Leadership in developmental disabilities: Where we've been, where we are, and where we're going. In G. Dybwad & H. J. Bersani (Eds.), *New voices self-advocacy by people with disabilities* (pp. 258–269). Cambridge, MA: Brookline Books.

Boyatzis, R. E. (1998). *Transforming qualitative information: Thematic analysis and code development.* Thousand Oaks, CA: Sage Publications.

Charmaz, K. (2006). *Constructing grounded theory: A practical guide through qualitative analysis.* London: Sage Publications.

Checkoway, B. (1998). Involving young people in neighborhood development. *Children and Youth Services Review, 20*(9–10), 765–795.

Cornwall, A. (2008). Unpacking 'participation': Models, meanings and practices. *Community Development Journal, 43*(3), 14.

Creswell, J. W. (2007). *Qualitative inquiry and research design, choosing among five approaches* (2nd ed.). Thousand Oaks, CA: Sage Publications.

Fox, C. (2003). Debating deinstitutionalisation: The fire at Kew Cottages in 1996 and the idea of community. *Health and History, 5*(2), 37–59.

Goffman, E. (1986). *Stigma: Notes on the management of spoiled identity.* New York, NY: Touchstone.

Gupta, A., & Blewett, J. (2008). Involving services users in social work training on the reality of family poverty: A case study of a collaborative project. *Social Work Education, 27*(5), 459–473.

Gupta, A., & Royal, H. (2015). Poverty and shame – messages for social work. *Critical and Radical Social Work, 3*(1), 131–139.

Happell, B., & Roper, C. (2008). Promoting genuine consumer participation in mental health education: A consumer academic role. *Nurse Education Today, 29*, 575–579.

Hart, R. A. (1992). *Children's participation: From tokenism to citizenship.* Florence: UNICEF. Retrieved from http://www.unicef-irc.org/

Heffernan, K. (2006). Social work, new public management and the language of service user. *British Journal of Social Work, 36*(1), 139–147.

Hernandez, L., Robson, P., & Sampson, A. (2010). Towards integrated participation: Involving seldom heard users of social care services. *British Journal of Social Work, 40*(3), 714–736.

Ife, J. W. (1997). *Rethinking social work: Towards critical practice.* Melbourne: Longman.

Kemmis, S., & Wilkinson, M. (1998). Participatory action research and the study of practice. In B. Atweh, S. Kemmis, & P. Weeks (Eds.), *Action research in practice: Partnerships for social justice in education* (pp. 21–36). New York, NY: Routledge.

Krueger, R. A., & Casey, M. A. (2009). *Focus groups: A practical guide for applied research* (4th ed.). Thousand Oaks, CA: Sage Publications.

Lardner, C. (2001a). *Exploring good practice in youth participation, a critical review.* Retrieved from http://www.clarity-scotland.co.uk

Manning, C. (2008). *Bye-bye Charlie: Stories from the vanishing world of Kew Cottages.* Sydney: University of New South Wales Press Ltd.

Manning, C. (2009). Imprisoned in state care? Life inside Kew Cottages 1925–2008. *Health and History, 11*(1), 149–171.

McNiff, J. (2013). *Action research: Principles and practice.* New York, NY: Routledge.

Padilla, M., Cabero, N., Parejo, S., & Gonza'lez, M. (2007). *Approaches to participation: Some neglected issues.* Paper presented at the Fifth Critical Management Studies Conference, Manchester, UK.

Schön, D. A. (2013). *The reflective practitioner: How professionals think in action.* Surrey: Ashgate.

Sheir, H. (2001). Pathways to participation: Openings, opportunities and obligations. *Children & Society, 15*, 107–115.

Simon, H. A. (1996). *The sciences of the artificial.* Retrieved September 26, 2016, from http://ieeexplore.ieee.org.ezproxy.lib.rmit.edu.au/xpl/bkabstractplus.jsp?bkn=6267338

Simon, H. A. (2000). Bounded rationality in social science: Today and tomorrow. *Mind & Society, 1*(1), 25–39.

Spence Laschinger, H. K., Leiter, M., Day, A., & Gilin, D. (2009). Workplace empowerment, incivility, and burnout: Impact on staff nurse recruitment and retention outcomes. *Journal of Nursing Management, 17*(3), 302–311.

Stoecklin, D. (2012). Theories of action in the field of child participation: In search of explicit frameworks. *Childhood, 20*(4), 443–457.

Strauss, A. L., & Corbin, J. (1998). *Basics of qualitative research: Techniques and procedures for developing grounded theory* (2nd ed.). Thousand Oaks, CA: Sage Publications.

Treseder, P. (1997). *Empowering children and young people.* London: Children's Rights Office/Save the Children.

Tritter, J. Q., & McCallum, A. (2006). The snakes and ladders of user involvement: Moving beyond Arnstein. *Health Policy, 76*(2), 156–168.

Webb, S. A. (2008). Modeling service user participation in social care. *Journal of Social Work, 8*(3), 269–290.

Wright, P., Turner, C., Clay, D., & Mills, H. (2006). *The Participation of children and young people in Developing Social Care* (Practice Guide 06). London: Social Care Institute for Excellence.
Yin, R. K. (2010). *Qualitative research from start to finish*. New York, NY: Guilford Publications.

Lou Iaquinto
RMIT University
Australia

PART 2

PLACE-MAKING – PRIVILEGES OF CULTURE AND IDENTITY

CHRISTOPHER C. SONN, KAREN JACKSON
AND REBECCA LYONS

6. EXPLORING MEANINGS AND PRACTICES OF INDIGENOUS PLACEMAKING IN MELBOURNE'S WEST

INTRODUCTION

In this chapter, we report on research with participants brought together by means of a community development project initiated in 2013–2014 by the City of Wyndham in collaboration with Aboriginal and Torres Strait Islander people in the Wyndham region and the subsequent establishment of the Wyndham Aboriginal Community Centre Committee (WACCC) (Western Suburbs Working Group, 2013). The collaboration between the City of Wyndham and representative groups of the Aboriginal and Torres Strait Islander communities has developed over several years and is responding to Aboriginal people's need "for permanent places in which they can strengthen cultural identity, build community connections and improve access to services" (p. 1). The specific study evolved from initial questions posed by Aboriginal community members from the WACCC and Care Connect's Aboriginal Planned Activity Group (PAG) as they seek to establish cultural safety and create new community narratives together. PAG provides high quality, culturally appropriate day activities for frail aged and disabled persons from the Aboriginal Community and provides participants an opportunity to maximise their quality of life through activities designed to enhance the skills required for daily living and to provide physical, intellectual, psychological and social wellbeing (CareConnect, 2017).

PAG members mostly come from and live in the Western suburbs and surrounds of Melbourne, although some have come from other parts of Australia. The group attends PAG four times a week from Monday to Thursday. The group consists of elders, mostly women. Although many suffer health issues, they are welcoming and give generously of their time. The group is close-knit and engages in many group and individual activities such as painting, knitting, making crafts, and planning group activities and outings. The group uses their time and skills to make crafts that they can sell and they reinvest the money that they earn into PAG. PAG also donates to other local Aboriginal community organisations. The PAG members expressed the need for a culturally safe space as the space they use in the mainstream community setting is a shared space, and they do not always feel that they can be free there. The group members expressed their excitement about a new planned Aboriginal Community Center opening in Wyndham.

© KONINKLIJKE BRILL NV, LEIDEN, 2018 | DOI:10.1163/9789004381407_006

Our collaboration builds on a longstanding relationship between the researcher team and researcher members and the Aboriginal community. Key to our collaboration is a shared commitment to documenting the experiences of Indigenous groups and other ethnic communities in order to promote empowerment and self-determination. As has been the case for other critics and Indigenous scholars (Dudgeon & Walker, 2015; Kovach, 2009; Smith, 2012) the values of reciprocity and mutual recognition guided our research. We describe in detail how we put these into practice. The processes for this research included: spending time in ongoing critical discussion and negotiation with relevant groups (both at the university and with the community groups); ensuring cultural safety and reciprocity; expanding our ways of knowing through multiple methods and modes of inquiry; and surfacing the stories of survival and resistance (Dutta et al., 2016; Sonn & Baker, 2015).

Colonisation and Displacement

The colonising experience of Aboriginal and Torres Strait Islander people in Australia has included the systematic dispossession of culture, land, language, family and community (Walter, 2010). Colonial projects in Australia and other countries were realised through "massive violence, forcing the history, culture, and genealogy of blacks into oblivion" (Bulhan, 1985, p. 297). The oppressive rule following dispossession and the wars that accompanied the taking of land, and the various forms of physical and cultural violence throughout the 19th and 20th century effectively constituted genocidal activity as defined by the United Nations definition of genocide (UNHRC, 1948). Dudgeon and Walker (2015) wrote that, "colonial disruptions to domains of family, spirituality, land and culture have ... produced a profound sense of grief and a deep longing to reconnect with their cultural heritage and ancestry" (p. 281). Various paternalistic policies and practices rooted in an ideology of white supremacy, ranging from protectionism and assimilation to forms of self-management in Victoria in the 1960s, were put in place to achieve this dispossession. These policies and the ideology of supremacy laid the foundations for the removal of Aboriginal and Torres Strait Islander children from their families that resulted in the group commonly referred to as the Stolen Generations (Human Rights and Equal Opportunity Commission [HREOC], 1997).

It has now been 20 years since the delivery of the *Bringing Them Home* Report (HREOC, 1997) based on a national inquiry into the removal of Aboriginal and Torres Strait Islander children from their families (Aboriginal and Torres Strait Islander Healing Foundation, 2017). The original report documented the devastating social, psychological, economic and cultural consequences of these practices for individuals and communities as evidenced in experiences such as trauma and grief, family breakdown and violence, discrimination and racism. The recent action plan for healing delivered by the Healing Foundation (2017) highlights the continuing negative health and wellbeing outcomes that are a result of past and current experiences of oppression on members of the Stolen Generations and their families. For Aboriginal people, and particularly for people who were removed and institutionalised as well as for their descendants, the effects of disruption have been further compounded by the removal of identity. This removal includes no access to legal documents such as birth certificates confirming identity (Lyons, 2014), disconnection from Aboriginality and racism, as well as institutionalised physical, sexual and emotional abuse (Atkinson, Nelson, Brooks, Atkinson, & Ryan, 2014; Dudgeon, Wright, Paradies, Garvey, & Walker, 2014). It is important to understand the effects of these policies and practices, but it also should not be assumed that all descendants of members of the Stolen Generations have lost their identity and connection to their Aboriginality, as many of the Stolen Generations did return home and ensured that their connection to their family and Aboriginality remained strong (Behrendt, 2009; Lyons, 2014).

Krieg (2009) argued that colonisation was not a moment but is an ongoing experience which finds expression in institutional and cultural practices in current contexts, as is signalled in Moreton-Robinson's (2003) reference to post-colonising Australia. Indigenous people continue to face various forms of exclusion, such as racism and marginalisation, which suggests that despite the removal of various oppressive policies and practices coloniality continues to constrain their lives. The history of colonial dispossession and current forms of oppression have implications for the health and social and emotional wellbeing of individuals and communities and require responses from them (Zubrick et al., 2014). This is the case for the growing Aboriginal population in Melbourne's western region, which has seen an increase from 703 in 2006 to 1,144 in 2011 (ABS, 2011). Many studies have shown the effects of oppressive practices on the health and wellbeing of individuals and communities, but researchers have also argued that people and communities develop strategies of survival and resistance to ensure cultural continuity and to protect identities. These strategies developed at the borders of exclusion form the basis for resilience and social and emotional wellbeing (Dudgeon et al., 2014; Quayle, 2017; Zubrick et al., 2014). These strategies are evident at individual, group and community levels and include practices such as story-telling and socialising children to know their family and community stories, deconstructing racism with significant others and drawing on local and traditional knowledge to assert positive identities (Behrendt, 2009; Quayle, 2017). In research with South Africans who have endured apartheid, Sonn (2012) argued that under changed circumstances people retell stories about racism and they actively engage in liberatory activities by retrieving family archives and histories to understand their personal and community experiences of dispossession. Along similar lines, Kirmayer et al. (2011) noted that collective forms of narrative "help people make sense of their experience and construct a valued identity but also ensure the continuity and vitality of a community or a people" (pp. 85–86).

Consultation with Aboriginal groups in the western region of Melbourne has identified a priority need for specific support for people who come to discover their identity as Aboriginal, particularly children and young people, and also people displaced through dispersal, and whose needs for understanding and care

are insufficiently acknowledged or satisfied at present (Balla, McCallum, Sonn, Jackson, McKenna, & Marion, 2009). This population is diverse, and people have moved into the area from other parts of Victoria and Australia for a host of reasons including to connect with family and to be closer to family members in prison, to have access to health services, and for work and study. What is not clear is the extent, and in what ways Indigenous people in the western suburbs experience a loss of identity and a sense of displacement as an outcome of colonialism and current forms of social oppression, but also how people are building community and constructing places for meaningful engagement and positive experiences of place, belonging, and community.

Through the research, we sought to gather stories of Aboriginal people who are seeking to establish cultural safety and create new community narratives together. The focus of this chapter is twofold. The first task is to outline the importance of stories and storytelling as a methodology to conduct research that is affirmative of Indigenous self-determination and cultural renewal. This is necessary given the criticisms of traditional mainstream approaches which are felt to be based on an underlying assumption of universality and objectivism, and whose ahistorical and decontextualised stance reinforces colonising research practices (Kovach, 2009; Smith, 2012). Indigenous methodologies anchored in different epistemologies see knowledge as situated and relational, and the process of knowledge production as dialogical and in response to the needs of the people (Tuck, 2009). The second task is to discuss the insights we developed through our decolonising approach to placemaking. Our analysis shows that placemaking involves material and social practices of emplacement – for instance, retrieving family histories and memory, and engaging cultural traditions and expression to create new narratives.

DECOLONISING APPROACHES AND INDIGENOUS METHODOLOGIES

Various areas of scholarship have called for critically oriented research (Montero, 2007, 2017; Montero, Sonn, & Burton, 2017; Teo, 2015). Central to this orientation is an epistemology that recognises the embeddedness of people in social cultural systems, and how people and the social world are co-constituting a view that challenges the epistemic violence inherent in individualistic, objectivist, decontextualised and ahistorical analysis (Gergen & Gergen, 2010; Montero, 2007, 2017; Rappaport, 2000; Teo, 2015). Importantly such approaches also emphasise the examination of issues within longer histories of colonialism that have shaped people's differential access to the resources required for living (Dutta, Sonn, & Lykes, 2016) and they bring under close scrutiny the way that Western scientific modes of knowing, doing and being have been implicated in colonialism and imperialism (Dudgeon & Walker, 2015; Reyes Cruz & Sonn, 2011; Smith, 1999). For Reyes Cruz and Sonn (2011; Sonn & Green, 2006) this has entailed a call for adopting a decolonising standpoint from which to engage in community research and action that is aimed at exposing the dynamics of oppression in research and in practice.

In Australia and other countries, Indigenous scholars and activists, alongside critical scholars of race have argued for Indigenous and Indigenist methodologies (Martin & Mirraboopa, 2003; Moreton Robinson & Walter, 2009; Kovach, 2009; Rigney, 2006, Tuck & McKenzie, 2015) based in indigenous knowledge. In a broad sense indigenous knowledge differs from Western scientific knowledge. It refers to local knowledge that is unique to a society or culture and is produced in social, political and historical contexts both on its own terms and in relation to colonialism. Typically knowledge is something to be shared and produced in context and places and in relationships through cultural means such as stories, storytelling, art, song, and dance.

Land, Country, and Place

The notions of land and country are central to how identity and belonging is constituted for Indigenous people. Moreton Robinson (2003) argued that Indigenous people's conceptions of place and belonging are different to those of the settlers: "the ways that country is constitutive of us, and therefore the inalienable nature of our relation to land, marks a radical, indeed incommensurable, difference between us and the non-Indigenous" (p. 31).

According to Bird Rose (1996, p. 7):

Country is a place that gives and receives life. Not just imagined or represented, it is lived in and lived with. Country in Aboriginal English is not only a common noun, but also a proper noun. People talk about country in the same way that they would talk about a person; they speak to country, sing to country, visit country, worry about country, feel sorry for country and long for country. Rather, country is a living entity with a yesterday, today and tomorrow with a consciousness, and a will toward life. Because of this richness, country is home and peace: nourishment for body, mind and spirit [...].

Scholars in various disciplines have advocated for a dialogical understanding of place, identity and community, contested and negotiated as always (Hodgetts, Drew, Sonn, Nikora, & Curtis, 2010; Massey, 2005). Advocates of critical place inquiry highlight the importance of indigenous understandings of land and country, and of lived experiences, for understanding places and placemaking (Somerville, 2007; Tuck & McKenzie, 2015). Places are not neutral. Places are contested and continuously made and remade and given meaning in local contexts and also within the broader history of colonialism and indigenous struggles for land rights and sovereignty (Fredericks, 2013; Moreton Robinson, 2003; Tuck & McKenzie, 2015). Somerville (2007) has proposed a place pedagogy that recognises that "our relationship to place is constituted in stories and other representations; place learning is local and embodied; and deep place learning occurs in a contact zone of contestation" (p. 342). Somerville emphasised the importance of undoing dominant stories of place as part of decolonisation, but also of engaging in the collective and relational process of creating new place stories.

Importantly, as noted by Fredericks (2013; Behrendt, 2009), because of dispossession many Aboriginal people are away from traditional country and instead are contesting and making places in urban settings. Counter to the narratives of invisibility in urban spaces, Aboriginal people through practices such as the recovery of historical memory and drawing on current histories are carving out places for communality and belonging. As Behrendt (2009) noted:

> The "traditional", the colonial, and the present are a fluid history connecting place and kin in our culture. Home is a special, specific place. Home is everywhere. Home is the long "lost" past. Home is like a perpetual present. ... wherever we have lived there is a newer imprint of history, one that meaningfully creates a sense of belonging within Aboriginal communities formed in urban areas. (p. 78)

Stories and Story-Telling

Dudgeon and Walker (2015) have provided an argument for the decolonisation of the science of psychology and provided several strategies for doing so. These strategies include: the development of new discourses and narratives that challenge mainstream conceptions of people and the origins of psychological and social problems; challenging privilege and whiteness; and promoting resources and strategies that are indigenous led that can support the development of critical reflexivity and culturally safe practice (Walker, Schultz, & Sonn, 2014). Along similar lines, informed by the postcolonial and critical scholarship of Frantz Fanon (1967, 1986) and Steve Bantu Biko (1988) among others, South African scholars Stevens, Duncan and Hook (2015) have advocated a psychosocial political approach to race, memory and history, and transformation. They argue that such an approach moves beyond traditional theories of the psychosocial and is:

> concerned more fundamentally with the type of conceptual and critical work a piece of research enables, and how a number of approaches and theories may be combined in helping us understand the interface between structural and psychical constituents in the production of 'race, racism and aligned forms of racialised power and oppression'. (Stevens et al., pp. 4–5)

In the model developed by them for the Apartheid Archive Project, stories from the margins matter (Sonn, Stevens, & Duncan, 2013). Stories are individual, social, and ideological and because they are produced in social contexts they often reflect narratives that are socially and culturally available (Sonn et al., 2013). Martin (2007), in Australia, wrote about the significance of stories for knowing and being in the world as Aboriginal people.

> Stories are our law. Stories give identity as they connect us and fulfill our sense of belonging. Stories are grounding, defining, comforting and embracing. Stories vary in their purpose and content and so stories can be political and

yet equally healing. They can be shared verbally, physically or visually. Their meanings and messages teach, admonish, tease, celebrate, entertain, provoke and challenge. (Martin, 2007, p. 45)

As Maori scholar Linda Tuhiwai Smith (1999) has noted about stories and storytelling: "Telling our stories from the past, reclaiming the past, giving testimony to the injustices of the past are all strategies which are commonly employed by indigenous peoples ..." (p. 34). Kirmayer, Dandeneau, Marshall, Phillips, and Williamson (2011) noted the importance of narrative and storytelling in their work with indigenous peoples in Canada. They wrote that collective forms of narrative "help people make sense of their experience and construct a valued identity but also ensure the continuity and vitality of a community or a people" (pp. 85–86). The authors discussed the notion of narrative resilience and its function in self-determination and cultural renewal. For them narrative resilience is not just about individual stories. Rather there is:

a communal or collective dimension, maintained by the circulation of stories invested with cultural power and authority, which the individual and groups can use to articulate and assert their identity, affirm core values and attitudes needed to face challenges, and generate creative solutions to new predicaments. (Kirmayer et al., 2011, pp. 85–86)

Moorhead and LaFromboise (2014) similarly emphasised that "if more resilience stories were told, people would reconnect with a sense of pride in their cultural identities and cultural practices" (p. 148).

This discussion of methodology has generated important questions about the psychosocial and cultural strategies and practices involved in making place away from traditional country in institutions, organisations, and other settings. In the next section we outline the study we conducted with a group of Aboriginal people who share this history of dispossession and displacement and who are making place in an urban context.

NEGOTIATING THE RESEARCH AND COLLECTING STORIES

We outline the research process in detail below because it was vital to our efforts to enact and contribute to critical and indigenous methodologies. These methodologies emphasise collaboration, reciprocity, empowerment and decolonisation (Moreton Robinson & Walter, 2009; Smith, 1999).

Making Links with the Groups

In order to document the experiences of place and placemaking by Aboriginal people we embarked on a small collaborative study working with Karen Jackson, Director of the Moondani Balluk, the Indigenous academic unit at Victoria University, who plays a key role in connecting Victoria University researchers with the local Indigenous communities.

Tony Birch, Rebecca and Tanaya Lyons, Karen Jackson (Indigenous researchers) and the first author (Christopher Sonn, a black South African settler) made up the research team for the project. Guided by a commitment to self-determination and reciprocity the study unfolded over time and involved various stages of linking up with two groups of Indigenous people and our own internal discussions. The first stage in this formal process included visiting the two groups, the WACCC and the Aboriginal Planned Activity Group (PAG). We visited the WACCC at one of its monthly meetings and PAG on a weekday when the group met. The purpose of the first visit was to introduce the researchers and the research and to gauge interest and support for the idea. At this stage, led by Karen Jackson, we discussed our roles, the project design and the group's ideas about the research. We highlighted the storytelling component and that we were interested in their stories of making place in Melbourne's West. We also offered the group a storytelling workshop that Tony Birch later delivered.

Cultural Safety and Spending Time

After this first meeting, the researchers agreed that Rebecca and Tanaya Lyons would make contact with people to make time for interviews. Rebecca and Tanaya are both emerging Indigenous researchers with experience in working with Aboriginal people including those who are members of the Stolen Generations. Their experience includes having conducted a collective auto-ethnographic study of their family history (Lyons, 2014) as well as gathering testimonies from members of the Stolen Generations for a project with the Victorian Aboriginal Legal Service into institutional cultural abuse. The State Government discussion paper defined 'cultural abuse' as "the cessation of the ability to continue cultural practices that would have been handed down by parents to children but for the fact of institutionalisation – including spiritual practices, language, cultural practices, understanding of kinship relations, and other traditions' (Victorian Aboriginal Legal Service, 2015, p. 9).

The two researchers spent time with the groups over several weeks in 2016 and, in a sense, took on the role of participant observers in the PAG setting and interviewed several people who expressed an interest. Out of the 18 PAG members we collected stories from seven people and two stories were collected out of 17 WACCC members. Four people belonged to both PAG and WACCC. So in total we collected nine stories from eight women and one man. Given the purpose of PAG, participants were older people ranging in age from 38–70. All the participants had moved into the local area west of Melbourne and were thus not traditional owners. The interviews were transcribed and copies of the transcripts returned to each of the interviewees for them to keep and to ensure that they were happy with the record.

Creative Writing Workshop and Ethnographic Observations

The next step was to organise and deliver the creative writing workshop. Prior to the writing workshop we shared lunch with the group. After this Tony Birch delivered the workshop to a small subgroup because other people were away on the day. He introduced strategies and techniques for writing, which included memory triggers and suggestions for writing – that is, mnemonic devices to help trigger memory and story writing. The workshop was informative for several reasons. Many people took the opportunity to tell and create short stories about their parents and about memories of particular places from their childhood that they recalled. One person relayed a story of growing up in a town on the riverbanks in New South Wales. This was the period when government officials took children from families and placed them in institutions. The narrator described how parents had to hurry to move their children to safety by crossing a river in a canoe as soon as they saw the dust clouds generated by cars approaching from a distance. These were the people coming to take children away.

The workshop dynamics were also revealing in and of themselves because of the interactions within the group, which included staff employed to support PAG. It became obvious to us that the workshop setting was a temporary Indigenous space within the broader non-Indigenous structure of the Community Centre, and the interactions within the workshop provided some insight into power dynamics within the setting. For example, non-Indigenous participants seemingly dominated opportunities to respond to provocations and invitations by Tony to share stories. There seemed to be a lack of awareness about how embodied practices such as turn-taking can influence the dynamics of the setting. PAG participants also disclosed to Rebecca some of their concerns about what they perceived as differential treatment, that they had their identity challenged by different people who use the Centre's facilities, and that Centre staff expected them, and no other groups, to pack away tables and chairs. These insights and observations provided additional information for understanding the stories that people shared about their experiences as members of PAG and their need for an Aboriginal controlled space.

Documenting, Organising and Representing Stories

We organised our interview questions more as conversation starters around a series of topics which included Identity, Family, Place, Country, Health, PAG/Community, Mob, Migration, Culture, Music, Next Generation, Removal, Stolen Generation and Services needed in the West. Guided by standard qualitative data management and analysis strategies, each person read the transcripts and summarised key aspects using a question-ordered matrix. The research group came together to discuss the initial readings and what each of us saw as key themes. Karen and Rebecca, who both have deeper insider knowledge because of their ongoing involvement and longer field work respectively, highlighted different aspects including nuanced insights about the politics within the group as well as some of the tensions and challenges the group members faced in making a community within the non-Indigenous controlled community setting. Yet, as a group, we agreed on the overall themes that people narrated. These themes were mostly positive and reflected the varied meanings and practices of place and placemaking for the PAG members. The themes that we generated through our group discussions focused on the meanings of PAG for a diverse group of Indigenous people. The primary meaning of PAG is as a place for being and becoming Aboriginal. In this place people are engaged in processes and material practices, such as art making, that draw on understandings of Aboriginal culture and traditions and that are central to their personal identities as well as to what they want to develop for future generations. In this place people also examine and deconstruct their family histories and the various challenges tied to the ongoing legacy of the forced removals, challenges such as getting the legal documents (e.g. birth certificates) required for formal identity recognition.

CREATING PLACES FOR BELONGING AND SELF DETERMINATION

Our analysis showed that within the broader historical and political realities around Indigenous sovereignty this group of people is constructing a place for belonging through being together and engaging in individual and group activities. They are all engaging in individual and group processes that involve sharing memories of family and home as they negotiate, in various ways, and learn about their Aboriginal ancestry and identities. They are countering the effects of dispossession and cultural removal, making place and community through arts and cultural activities, and sharing memories and stories. These processes are part of placemaking and the rearticulation of important values and practices that inform Aboriginal identities and ways of being. Importantly the ways in which people described their experiences suggests that coming together with and as Aboriginal people is a very important foundation for experiences of belonging, support and communing. These experiences, and the various practices the members use, are central to laying foundations for the Wyndham Aboriginal Community Centre.

Placemaking as Shared Experiential Communality and Embodied Practice

Our initial analysis of the data as a research group suggests that the PAG setting is central to the everyday life of this group. PAG is where people are learning and showing how they imagine their own culturally safe place. Participation is meaningful in different ways for different people as it fosters a sense of belonging derived from strong family and social relationships and from an "experiential communality" (Nobles, 1972, p. 286) as Aboriginal people. The setting that people have created is productive and linked with other community settings and Indigenous community networks in the west of Melbourne and beyond. Participants mostly spoke positively about PAG. They described it as a place to belong, where they fit in, and where they can meet other Aboriginal people and feel safe and like a family. For some it also meant more. For example, Joan said, "it's a support group which helps me discover me-self" and Terry said, "I feel a part of the community in the West. I like PAG. I get to meet more people. It helps me to open up more and that way I can pass that onto my grandchildren and great grandkids".

Two participants highlighted the other support derived from the group. For Stacey PAG is important: "because I can't do much. It gets me out of the house. At the moment I can't for a long time I haven't been able to use my hands, my husband can't use his hands so we have a meal, we go out, we mix in the Aboriginal community". Sara commented: "I get out of the house. I like PAG because I got friends. I come here 4 days a week for 3 years. It is very important to me. The west has a good community. I fit in more than Fitzroy". Lilly expressed her deep affection for the group in the following way: "PAG group, I love it. I have my ups and downs about it but then hey I'm the eldest one in the group. So I feel it's up to me to talk to them about the values that I see as an Aboriginal woman".

People spoke of the importance of being with other Aboriginal people and they highlighted the role of making arts and crafts, especially artefacts based in Aboriginal history, culture and traditions. The stories also showed that participants engage in arts and creative practices that are personally fulfilling, a means of self-expression and linked with getting back to 'cultural roots'. The getting back to cultural roots involves imagination and reconstruction of symbols, signs and memories as the basis for collective identity in place. These activities included knitting various items using coloured wool, typically black, yellow and red symbolising Aboriginality, and creating paintings of landscapes and of places using dot-painting techniques. Some participants made jewelry such as necklaces and bracelets using black, yellow and red beads or engaged in other crafts. For example, Nelly stated, "I don't know where I'd be without the PAG group. When I came out of hospital I couldn't do anything but when I joined here I found I could make jewelry, crochet, I made hats yeah it just felt like my family". She made a possum skin bag, which she gave away "because I don't believe in making money off things, everywhere I go I give away things".

Joan spoke about the meaning of painting and coming to realise her own talent. "I enjoy painting. I didn't realise I was so talent, gifted, I've been painting I've been doing a lot of stuff, I've been doing a lot of craft stuff which I knew I was good at craft but sorta coming here and helping the girls and doing". For Stacey the opportunity for connection with other Aboriginal people and learning with each other took on a deep meaning of reconnecting with roots: "I believe by moving to the west it has helped me to get back to my roots. Things and we here with the girls and getting the idea from each other I've done it more".

The group members sometimes sell the artefacts that they make through networks at different venues and they use the funds to support other initiatives. PAG fundraising goes to various groups such as the Men's Shed in Altona, a shed that many of the PAG women and men attend, the Deadly community kitchen, Wangal United Aboriginal Corporation Dance Group, local Community Day functions, Baroona

Youth Healing Place, Juvenile Detention Centre's Boys Prison Group and the Dame Phyllis Frost Women's Prison. Terry noted, "I sold paintings and the money goes back into the PAG. I am happy that I can help others in the group. Funding goes to teaching courses and the kids cultural dance group". Through this practice of sharing, the group members enacted support, reciprocity, and solidarity – important cultural values and responsibilities. They communicated messages to remind the young people that their Aunties and Uncles are thinking of them and love them and that they are not alone. Another participant, Stacey, noted, "So we try to do things that are culturally aware in the group. We are trying to make culturally aware stuff you know knitting and stuff. We make scarfs, hats and you know. And we supply stuff to the Aboriginal women that are in prison so that's a thing too".

Dispossession, Institutional Barriers, and Being Aboriginal

Another aspect of placemaking in the stories that people related is about the impact of forced removals and the dispossession of culture and identity. Several of the participants said that they only affirmed their Aboriginal identities later in their lives because it was hidden or concealed until then. This is typical of responses created to survive oppressive realities (Sonn & Fisher, 2003). One person shared a story that showed how she was othered as a young person – referred to as different and needing to be with "your kind". Some participants described the importance of this affirmation but also the painful task of reconnecting and restoring these aspects of self and culture denied to them. Joan noted the deep hurt at being denied their ancestral story. "The Stolen Generation had a lot to do with it. That's why mum used to … mum denied it to the very end denied it on her death bed. She denied it we asked her then she still denied it. So we don't know, we don't know".

Another participant said, "I went to the Elders and they said no we can't do it [trace her family roots] at the moment because you've got no birth certificate. I know who I am I don't need them to tell me who I am and so that made my grandmother one of the Stolen Generation" (Nelly).

For some participants, the struggles inherent in reclaiming identity are particularly complicated as they live in a different state to where they were born or they don't know where to get access to documents, and the institutional requirements function as barriers. Joan for example said:

I found one person that wanting to help me and I never turned back from then. Cause they tried to turn me off doing it because there're that many people applying for Aboriginality papers and are not actually Aboriginal. Where I was getting upset because I knew I was Aboriginal and couldn't get me papers and the more they said no the more determine I was to get them. So, got them and so did me children and grandchildren I did the same thing with them because the problem was I had to go back up to Queensland to get mine because I was born in Queensland. You got to get them from where you were born. My children were born in Victoria but they weren't known in Victoria. The family is only known in Queensland so the Victoria people wouldn't give me the papers because they are not known in Victoria, they are only known in Queensland.

Joan continued stating how difficult the process has been for her and her family: "Different Aboriginal organisations no one will help me. I got a few nasty phone calls from a few people I know and I told them what I thought of them since they try to put me off saying that it's not like getting a piece of candy you got to earn the right to get your papers. So that all happens, so it took me quite a few years".

DISCUSSION

In this chapter we have reported research that we developed to examine place and placemaking for Aboriginal people in the West of Melbourne. We worked in a collaborative way informed by critical theory and Indigenous methodologies, which have been central to doing research that supports decolonisation and self-determination. At a foundational level this entails a critical stance and a decolonising standpoint that seeks to expand ways of knowing and that legitimises the lived realities and experiences of groups relegated to the margins or made appendages to the stories of dominant cultural groups (Bulhan, 1985; Reyes Cruz & Sonn, 2011). Vital to our process has been a commitment to relationships and dialogue and developing research that will serve the needs of Moondani Balluk and the broader Indigenous community in the west of Melbourne. We have drawn out the importance of relationships and ethics reflected in the seemingly small yet significant acts of sharing, reciprocation and mutuality. We have gathered stories that we returned to the people who told the stories, we delivered a writing workshop and we spent time sharing lunch with the group. These aspects of the embodied cultural practices of sharing were, in our view, vital to building the research relationship. As Bulhan (1985) warned, a psychology of oppression that does not concern itself with space, time, mobility and bonds that people form in place and that does not nurture or sustain a positive sense of self and community will be "misleading and evasive" (p. 125).

Given that participants or their families were members of the Stolen Generations, we needed to be sure that a person with links to, cultural knowledge of, and experience with this group could do the story collection. This is being respectful and supportive. Storytelling and dialogue by those typically excluded as knowledge producers are key methods in critical and indigenous approaches as well as in liberation psychology (Montero, Sonn, & Burton, 2017). We collected stories from people using conversational interviews and creative writing. These stories are important for the recovery of historical memory and give insight into how people make sense of individual and family histories (Stevens et al., 2013). The stories also attest to how through place making people are constructing complex subjectivities that challenge the dominant stories of damage and dependency. Instead we heard stories of family, friendship, creativity and belonging as characteristic of the social bonds and experiences in the group and as evidence of the ways people make places in urban contexts (Behrendt, 2009). As Kirmayer et al. (2011) noted in their work in Canada, these stories of strength, connectedness and support are very important narratives for community building. Thus, as Sonn et al. (2013) have noted, these personal stories are a powerful mode to document everyday lives and through this to build information to contest the over-determining discourses of deficit and damage that continue to constrain the lives of racialised people. The important task is to capture the "complexity, contradictions and self-determination of lived lives" (Tuck, 2009, p. 415).

Through this project we have been able to identify how members of PAG are engaged in placemaking, that is in giving meaning to the PAG space in their everyday lives. The findings show that PAG is a primary social setting where people come to connect with other Aboriginal people, and where they feel safe and supported to share memories about their families and communities. The setting is no longer just a space within a Center, but a space where they engage in creative and social activities. Through these activities PAG becomes a place for healing and reconnection, a place where people can engage in the delicate process of examining histories as they go about making sense of personal and group identities disrupted by colonialism, by forced removals from families and country and by contemporary urban migration between states and suburbs. These processes of displacement, place making and establishing identity are not straightforward. They are complicated by institutional barriers and limited access to the legal documents that some people need to establish family (Lyons, 2014). The stories told about placemaking signal strengths derived from Aboriginal people's understandings of family and reciprocity, and ways of being that are produced through memory and are central to placemaking in different contexts. Other researchers have suggested in their research that settings such as these are vital because they enable "access to such group-based resources that include but are not limited to instrumental support for action, leadership, channels of communication, trust and solidarity" (Cakal, Eller, Sirpolu, & Perez, 2016, p. 356).

While people are making a place that is significant to them, the space within which they are making a place sits within an organisation and the institutional power relations of the Community Centre. People commented about their treatment and concerns that they perceive themselves as being treated differently. These perceptions speak to how 'white' spaces and institutions are experienced and felt by Aboriginal people, and the subsequent implications for belonging, being and self-determination (Fredericks, 2009). This information has opened up another angle for our research and points to the importance of providing space, support and opportunities for people to have assistance in their efforts to establish links with different Aboriginal groups as part of the process of making community and reclaiming identities. Placemaking is a delicate, fraught and significant process for Aboriginal people. The process involves the negotiation both of history in the present, and also of various ongoing forms of displacement and structural violence. Importantly the process draws on a knowledge of country, culture and family history, which are all vital to belonging, identity construction and individual and community self-determination.

REFERENCES

Australia Institute of Health and Welfare. (2014). *The health and welfare of Australia's Aboriginal and Torres Strait Islander peoples 2015*. Retrieved August 29, 2016, from http://www.aihw.gov.au/indigenous-observatory/reports/health-and-welfare-2015/

Australian Bureau of Statistics (ABS). (2011). *Community profiles: Wyndham (C)*. Retrieved August 28, 2015, from http://www.censusdata.abs.gov.au/census_services/getproduct/census/2011/communityprofile/LGA27260?opendocument&navpos=220

Balla, P., McCallum, D., Sonn, C., Jackson, K., McKenna, T., & Marion, C. (2009). *Interventions in Aboriginal child removal in Melbourne's West: A scoping study*. Melbourne: ARACY.

Behrendt, L. (2009). Home: The importance of place to the dispossessed. *South Atlantic Quarterly, 108*(1), 71–85. doi:10.1215/00382876-2008-023

Biko, S. (1988). *I write what I like: A selection of his essays*. Ringwood: Penguin Books.

Bird Rose, D. (1996). *Nourishing terrains: Australian Aboriginal views of landscape and wilderness*. Canberra: Australian Heritage Commission.

Bulhan, H. A. (1985). *Frantz Fanon and the psychology of oppression*. New York, NY: Plenum Press.

Care Connect. (2016). *Aboriginal planned activity group PAG*. Abbotsford: Care Connect. Retrieved May 1, 2017, from http://www.careconnect.org.au/wp-content/uploads/2016/.../PAG-Support-Worker-PP.docx

Cochran, P., Marshall, C., Garcia-Downing, C., Elizabeth Kendall, E., Cook, D., McCubbin, L., & Gover, R. (2008). Indigenous ways of knowing: Implications for participatory research and community. *American Journal of Public Health, 98*(1), 22–27.

Dudgeon, P., & Walker, R. (2015). Decolonising Australian psychology: Discourses. strategies, and practice. *Journal of Social and Political Psychology, 3*(1), 276–297. doi:10.5964/jspp.v3i1.126

Dudgeon, P., Wright, M., Paradies, Y., Garvey, D., & Walker, I. (2014). Aboriginal social, cultural and historical contexts. In P. Dudgeon, H. Milroy, & R. Walker (Eds.), *Working together: Aboriginal and Torres Strait Islander mental health and wellbeing principles and practice* (2nd ed., pp. 3–24). Retrieved from http://aboriginal.telethonkids.org.au/media/699863/Working-Together-Book.pdf

Fanon, F. (1967). *The wretched of the earth*. Ringwood: Penguin Books.

Fanon, F. (1986). *Black skins, White masks*. New York, NY: Grove Press.

Fredericks, B. (2013). 'We don't leave our identities at the city limits': Aboriginal and Torres Strait Islander people living in urban localities. *Australian Aboriginal Studies, 1*, 4–16.

Gergen, K. J., & Gergen, M. M. (2010). Scanning the landscape of narrative inquiry. *Social and Personality Psychology Compass, 4*(9), 728–735.

Healing Foundation. (2017). *Bringing them home 20 years on: An action plan for healing*. Retrieved June 7, 2017, from http://healingfoundation.org.au//app/uploads/2017/05/Bringing-Them-Home-20-years-on-FINAL-SCREEN-1.pdf

Hodgetts, D., Drew, N., Sonn, C. C., Stolte, O., Nikora, L., & Curtis, K. (2010). *Social psychology and everyday life*. Basingstoke: Palgrave Macmillan.

Human Rights and Equal Opportunity Commision. (1997). *Bringing them home*. Report of the National Inquiry into the Separation of Aboriginal and Torres Strait Islander Children from Their Families. Retrieved June 13, 2017, from https://www.humanrights.gov.au/publications/bringing-them-home-report-1997

Kirmayer, L. J., Dandeneau, S., Marshall, E., Phillips, M. K., & Williamson, K. J. (2011). Rethinking resilience from indigenous perspectives. *The Canadian Journal of Psychiatry, 56*(2), 84–91.

Kovach, M. E. (2009). *Indigenous methodologies: Characteristics, conversations, and contexts*. Toronto: University of Toronto Press.

Krieg, A. (2009). The experience of collective trauma in Australian indigenous communities. *Australasian Psychiatry, 17*, 28–32. doi:10.1080/10398560902948621

Lyons, R. (2014). *Terra Nullius: A personal family perspective of the stolen generations* (Honours thesis). Victoria University, Melbourne.

Martin, K. (2007). *Aboriginal people, Aboriginal lands and indigenist research: A discussion of re-search pasts and neo-colonial research futures* (Unpublished dissertation). James Cook University, Cairns, Queensland, Australia.

Martin, K., & Mirraboopa, B. (2003). Ways of knowing, being and doing: A theoretical framework and methods for indigenous and indigenist research. *Journal of Australian Studies, 27*(76), 203–214.

Massey, D. (2005). *For space*. Thousand Oaks, CA: Sage Publications.

Montero, M. (2007). The political psychology of liberation: From politics to ethics and back. *Political Psychology, 28*(5), 517–533. doi:10.1111/j.1467-9221.2007.00588.x

Montero, M. (2017). Psychology of liberation revised (A critique of critique). In B. Gough (Ed.), *The Palgrave handbook of critical social psychology* (pp. 147–180). Houndsmills: Palgrave Macmillan.

Montero, M., Sonn, C. C., & Burton, M. (2016). Community psychology and liberation psychology: A creative synergy for an ethical and transformative praxis. In M. A. Bond, I. Serrano-García, & C. B. Keys (Eds.), *APA handbook of community psychology: Theoretical foundations, core concepts, and emerging challenges* (Vol. 1, pp. 149–167). Washington, DC: American Psychological Association.

Moorehead, V., & LaFromboise, T. D. (2014). Healing one story at a time: American Indian/Alaska native social justice. In C. Johnson & H. Friedman (Eds.), *The Praeger handbook of social justice and psychology* (Vol. 3, p. 135). Retrieved from http://publisher.abc-clio.com/9781440803796

Nobles, W. W. (1972). African philosophy: Foundations for Black psychology. In R. Jones (Ed.), *Black psychology* (pp. 18–32). New York, NY: Harper & Row.

Quayle, A. (2017). *Narrating oppression, psychosocial suffering and survival through the bush babies project* (Unpublished doctoral dissertation). Victoria University, Melbourne.

Rappaport, J. (2000). Community narratives: Tales of terror and joy. *American Journal of Community Psychology, 28*(1), 1–24.

Reyes Cruz, M., & Sonn, C. C. 2011. (De)colonizing culture in community psychology: Reflections from critical social science. *American Journal of Community Psychology, 47*(1–2), 203–214.

Rigney, L.-I. (2006). Indigenist research and aboriginal Australia. In J. Kunnie & N. Goduka (Eds.), *Indigenous peoples' wisdom and power: Affirming our knowledge through narratives* (pp. 32–50). Aldershot: Ashgate.

Smith, L. T. (1999). *Decolonizing methodologies: Research and indigenous peoples*. London: Zed Books.

Sonn, C. C. (2012). Speaking unspoken memories: Remembering apartheid racism in Australia. *Peace and Conflict: Journal of Peace Psychology, 18*(3), 240.

Sonn, C., & Baker, A. (2016). Creating inclusive knowledges: Exploring the transformative potential of arts and cultural practice. *International Journal of Inclusive Education, 20*(3), 215–228. doi:10.1080/13603116.2015.1047663

Sonn, C. C., & Fisher, A. T. (2003). Identity and oppression: Differential responses to and in between status. *American Journal of Community Psychology, 31*, 117–128.

Sonn, C. C., Stevens, G., & Duncan, N. (2013). Decolonisation, critical methodologies, and why stories matter. In G. Stevens, N. Duncan, & D. Hook (Eds.), *Race, memory and the apartheid archive: Towards a transformative psychosocial praxis* (pp. 295–314). Hampshire: Palgrave Macmillan.

Stevens, G., Duncan, N., & Hook, D. (2013). The apartheid archive project, the psychosocial and political praxis. In G. Stevens, N. Duncan, & D. Hook (Eds.), *Race, memory and the apartheid archive: Towards a transformative psychosocial praxis* (pp. 1–24). Hampshire: Palgrave Macmillan.

Tuck, E. (2009). Suspending damage: A letter to communities. *Harvard Educational Review, 79*(3), 409–427.

United Nations Office on Genocide Prevention and the Responsibility to Protect. (1948). *Article II of the genocide convention*. Retrieved October 17, 2015, from http://www.un.org/en/genocideprevention/genocide.html

Victorian Aboriginal Legal Service. (2015). *A Victoria redress scheme for institutional child abuse: Public consultation paper Victorian Aboriginal community response, Victorian Aboriginal community state redress submission 19 october 2015*. Victoria: Victorian Aboriginal Legal Service.

Walker, R., Schultz, C., & Sonn, C. (2014). Cultural competence: Transforming policy, services, programs and practice. In P. Dudgeon, H. Milroy, & R. Walker (Eds.), *Working together: Aboriginal and Torres*

Strait Islander mental health and wellbeing principles and practice (2nd ed., pp. 195–220). Retrieved from http://aboriginal.telethonkids.org.au/media/699863/Working-Together-Book.pdf

Walter, M. (2010). Market forces and indigenous resistance paradigms. *Social Movement Studies, 9*(2), 121–137.

Wyndham City Council. (2015). *Wyndham City Council statement of commitment 2015 Aboriginal people in Wyndham leading communities – Statement of commitment.* Retrieved from https://www.wyndham.vic.gov.au/sites/default/files/2016-06/Leading%20Communities%20%20 Statement%20of%20Commitment%20FINAL%20for%20web%20or%20email%20smaller_5.pdf

Zubrick, S. R., Shepherd, C. J., Dudgeon, P., Gee, G., Paradies, Y., Scrine, C., & Walker, R. (2014). Social determinants of social and emotional wellbeing. In P. Dudgeon, H. Milroy, & R. Walker (Eds.), *Working together: Aboriginal and Torres Strait Islander mental health and wellbeing principles and practice* (2nd ed., pp. 93–112). Barton: Commonwealth of Australia.

Christopher C. Sonn
Victoria University
Australia

Karen Jackson
Victoria University
Australia

Rebecca Lyons
Victoria University
Australia

RAMÓN SPAAIJ AND JORA BROERSE

7. SPORT AND THE POLITICS OF BELONGING

The Experiences of Australian and Dutch Somalis

INTRODUCTION

Contemporary policy and academic debates on the settlement and integration of recently arrived migrants and refugees draw attention to migrants' negotiation of identity and belonging in relation to the receiving community. Recent research suggests that this process is shaped by the interplay between the aspirations and resources of migrants and the structural forces and social norms to which they are expected to conform within the country in which they live (Bhatia & Ram, 2009; Hammond, 2013). Critical academic work indicates the unintended consequences that integration policies can have on migrants' and refugees' feelings of national belonging and identification (Valentine, Sporton, & Nielsen, 2009). That is, prevailing notions of nationhood and national citizenship tend to constrain the social and discursive space available to recently arrived migrants as they define their identities and their sense of belonging to the nation as well as to their homeland or a diasporic community (Ager & Strang, 2010; Valentine et al., 2009). Yet research also suggests important trajectories of identity construction beyond or parallel to the mould of narrowly defined national identities (Cohen, 2010) that present possibilities for unfixing identities, particularly nation-derived ones (Vertovec, 2001). This potentially creates space for more hybrid, plural and fluid forms of identity and belonging (Hall, 1990).

In this chapter we interpret cultural forms such as sport as a critical aspect or space in the politics of belonging and identity formation (Werbner, 1996; Bradbury, 2011; Burdsey, 2006, 2008; Joseph, 2011; Spaaij, 2012a, 2015). These processes and practices do not occur in a social vacuum; rather, they are enacted within and through different spaces. We will focus specifically on the lived experiences of Australian and Dutch Somalis in relation to community-based sports clubs and events in order to address two questions: What kinds of belonging are constructed by Australian and Dutch Somalis in community-based sport? What social processes facilitate or impede these belongings? In this chapter we extend our previous research that focused specifically on the Australian context (Spaaij, 2011, 2012a, 2013, 2015) by offering a more comparative and multi-sited perspective on these questions. In the next section we first discuss the concept of belonging and then follow that with an overview of the ethnographic research that underpins our analysis.

THE POLITICS OF BELONGING

The concept of belonging provides the overarching framework for this chapter. We build on contemporary sociological theory to conceptualise belonging as a dynamic dialectic of the (inter)personal experience of belonging on the one hand and the politics of belonging on the other hand. The subjective experience of belonging can be defined broadly as the development of some form of emotional attachment that relates individuals to other people, places or modes of being (Anthias, 2005; Probyn, 1996; Wood & Waite, 2011). From this perspective belonging is a personal, intimate feeling of being or becoming part of, or at home in, a place or particular set of collectivities (Antonsich, 2010). Yet belonging is inherently relational, laden with power and contested (Krzyzanowski & Wodak, 2007). Understanding belonging requires a focus not only on an individual's or a group's claims to belonging, but also on how their ability to claim belonging is affected by discourses and practices of social inclusion/exclusion.

Yuval-Davis's (2006, 2011) theory of belonging as a multi-layered social process is particularly instructive in this regard. She constructs belonging along three major analytical levels. The first level concerns categories of social location, which have "a certain positionality along an axis of power, higher or lower than other such categories" (Yuval-Davis, 2006, p. 199). Categories of social location are often structured around dualistic norms, such as man/woman, heterosexual/homosexual or White/Black. The implications of these social locations vis-à-vis the grids of power relations in society are historically specific and subject to change. Moreover social locations are fluid and contested, and constructed along multiple axes of difference, such as gender, class, race and ethnicity, simultaneously; that is, they are intersectional.

The second level refers to belonging as an affective and personalised experience. This level focuses on individual and group identifications and emotional attachments, based on the narratives people tell themselves and others about who they are and who they are not (Yuval-Davis, 2006). Belonging is not just cognitive but also emotional. Affective dimensions may become more decisive or salient in shaping experiences of belonging when people's belonging is threatened or less secure. Thus experiences of social exclusion and marginalisation may generate an increased longing for emotional belonging to an accepting community where they can feel safe and at home.

The third level concerns the politics of belonging, that is, the way social locations and individual and group identifications and attachments are valued and judged. This process involves public policy and media discourses that communicate which identities do and do not belong in a place. The politics of belonging, then, concerns the evolving boundary discourses and practices that separate "us" from "them". Yuval-Davis's (2006, 2011) theory of belonging posits that control over the construction of belonging is not located within the individual or group but inheres in a complex interplay between the side that seeks or claims belonging and the side that has the power to 'grant' belonging (Antonsich, 2010). This 'granting' power involves what Hage (1998) refers to as "governmental belonging" (p. 46), which is claimed by those who are in a dominant position and can lead to individuals or groups being silenced and positioned as 'Other'. Belonging, then, occurs at the intersection of individual affective experience and the structural process of (not) becoming a member; it involves ongoing negotiation and (re)construction through the inclusion of some and the exclusion of others (Krzyzanowski & Wodak, 2007).

As the above shows, belonging is a multi-faceted and multi-scalar phenomenon. In *The Politics of Home* Duyvendak (2011) distinguishes four spheres of "home": the sphere of the individual household, the economic sphere of the workplace, the associational sphere of the community and the politico-cultural sphere of the nation-state. Belonging tends to be constituted and experienced differently in these different spatial contexts, such that particular subject positions and emotional attachments may become salient or irrelevant in particular spaces (Valentine et al., 2009). Key differences across different spheres and spaces of belonging may include, for instance, the degree of dynamism and porosity of boundaries of inclusion/exclusion and the specific modes of performance and signification (Antonsich, 2010; Nunn, 2014). However different spaces of belonging are also simultaneously tied together by processes that exert influence across various scales, such as globalisation, migration, the gender revolution and attendant changes to international or national laws (Duyvendak, 2011).

Sport may also be viewed in this way. Community sports practices are a significant associational sphere where the experience of belonging and the politics of belonging intersect. Like other potential spaces of belonging sport is situated within, and reflects, wider social structures and discourses yet it is also a site where such structures and discourses are mediated and contested. The particular context and research methods used to address these issues, with a focus on the experiences of Australian and Dutch Somalis, are discussed in the next section.

SPORT AND BELONGING IN CONTEXT: SOMALIS IN AUSTRALIA AND THE NETHERLANDS

The emergence and meaning of the community-based sports practices of Australian and Dutch Somalis examined in this chapter should be understood within the context of forced migration, resettlement and diaspora formation. Prolonged violent conflicts between government forces and armed opposition in Somalia culminated in the collapse of the Somali state in 1991 with the overthrow of Siyad Barre's military rule. This resulted in the intensification of conflict between clan-based military factions in many parts of the country. By 2017 more than two million Somalis had been displaced by a conflict that has lasted over two decades. An estimated 1.5 million people are internally displaced within Somalia and nearly 900,000 are refugees in the region nearby which includes Kenya, Yemen and Ethiopia (UNHCR, 2017). It should be noted, however, that Somali migrants are a highly diverse population in terms of educational attainment, employment, region of origin, family arrangements and so on (Horst, 2007). Their resettlement experiences are also highly diverse.

Somalis currently constitute one of the largest refugee-background populations from Africa in Australia. Somali refugees began to arrive in Australia in significant numbers from the late 1980s primarily under the Refugee and Special Humanitarian Program. The second half of the 1990s was the peak period for Somali arrivals in Australia, many of whom arrived indirectly via refugee camps in Kenya, Ethiopia, Yemen and Djibouti. The 2016 Census of the Australian Bureau of Statistics recorded 8,960 Somalia-born people in Australia. Although Somalis are mostly nomadic pastoralists, in Australia they have become one of the most urbanised population groups in Australia with 98 per cent living in urban areas (ABS, 2017). The 2011 Census showed that 30 per cent of Somalia-born people in Australia were aged below 25 (ABS, 2012).

The Netherlands became a popular destination for Somali refugees and asylum seekers fleeing the Siyad Barre regime in the late 1980s and early 1990s. Currently there are 39,465 Somalis officially registered in the Netherlands, 26,803 (68 per cent) of whom are first-generation migrants (CBS Statline, 2016). However, this number fluctuates considerably due in part to subsequent onward migration to cities in the United Kingdom with much higher concentrations of Somalis. It is estimated that since 2000 more than 20,000 Somali migrants have left the Netherlands for the UK (van Liempt, 2011a). At the same time the Somali community in the Netherlands is scattered across cities and small towns in different parts of the country due in part to the Dutch policy of dispersing asylum seekers. While asylum seekers were housed in relatively high-quality housing they were spread all over the Netherlands and often isolated from family members and friends (van Liempt, 2011b).

A distinctive feature of the Dutch Somali population is its internal diversity in terms of the period of arrival. The first cohort, which arrived in the late 1980s and in the 1990s, consists mainly of people with relatively high levels of educational attainment who are more likely to have subsequently migrated to countries such as the United Kingdom to pursue economic and educational opportunities. The second cohort, the so-called *nieuwkomers* (new arrivals), arrived after 2007 and have lower levels of educational attainment due to the prolonged conflict in Somalia. A relatively large proportion of these newcomers are minors. As a result Somalis in the Netherlands are relatively young as compared to other asylum seeker groups and have become increasingly so in the past six years (CBS Statline, 2016). Two-thirds are below the age of 30. In 2010 58 per cent of Somali asylum seekers were below the age of 18, and 48 per cent were under the age of 15 (Nijenhuis & van Liempt, 2014).

Challenges associated with integration and wellbeing are well documented in both countries, including the Australian and Dutch Somali populations' vulnerable socioeconomic status (including low educational attainment and high unemployment and underemployment rates), family separation and social disconnectedness. Moreover research suggests that many Somalis feel marginalised in terms of service provision (Hopkins, 2006) and that mainstream community associations do not necessarily meet their needs (Griffiths, 2002; Spaaij, 2011). Within this context community-based sports clubs and events have emerged in order to partially fill this void. Youth worker Yunus (male, 40s) describes this need as follows with specific reference to a Somali-based football (soccer) club in Melbourne, Australia:

> Well, the whole welfare and trying to educate the community, the kids, and also the parents who are not involved with the kids ... trying to bring the community together. Have that link. Because we don't have, you know, any association or any activity for the kids, and the kids will not see one another. We are having this club so they are having an awareness of who is who.

In a similar vein the Amsterdam Futsal Tournament (AFT), established in 2005 within the Dutch Somali community, aims to offer a space to empower and improve the settlement and social networks of Somali youth in Europe. The AFT is currently held twice a year – a 32-team international Winter event and a smaller, 16-team Summer futsal (indoor, five-a-side football) tournament. Its organisers view sport as a platform for fostering social connectedness and for cultivating a sense of belonging to others with a similar cultural heritage.

In examining the experiences of Somalis in two nation-states – Australia and the Netherlands – it is important to consider the specificities of the political and social contexts. Both countries feature a complex and changing relationship between multiculturalism and national identity. While the differences between the two political and ideological contexts should not be exaggerated, scholars such as Van Krieken (2012) distinguish between the relative homogeneity of the Netherlands and the situation in Australia. According to Van Krieken (2012), the Netherlands has a "thick" but also "cool" (implicit) national culture within a more or less ethnically homogenous nation. The country is characterised by relatively exclusionary conceptions of citizenship and national identity and their "lack of porousness for newcomers" (Van Krieken, 2010, p. 16). This is reflected in, for instance, the linguistic distinction still made between *autochtoon* (native, indigenous) and *allochtoon* (of foreign origin, "not from here") within the category of "Dutch citizen". Autochtony can only be claimed when cultural and racial difference has been more or less eliminated; as long as one looks racially different, as in the case of Dutch Somalis, one remains an allochtoon, a non-native (Van Krieken, 2012). In contrast, Australia is characterised by the dominance of a "thinner" conception of national culture, even if it may be more explicit and enthusiastic ("hot"). The "thick" conception of culture is less self-evident in Australia and "its defenders have to work a lot harder to sustain it" (Van Krieken, 2012, p. 14).

METHODS

This chapter draws upon five years of ethnographic research that commenced in 2008 in Australia. The research initially sought to explore Australian Somalis' participation in and experiences of team sports with a particular focus on football

109

(soccer), which is the most popular sport among Somalis. The research approach in this project flowed from its objective to capture participant voices, experiences and meaning-making processes. The primary research site was Melbourne, Australia, which has a sizeable concentration of Somalia-born people. The research initially focused on a single football club in Melbourne but over time the study developed into a multi-sited ethnography in order to trace participants, their relationships and their experiences across multiple sites in Australia which include other sports clubs and events. The research combined multiple data collection strategies with a focus on ethnographic observations and interviews (Spaaij, 2012a, 2013, 2015). This approach involved spending time and sharing space with participants, and watching, observing and talking with them in order to discover their interpretations, meanings and relationships.

In 2015, this research shifted to Europe. A number of Australian-based participants reported that they had previously lived, or had family or friends, in Europe. They described diasporic sports events organised in countries such as the Netherlands, Sweden and the United Kingdom that they or their family members had participated in. One event that featured in the narratives of Australian Somali participants was the AFT. The authors therefore decided to conduct qualitative research at this event. This study too comprised ethnographic observations and interviews with players, coaches, referees, volunteers, spectators, and representatives of Somali community organisations.

In both settings research protocols and interview guides were developed in close consultation with members of the Somali communities to ensure cultural appropriateness and relevance. Interview questions and observation guides were designed to capture the participants' perceptions and experiences of identity and belonging in general, and of the sports activities under study in particular. The interviews were conducted at sports facilities, at local cafés, in people's homes and in the offices of Somali community organisations located in different parts of Melbourne and Amsterdam.

Interview transcripts and field notes were analysed using thematic analysis techniques. The authors independently read the transcripts, field notes and social media messages and coded passages of text firstly using an open (or initial meaning code) and secondly an axial (or categorisation of open codes) coding scheme. Dialogue between the authors resulted in intersubjective agreement on the interpretation of the identified passages and codes. The first author then coded the transcripts line by line and the second author reviewed the coding.

The research approach outlined above constitutes a form of "conventional humanist qualitative methodology" that has been subject to critique (e.g., St Pierre, 2012, 2014). This critique invites us to think reflexively about the ontological dimensions of the researcher and research practices. We acknowledge that the research practices conducted in this study have a constructive dimension in terms of both the discursive framing of the research and participants' narratives elicited within the interviews and observations. For example, the research questions we posed were informed by a strengths-based approach as opposed to a deficit model, as well as by a conceptualisation of belonging as multiple, dynamic and hybrid, in contrast to the static, monolithic and binary notion of belonging that is enacted in the dominant political and media discourses in both countries. These orientations shaped the data collection and analytical procedures in terms of, *inter alia*, focus and the identification of salient themes.

In the next sections we use the data elicited via these methods to examine how participation in community-based sport affects participants' sense of belonging. We foreground two themes that emerge from the data: first, the multiple forms of belonging that are enacted in community sports spaces; and second, how such experiences of belonging are affected by, and negotiated in relation to, the politics of belonging. All participant names referred to in this chapter are pseudonyms.

FORMS OF BELONGING

The forms of belonging created or enacted in and through participation in community sports activities and events are best understood as situated and situational accomplishments (Ajrouch & Kusow, 2007; Valentine et al., 2009). They tend to be fluid, hybrid, multiform and performed within specific contexts and moments, but can also transcend particular situations to affect individual and collective belonging in their everyday lives. As shown below these forms of belonging operate at a plurality of scales (Antonsich, 2010; Wood & Waite, 2011), from local to global. Within the limited space of this chapter we are unable to discuss in any detail all of the different forms of belonging that emerged from the data. Instead we foreground three salient, inter-related dimensions of belonging experienced and narrated by participants: being Somali, transnational belonging and belonging to the nation.

Being Somali: Roots, Connections and Practices

Participants appear to be more consciously aware and proud of their Somali identity and heritage during the community sports activities and events observed in this research. Their engagement with and experience within these practices increases their sense of belonging to, and 'roots' in, the homeland and Somali diasporic communities. Hala, a female player and volunteer in her 20s, expresses this as follows:

> I am Dutch. I was born here but it is still important to me to know where I come from. Because we are so dispersed it is difficult to find anyone who reminds you of your roots. I believe that is a very essential thing.

Her friend Aicha (early 20s) elaborates:

> The mentality that I used to have was, like, Somali music and culture is annoying. No, I don't need any of that. And I see that now with my nieces and

111

nephews who say, "It's so boring". But now I think: it's your culture. You have to know it. And I immerse myself in it. It's a part of yourself, it's a piece of your roots. It's important to know yourself, who you are.

Both women explain that they enjoy spending time and sharing space with fellow Somalis within the context of the sports activities. These activities offer a space where they can be with "people like me", where they can speak Somali, eat Somali food and enjoy Somali cultural performances. Such interactions enable them to "feel more Somali" and to "get to know my heritage". During the AFT participants share stories and memories about Somali society, politics and sport. They also indulge in Somali music, poetry and food and have the opportunity to participate in organised debates on the current situation and future of Somalia as well as the circumstances and experiences of Somalis in their receiving communities. A female volunteer (Fatima, late teens) explains:

> Well, for example, when I speak Somali, I know that the other will answer in Somali … the communication is different when you're with Somalis than when it is mixed. I think it's because you understand each other better. I'm not sure … it could be that when you have different backgrounds you can get misunderstandings. And when you're both Somali it's easier and smoother.

In a similar vein, male referee Abdi (30s) notes that: "It makes me feel more Somali. Yeah. And like I'm involved here … with other people who also speak Somali as their first language. It makes me proud". And Ahmed, a British Somali coach in his 60s, explains: "It broadens your family. They get to know each other, they care for each other, so it opens that aspect of trusting and having, yeah, dialogue and communication".

In the Dutch context an important aspect of this is the opportunity AFT and other sports activities provide for social interaction and learning between established Dutch Somalis and recent arrivals. Hala (female, 20s) explains:

> The past few years we have seen many new arrivals. They don't come here because they like it but because they were forced to flee their homeland. It's easier to help them when you speak the same language and when you understand where they come from. … That can be an important source of support, that they feel safer and also to participate in sport and to get to know many people who can teach them the [Dutch] language and make friends. You simply feel better understood by someone who knows where you come from. I have many people in my environment who are new arrivals and I always try to motivate them.

We observed similar dynamics in Melbourne. During one of the first author's observations at a Melbourne-based football club, an established club member introduced him to Khalid (male, 40s), who had recently arrived in Australia after living in Europe for the last 20 years. Khalid moved to Australia to seek better employment opportunities. In London he had been playing football in a Horn of Africa team. He explained that upon his arrival in Melbourne he began to play casual football with other recently arrived migrants in a local park, which provided him with opportunities to meet new people as well as to maintain a sense of continuity in his life. For him and many other (young) men football is regarded with fondness and produced feelings of nostalgia and a deep connection to life in both the homeland and the diaspora (Dukic, McDonald, & Spaaij, 2017).

Hala and Aicha's earlier reference to 'roots' is insightful for the purpose of this chapter. Some participants explicitly compare their participation in events like AFT to return visits they have undertaken to Somalia. Roble, Dutch Somali player (male, late teens), voices how "having Somalis together is important. All those people who you see there, it makes you feel like a real Somali, so to speak". When asked how that experience affects his sense of belonging, he replies:

> As a Somali, quite a lot actually. 'Coz most people [at AFT] are Somalis so you learn how to deal with your own culture. The last time I was in Somalia was eight years ago. When I'm over there, I can quite easily regain the Somali language or culture, it brings back the memory.

Yet their experiences of return visits also reveal complexities regarding the negotiation of belonging. A number of participants point out that when they visit Somalia they are not necessarily recognised as being "fully Somali" and often stand out as European or Australian Somalis in terms of dress, language or customs. Haji (male, 20s) relays the following experience:

> Look, when I'm abroad [in Somalia] and someone asks me, "Where are you from?" I always say "The Netherlands". They can tell by your language that you're not 100% Somali. Or that you mix in Dutch words and so they think, "He's not from this country". But I always say: "I'm from the Netherlands".

Haji's comment reveals the multiple and hybrid identities that many Dutch and Australian Somalis enact situationally. It is to this issue that we now turn, with specific reference to both transnational belonging and belonging to the nation.

Transnational Belonging: Diaspora Formation in Action

In addition to a sense of belonging to homeland, participants possess a strong sense of transnational belonging that is closely associated with diaspora formation. As Burdsey (2006) points out sports clubs or events can act as cultural intermediaries or flows between the homeland and the dispersed diasporic community. He gives the example of a British Asian football player who spoke of "how his federation intends to establish links, partnerships and exchanges with clubs in Bangladesh through actually entering a club in a tournament in that country" (p. 490). We observe similar processes among both Dutch and Australian Somalis. For example, football teams composed of young Somali Australian men have traveled to Europe and North America to compete in international tournaments and this offers them an opportunity to engage with Somali diasporas which include their relatives and kin around the world. These global sporting encounters are but one aspect of the transnational lives that many Somali Australians lead. In the same vein some young Dutch Somalis had participated in or helped organise diasporic sports events in European countries with sizeable Somali diasporas, including Sweden, Finland, Norway, Germany, United Kingdom, Switzerland and Turkey. Conversely teams and individuals from six different European countries participated in the 2015 edition of the AFT. Musa, a Swedish participant in his 20s, explains this transnational engagement as follows:

> Because they connect each other … I can tell you that when I am in Sweden … the nearest Somali community is like 30 minutes by car from my home. Sometimes I play with them, sometimes I arrange a big tournament which involves many teams … from other cities. So when they play each other, meet each other, play against each other, they connect with them, or connect, make a connection. And this connection, after the tournament they connect with each other, they contact each other, to make another games between themselves.

Asad, a visiting player from Finland in his 20s, specifically addresses the meaning of such connections:

> It's always nice to meet other people from other countries. I guess that when we see some youngsters from different countries and you chat with them, and you ask where they are originally from, and some people are born and raised here in Europe. And there are some people who have gone back to Somalia and they have their own story, and it's quite fascinating to hear each story of everyone. For example, last year I met so many people and still we are friends, and we are sitting here and hey, I remember you. I think it's very important, because even though we have the same culture, you see some differences when you talk to like another Somali who came from different country … like when you start to talking to him you see some little differences.

Dutch Somali player Abdi (male, 20s) gives another example:

> Last year I met [a Swedish player] in the dressing room and we had a short conversation. We asked: how is it there? How is the nationality? How is life there? And what do you think of the Netherlands as an outsider? That's super interesting to hear from someone from that country. He told us that the first Somali tournament in Sweden was a huge success, and many in the Netherlands don't know about this. I find that very interesting to learn about.

These kinds of transnational connection, whether fleeting or more durable, contribute to a sense of belonging to the global Somali diaspora. While for some participants such transnational belonging is primarily enacted within and through sports activities, for others the transnational engagement extends well beyond sport into media, music, political engagement and transnational activism (Kleist, 2008; Hammond, 2013).

Transnational belonging and more place-based or nation-based forms of belonging are not mutually exclusive but rather intersect and co-exist in complementary ways. As Hammond (2013) explains, transnational engagement can be a way to bridge between the Somali, diaspora and 'host' cultures. Her research suggests that transnational engagement may actually support belonging to the nation, and vice versa. It is to this issue of national belonging that we now turn.

Being Dutch, Being Australian: Belonging to the Nation

The sociocultural meanings of the experiences discussed in the previous sections are often misrecognised by policymakers who view mono-ethnic sports spaces as antithetical to the political objective of social integration (Krouwel et al., 2006; Spaaij, 2012a). Organised sport has been identified by policymakers as a sphere for social 'mixing' between different cultural groups. An assumption is that ethnically diverse sports activities stimulate the social integration of minority ethnic groups in ways that mono-ethnic sports spaces do not (e.g. Pooley, 1976; Krouwel et al., 2006). The lived experiences of Dutch and Australian Somalis reveal the flaws of this integration/self-exclusion binary and instead suggest that the activities they participate in can simultaneously elicit belonging to both homeland and receiving communities.

This is evident, for example, in the ways AFT participants describe how they represent their nation or city during the competition. Identification with their country and city of residence is a source of pride for many of the participating teams. Haji and Hasan, whose team 'represents' a Dutch city, reflect upon this as follows:

> You have to put [your city] on the map [during the event]. Yes, you can just play for another team that represents a different city, but you have to represent your own city. You go back home and the people in your city are proud of you. They watch you on the livestream, our mothers and siblings. And they tell us that: "Hey, great that you got that far [in the tournament]".

In a similar vein two players (both in their 20s) representing one of the Finnish teams that participate in the AFT stated:

> *Asad:* We are representing Finland and you can play against Norway, and there's always a little battle against each other ...

> *Warsame:* And people in Finland also know that these guys are selected from Finland so they are here for representing a Finland team and also when we are posting something to Facebook and we are saying like we are the Finnish team coming to Netherlands playing for the futsal. So they are supporting us and watching the live[stream] on YouTube.

115

Another important aspect of participants' sense of belonging to the nation is their engagement in sport, and in organised team sport in particular, as a cultural activity that is itself a powerful manifestation of the receiving community's culture. Sport assumes great social, cultural and economic importance in countries like Australia and the Netherlands, and it is at the centre of popular culture in both countries (Spaaij, 2012b). It is also a key site for the production, shaping and regulation of national identity (Ward, 2010). In the Netherlands, football is the dominant national participation and spectator sport and is commonly viewed as a vehicle for multicultural and societal integration (Krouwel et al., 2006; Müller et al., 2008). For many migrant-background young males participation in football is a way to claim belonging to the Dutch nation, even though in reality Dutch football is fraught with racialised and ethnicised discourses and practices (Van Sterkenburg, Knoppers, & De Leeuw, 2012).

The status of football is somewhat different in the Australian context. As part of their negotiation of national belonging in and through sport participation, Australian Somalis tend to develop a tacit awareness of the ways different sports are perceived within Australian society. For example most are readily aware of football's historical association with migrant communities. Football in Australia has long been distinguished by its popularity among sections of minority ethnic groups. Many football clubs were founded and organised along non-Anglo lines and these clubs remain a vital power base for the game at both the grassroots and semi-professional level (Hallinan et al., 2007). Football clubs and teams preceded formal community organisations for at least some migrant groups (Hay, 2009). For Australian Somalis like Mohamed, a former player and coach in his 20s, history shows that community-based sports clubs and events that cater to specific cultural groups can serve as a stepping stone towards more culturally diverse sports activities:

> [O]bviously I think even if you go back to other generations that were before us, the Greeks and people with different identities, they would have had clubs that were just based on Italians and Greeks. We are just going through that phase now, but down the track I don't see the reason why it shouldn't open up, and it will open up.

Moreover respondents recognise that – in Melbourne at least – Australian football, as a hegemonic team sport, is an ideal way to claim belonging to the Australian nation through the symbolic capital it bestows upon participants. The following conversation between Samatar, an Australian Somali man in his 20s, and the first author about the differences between football (soccer) and Australian football illustrates this tacit understanding:

> *RS:* Would it be different if you were involved in Australian football? Would that be different from being a soccer club?

> *Samatar:* I think Australians have to protect their Australian Rules, that's a national sport, you know. It's Australian identity, and yes soccer is seen as a violent thing because of as we know, soccer is a very passionate sport.

You know? I come from a soccer background. Somalia is based on soccer, that's the national sport. And you're from Europe you understand that soccer's like it's more emotional than footy. And that's why people are like "I just hate it".

RS: But you and quite a lot of Somalis are very interested in Australian football?

Samatar: We are. I always say: "why not, why don't they [play]". My brother plays AFL (Australian Football League) footy, you know he plays for [a club]. They kind of drove 40 minutes from here to play on the weekends and they train twice a week. And I used to play footy. I used to play for a club. I love playing footy, but that doesn't mean I have to leave soccer behind. If there's younger people who, the younger people that want to play soccer, play soccer. The younger people who want to play footy, play footy. There's no discrimination. We don't say "don't play footy because it's their sport". It's sport you know, the boys love it, they play it and that's why I said that's why now, even me, I put my hand up to work with the AFL to build this African team to play in the international competition. I put my hand up you know, a lot of people put their hands up. Ahmed put their hand up, Yusuf put their, his hand up. They don't come to the trainings, but I am at every training … You know my friends, the younger people, it's a way of saying to them, we can achieve anywhere anything, you know and just going to what's it called, uncharted territory. You know, going to footy for a lot of Africans is uncharted territory.

RS: How so?

Samatar: Why not go into it, integrate or assimilate? I don't mind, as long as you are going to benefit. At the end of the day it's all about being benefit. Our parents want us to benefit. Australia I am assuming wants the Africans to benefit, to move forward, because that's the reason why they invited us in this country. At the end of the day it's just people have different ideas about how you benefit.

Samatar's comments reveal his awareness of how engagement in Australian football can be interpreted as being symbolic or a reflection of integration and belonging to the nation. Taking up "their sport", a sport that embodies "Australian identity", provides "uncharted territory" for migrants like Samatar to "benefit, to move forward", and to seek and be granted a sense of belonging to the Australian nation. Yet this quest for belonging in and through sport participation is anything but straightforward; instead, it is typically fraught with tensions and constraints. It is to this issue that we now turn.

THE POLITICS OF BELONGING IN ACTION

The aforementioned forms and scales of belonging cannot be divorced from the historical, social and political contexts in which they are situated. As noted earlier, prevailing notions of nationhood and national citizenship shape the social and discursive space available to recently arrived migrants to create and enact their sense of belonging. The politics of belonging thus affect the process of identity formation which can be fraught with insecurities and ambiguities, especially for young Somalis in the West. Ahmed, the aforementioned British Somali coach (male, 60s), explains this as follows:

Questioning identity is very, very strong for lots of young Somalis [in the West]. For some of them it becomes really painful to understand or accept who they are, because one country gave me everything that I have now, and another one I came from. ... I think [the AFT] is one of those things that can make that process easier, especially some of the debates that happened last night ... There was one was born here, he's never seen Somalia; one who came from Somalia young then grew up most of his life in Sweden, so he's kind of Swedish, and that's his feeling; and some who recently came to Somalia or visited Somalia. I hope lots of the others will listen and could learn something from it.

He goes on to reflect:

If they realise their identity and accept that they can be different people, and wear different hats at different times, that will make it easier for them. So identity, the questions are not going to end now, it's going to continue for a long time. Even for me, sometimes I don't know which of my hats I'm wearing, and it's something that will stay with them probably for the rest of their lives.

In this context, experiences of racialisation and social exclusion can have a major impact on participants' sense of (not) belonging. For example, Farah, an Australian Somali football player and social worker in his 30s, expresses:

It puts you in sort of an isolation thing. That's like sometimes when they live in the high-rises [housing commission flats] they feel that sharing language ... if they're living next to each other and they see each other every day and it's sort of like OK. But the thing is, if you live in the middle of nowhere, like, if I was supposed to be living in Hawthorn in a suburban rich area and I've got kids, now I would struggle. They're gonna be isolated. The Hawthorn community doesn't want to accept them, people living there, you know. They're not accepted by that community, therefore you may as well live in these high-rises where you feel you're accepted, where you feel you're happy and belonging in there.

Sport itself is not immune from such experiences. Some participants report that they are regularly subjected to discriminatory remarks relating to their skin color or their cultural or religious background (Spaaij, 2012a). Yusuf, a Melbourne-based coach in his 40s, explains:

We suffer a lot of abuse. Last weekend a women at [an away game] hurled about at my players things like "monkey" and "terrorist". I told her that if she continued I would make life very difficult for her. And the players nearly got into a fight with the opposing players. This is unacceptable. Their behaviour was really inappropriate. And you see our kids, if one is attacked they all go over there and back him up. That's the sense of sameness that emerges in those situations. Though it is wrong to react to provocations.

Yusuf's reference to a situationally produced "sense of sameness" is significant here. Although this notion is often evoked in team sports contexts, such as in the phrase "backing up your mates", it holds a specific meaning in the face of racial or religious vilification. Yusuf notes that, in part as a consequence of such experiences, players at his club tend to "live in their own little world, and it's difficult for them break through this". Or, as Abdullahi, a university graduate in his late 20s, puts it: "Most clubs can call you any name they like, like 'chocolate'. You want another person to say, like, 'I'm chocolate too'". He explains how socialising with other Africans in sport makes him feel "more comfortable, because we're the same color and everything". Other participants in Australia similarly report how engaging with "other Africans or Muslims" in sport is "more comfortable" or "easier" because "you have something in common" and "have experienced the same things".

The experiences of their Dutch counterparts are broadly similar. For example, Hala states: "I can be myself more when I am around other Somalis". Haji and Hasan, two male players (in their 20s) of a team that participates in the AFT elaborate on this issue as follows:

Haji: You feel at home here.

Hasan: It's a different feeling. I have to say that when I'm here, every year, it's different ... We sometimes play in different tournaments but that's ... you don't see people like yourself and that's frustrating. Of course, you are in a foreign country [the Netherlands] so it's logical. But to be able to experience an event like [AFT] is fun, it's attractive. Everyone is black. That gives you a different kind of feeling, I must confess.

These experiences speak to Australian and Dutch Somalis' ongoing negotiation of the effects of 'Othering' processes based on race/ethnicity, religion and nation, and how these affect their sense of (not) belonging in and beyond sports spaces. Some Australian and Dutch Somalis may thus prefer to play sport with other Somali migrants or minority ethnic groups because they feel more comfortable and secure within these spaces (Bradbury, 2011; Spaaij, 2013). Yet the space available for such co-ethnic interaction has become more constrained due to concerted governmental efforts to enhance cultural "mixing" in sport (for the Dutch context see Krouwel et al., 2006; Müller et al., 2008) and, in the Australian context, to "de-ethnicise" the game of football (Hallinan et al., 2007). In political and public discourse co-ethnic sport participation has been likened to "cultural separatism" and "self-exclusion", rather than being seen as a haven from prejudice that facilitates the negotiation of multiple and hybrid forms of belonging.

CONCLUSION

In this chapter, we have sought to explore the negotiation and politics of belonging through the lens of community-based sports activities. Drawing on ethnographic fieldwork with Australian and Dutch Somalis within and across several sports spaces, we have shown how participants enact and negotiate multiple situated forms of belonging that intersect in complex and dynamic ways. Despite political and ideological contextual differences concerning multiculturalism and integration between the Netherlands and Australia (see Van Krieken, 2012), we identified similar experiences of belonging by Dutch and Australian Somalis. The different forms and scales of belonging – homeland, transnational/diasporic and national – performed within these spaces are not mutually exclusive. On the contrary they can support and complement each other by bridging Somali, diaspora and "host" cultures (Hammond, 2013), and thereby offer potent sources for the construction of plural and hybrid identities that are betwixt and between. Yet our findings also suggest that the space available for Australian and Dutch Somalis to claim these forms of belonging is shaped by the politics of belonging and, specifically, by the narrow confines of governmental belonging (Hage, 1998). This governmental belonging is evidenced in, for example, the ways Australian and Dutch Somalis are urged to play sport in mixed, mainstream settings rather than within their own communities or with other minority ethnic groups. It is also evidenced in the way Australian Somalis are sensitised into an awareness and appreciation of the dominant discourse that positions certain sports, like Australian football, as being more socially acceptable as a space for belonging to the nation despite historical evidence to the contrary.

Our findings highlight the importance of community spaces for migrant groups, such as Australian and Dutch Somalis, to claim a sense of belonging to each other and to the nation. As such this chapter reinforces Sporton and Valentine's (2007) conclusion that "a sense of 'belonging' in a country develops where a community has a sense of security and space to define its own identity beyond or alongside narrow prescriptions of national identity" (p. 19). It is therefore imperative that sport and social policies support migrants to retain and develop a sense of belonging to homeland and to their own diasporic community, while also supporting them to simultaneously access belonging to the nation without prejudice or discrimination.

REFERENCES

Ajrouch, K., & Kusow, A. (2007). Racial and religious contexts: Situational identities among Lebanese and Somali Muslim immigrants. *Ethnic and Racial Studies, 30*(1), 72–94.
Anthias, F. (2006). Belongings in a globalising and unequal world: Rethinking translocations. In N. Yuval-Davis, K. Kannabiran, & U. Vieten (Eds.), *The situated politics of belonging* (pp. 17–31). London: Sage Publications.

Antonsich, M. (2010). Searching for belonging: An analytical framework. *Geography Compass, 4*(6), 644–659.

Australian Bureau of Statistics. (2012). *Census of population and housing 2011.* Canberra: ABS.

Australian Bureau of Statistics. (2017). *Census of population and housing 2016.* Canberra: ABS.

Bhatia, S., & Ram, A. (2009). Theorizing identity in transnational and diaspora cultures: A critical approach to acculturation. *International Journal of Intercultural Relations, 33*(2), 140–149.

Bradbury, S. (2011). From racial exclusions to new inclusions: Black and minority ethnic participation in football clubs in the East Midlands of England. *International Review for the Sociology of Sport, 46*(1), 23–44.

Burdsey, D. (2006). No ball games allowed? A socio-historical examination of the development and social significance of British Asian football clubs. *Journal of Ethnic and Migration Studies, 32*(3), 477–496.

Burdsey, D. (2008). Contested conceptions of identity, community and multiculturalism in the staging of alternative sport events: A case study of the Amsterdam world cup football tournament. *Leisure Studies, 27*(3), 259–277.

CBS Statline. (2016). *Bevolking; generatie, geslacht, leeftijd en herkomstgroepering, 1 januari.* The Hague: Central Bureau of Statistics. Retrieved August 10, 2016, from http://statline.cbs.nl/Statweb/publication/?DM=SLNL&PA=37325&D1=a&D2=a&D3=0&D4=a&D5=199&D6=17-20&VW=T

Dukic, D., McDonald, B., & Spaaij, R. (2017). Being able to play: Experiences of social inclusion and exclusion within a football team of people seeking asylum. *Social Inclusion, 5*(2), 101–110.

Griffiths, D. (2002). *Somali and Kurdish refugees in London: New identities in the diaspora.* Aldershot: Ashgate.

Hage, G. (1998). *White nation: Fantasies of white supremacy in a multicultural society.* Annandale: Pluto Press.

Hall, S. (1990). Cultural identity and diaspora. In J. Rutherford (Ed.), *Identity: Community, culture, difference* (pp. 222–237). London: Lawrence & Wishart.

Hallinan, C., Hughson, J., & Burke, M. (2007). Supporting the "world game" in Australia: A case study of fandom at national and club level. *Soccer & Society, 8*(2), 283–297.

Hammond, L. (2013). Somali transnational activism and integration in the K: Mutually supporting strategies. *Journal of Ethnic and Migration Studies, 39*(6), 1001–1017.

Hay, R. (2009). No single pattern: Australian migrant minorities and the round ball code in Australia. *Soccer & Society, 10*(6), 823–842.

Hopkins, G. (2006). Somali community organizations in London and Toronto: Collaboration and effectiveness. *Journal of Refugee Studies, 19*(3), 361–380.

Joseph, J. (2011). A diaspora approach to sport tourism. *Journal of Sport and Social Issues, 35*(2), 146–167.

Kleist, N. (2008). In the name of diaspora: Between struggles for recognition and political aspirations. *Journal of Ethnic and Migration Studies, 34*(7), 1127–1143.

Krouwel, A., Boonstra, N., Duyvendak, J. W., & Veldboer, L. (2006). A good sport? Research into the capacity of recreational sport to integrate Dutch minorities. *International Review for the Sociology of Sport, 41*(2), 165–180.

Krzyzanowski, M., & Wodak, R. (2007). Multiple identities, migration and belonging: Voices of migrants. In C. R. Caldas-Coulthard & R. Iedema (Eds.), *Identity trouble* (pp. 95–119). Houndmills: Palgrave Macmillan.

Müller, F., van Zoonen, L., & de Roode, L. (2008). The integrative power of sport: Imagined and real effects of sport events on multicultural integration. *Sociology of Sport Journal, 25*(3), 387–401.

Nijenhuis, G., & van Liempt, I. (2014). *Somaliërs in Amsterdam.* New York, NY: Open Society Foundations.

Nunn, C. (2014). Introduction: The belonging issue. *New Scholar: An International Journal of the Humanities, Creative Arts and Social Sciences, 3*(1), i–vi.

Pooley, J. (1976). Ethnic soccer clubs in Milwaukee: A study of assimilation. In M. Hart (Ed.), *Sport in the socio-cultural process* (pp. 475–492). Dubuque, IA: W. C. Brown.

Probyn, E. (1996). *Outside belongings.* New York, NY: Routledge.

Spaaij, R. (2011). *Sport and social mobility: Crossing boundaries.* New York, NY: Routledge.

Spaaij, R. (2012a). Beyond the playing field: Experiences of sport, social capital and integration among Somalis in Australia. *Ethnic and Racial Studies, 35*(9), 1519–1538.
Spaaij, R. (2012b). Sport. In P. Beilharz & T. Hogan (Eds.), *Sociology: Antipodean perspectives* (pp. 347–352). Oxford: Oxford University Press.
Spaaij, R. (2013). Cultural diversity in community sport: An ethnographic inquiry of Somali Australians' experiences. *Sport Management Review, 16*(1), 29–40.
Spaaij, R. (2015). Refugee youth, belonging and community sport. *Leisure Studies, 34*(3), 303–318.
Sporton, D., & Valentine, G. (2007). *Identities on the move: The integration experiences of Somali refugee and asylum seeker young people.* Sheffield & Leeds: University of Sheffield & University of Leeds.
St. Pierre, E. A. (2012). Post-qualitative research: The critique and the coming after. In N. K. Denzin & Y. S. Lincoln (Eds.), *Collecting and interpreting qualitative materials* (4th ed., pp. 611–625). Thousand Oaks, CA: Sage Publications.
St. Pierre, E. A. (2014). A brief and personal history of post qualitative research: Toward "post inquiry". *Journal of Curriculum Theorizing, 30*(2), 1–19.
Strang, A., & Ager, A. (2010). Refugee integration: Emerging trends and remaining agendas. *Journal of Refugee Studies, 23*(4), 589–607.
UNHCR. (2017). *Somalia situation 2017.* Geneva: UNHCR.
Valentine, G., Sporton, D., & Nielsen, K. B. (2009). Identities and belonging: A study of Somali refugees and asylum seekers living in the UK and Denmark. *Environment and Planning D: Society and Space, 27*, 234–250.
Van Krieken, R. (2012). Between assimilation and multiculturalism: Models of integration in Australia. *Patterns of Prejudice, 46*(5), 500–517.
van Liempt, I. (2011a). Young Dutch Somalis in the UK: Citizenship, identities and belonging in a transnational triangle. *Mobilities, 6*(4), 569–583.
van Liempt, I. (2011b). From Dutch dispersal to ethnic enclaves in the UK: The relationship between segregation and integration examined through the eyes of Somalis. *Urban Studies, 48*(16), 3385–3398.
Van Sterkenburg, J., Knoppers, A., & de Leeuw, S. (2012). Constructing racial/ethnic difference in and through Dutch televised soccer commentary. *Journal of Sport and Social Issues, 36*(4), 422–442.
Vertovec, S. (2001). Transnationalism and identity. *Journal of Ethnic and Migration Studies, 27*(4), 573–582.
Ward, T. (2010). *Sport and national identity: Kicking goals.* London: Routledge.
Werbner, P. (1996). "Our blood is green": Cricket, identity and social empowerment among British Pakistanis. In J. MacClancy (Ed.), *Sport, identity and ethnicity* (pp. 87–111). Oxford: Berg.
Wood, N., & Waite, L. (2011). Editorial: Scales of belonging. *Emotion, Space and Society, 4*, 201–202.
Yuval-Davis, N. (2006). Belonging and the politics of belonging. *Patterns of Prejudice, 40*(3), 197–214.
Yuval-Davis, N. (2011). *The politics of belonging: Intersectional contestations.* London: Sage Publications.

Ramón Spaaij
Victoria University
Australia

Jora Broerse
Victoria University
Australia

CHRIS MCCONVILLE AND NICOLE OKE

8. GENTRIFICATION

Power and Privilege in Footscray

What can the post-industrial Melbourne suburb of Footscray reveal to us about the political economy of gentrification? This political economy is symbolised in three key recent moments. In one, in early 2017, squatters died in a fire at the former Kinnear's Ropeworks, a manufacturing site, now out of production, and slated for one of the many high-rise residential developments changing the face of the suburb. In the second event, in late 2017, so-called 'hipster' cafes in Footscray were vandalised. These cafes, newcomers to the Footscray retail precinct, drew much of their clientele from the residents living in new high-rise apartments. In the third and earlier event, the Little Saigon Market, a hub for Footscray's everyday multiculturalism, burnt down just before Christmas 2016. In commonplace reflections, the three incidents all point to a wave of gentrification that is unstoppable. Gentrification can only, as one recent commentary suggests, mean that 'diversity is swapped for exclusionary, culturally homogenous spaces, and the area as we know it disappears' (ABC Radio Breakfast, 2017, May 5).

There are three fundamental problems with the current debate about Footscray's future and with gentrification discourse more broadly. In the first instance the assumption is that gentrification is entirely a negative process. Studies that emphasise the expertise and communal integration brought by gentrifiers remain the exception rather than the rule (Murdie & Teixeira, 2011; Shaw, 2004; Shaw & Hagemans, 2015). Secondly the discussion assumes that gentrification's displacement effect is irreversible and overwhelming; and thirdly almost any sign of change in an inner urban area that is not accompanied by economic collapse is described as gentrification. So, for example, transnational corporatised high rise apartment construction (better understood as urban renewal) is discussed in the same context as autonomous single dwelling renovation by owner-occupiers. As Van Criekingen and Decroly (2003) pointed out, the "persistence of the chaotic nature of the gentrification concept is particularly problematic in a geographical perspective. Indeed the diverse processes commonly referred to as 'gentrification' in the literature are very likely to display contrasting geographies" (Van Criekingen & Decroly, 2003). This is more than a problem of labelling. By collapsing a range of urban changes together under the banner of 'gentrification', any displacement driven by neoliberal urban 'management' can easily be overlooked and the circumscribed political influences of a small class of gentrifiers are made to carry the blame for urban inequalities. Here we seek to return gentrification to the quite specific processes described initially by Ruth Glass (Glass, 1964; Slater, 2006). In these Glass identified gentrification as a process of class displacement in which owner-occupiers, drawn from amongst middle class professions, 'invade' deteriorated nineteenth or early twentieth century residential districts inhabited by working-class renters. These 'gentrifiers' buy houses, restore and extend them. Subsequently the commercial activities and cultural character of an area are completely transformed. Gentrification is seen to remake a locality through a cultural shift, with the cultural style of the gentrifiers, usually Anglo or 'white' professionals, imposing their own aesthetic and moral values on both public space and communal events. Glass's gentrification is obviously describing a process distinct from the developer-driven high-rise construction physically transforming much of Footscray. We would expect then that the cultural effects of what is best called urban renewal in Footscray would be quite different. Lumping the two processes of change together obscures the political forces at work. Perhaps the most worrying aspect of this confusion is that it weakens any attempt to redress inequalities and displacement at a local level. Conveniently, the social class which has benefited most from global neoliberalism, the real estate investors and their supportive financial corporations, are able to deflect any challenge onto a small though visible class of home renovators in inner cities.

Our chapter here is not so much designed to defend gentrification from charges of privilege and displacement, but to see how the phenomenon fits within an urban political economy at metropolitan, local government authority (LGA) and neighbourhood scales. We explore political gentrification from a starting point in the politics of housing before turning to the political structures of commerce and then to transitions in cultural power. Ultimately we suggest that whilst gentrification does have a displacement effect in Footscray, this is far from being the dominant force in changing the suburb or in the politics emerging from that change. Gentrifiers themselves have a limited ability to change political decision-making about their suburb, and in fact they are generally only successful in coalition with neighbours who do not fit any commonly held image of gentrifiers. The transitions in power relations in Footscray direct us towards understanding gentrification less as an agent driving class and ethnic displacement and more as a material and cultural process sharing in networks of ethnicity, class and gender in Footscray. These changes need also be located with politics and political economies broader than the neighbourhood scale. Current changes, and the resilience demonstrated by long-term residents and others who have maintained close connections to the suburb over a long period of time, indicate that the suburb will be different but that it can retain its diversity.

The chapter draws on urban planning and property industry documents, and a series of 30 interviews. Documents analysed include state government planning documents, the masterplans of the local council (the City of Maribyrnong), as well as promotional material from the property industry. In conjunction with the

30 interviews, which were undertaken in 2015 with residents and others who frequent Footscray (Oke, Sonn, & McConville, 2016), these allow us to analyse the politics of gentrification and displacement in this suburb of Melbourne.

GENTRIFICATION AND THE FOOTSCRAY LANDSCAPE

Gentrification has generated a vast literature in academic and policy areas (Blasiu, Friedrichs, & Rühl, 2016; Grodach, Foster, & Murdoch, 2016). What is more, gentrification is (perhaps, along with Herbert Gans' and Jane Jacobs' associated concept of an 'urban village' (see Rex, 1971)), the one term from academic discussions of urban life to have been taken up without hesitation by the property industry and in popular discourse. So much so, that it has come to seem a normal phase in urban transitions around the globe. Observers only occasionally explore further and see gentrification in relation to the neoliberal ideology driving urban change (see Otuoğlu-Cook, 2006; Smith, 2002).

Typically academic observers see the politics of gentrification through the lens of street level, localised resistance to change in land use. Such resistance is expressed through vandalism of shops associated with the 'gentrifiers', the defacing of so-called 'hipster cafes' in Footscray being one recent and widely-publicised instance of such 'resistance' (Spark, 2017). These events, interesting though they are, remain in their very nature reactive (Newman & Wyly, 2006; Pearsall, 2013; Robinson, 1995). By the time these acts of resistance occur, decisions about demolition, new land uses and controls of public space have already worked their way through the political system. There are some exceptions to this focus but they are infrequent (see Choi, 2016; Slater, 2006). It thus becomes difficult to disentangle neighbourhood gentrification and its effects from wider global and metropolitan processes.

The Melbourne suburb of Footscray provides a good locale to investigate these themes since it has for so long resisted gentrification, whilst the neighbouring localities (West Footscray, Yarraville, Seddon, Kensington) have been largely gentrified since the later twentieth century. Footscray instead has been changed by successive immigrant settlement, beginning with European immigrants in the immediate post-war decades and followed by new settlers from Vietnam from the later 1970s. In more recent years the suburb has become a place of first settlement for recent arrivals from India. The retail centre reflects these transitions and in addition serves several African communities whose members live in the broader western suburban region of Melbourne. When Bill Logan wrote his seminal account of gentrification in Melbourne, Footscray did not appear as significant (Logan, 1985). The social geography and history of Footscray explains such an absence. Footscray has been physically separated from central Melbourne by a river, a swamp reconstructed into shipping berths, major roadways and then by the railyards and container terminals abutting the Port of Melbourne. Footscray's housing stock is rarely uniform so that the suburb lacks that imagined historic 'urban village' ambience attractive to gentrifiers. Footscray does have surviving pockets of nineteenth-century workers' cottages, though these are rarely grouped into potential heritage zones. As a result the heritage precincts identified in the City of Maribyrnong's Planning Scheme are less uniform than are those in nearby gentrified localities (Graeme Butler & Associates, 1991). Footscray again differs from hipsterised commercial zones in the inner suburbs of Melbourne, such as Fitzroy or Carlton, since it has a grid of shopping streets rather than one strip. This central business district is largely built up with cheap, medium rise and bland two- or three-storey modern commercial blocks without appeal to the hipster/gentrifier aesthetic. Furthermore Footscray has found it difficult to shake off a reputation for crime, industrial pollution and lack of open space. The crowding of even minor streets with heavy traffic shuttling between docks, railway yards and urban fringe warehouse complexes is the most obvious and destructive legacy (Cooper & Lanza, 2015).

Beyond these circumstances, the riverside frontage of Footscray was identified as an urban renewal site in 1983 with a local government-driven 'City Link-Quay West' redevelopment planned. As John Lack pointed out, this was 'tainted' by the then Victorian state government's financial catastrophes (Lack, 1991, pp. 106–107). The river frontage was largely left ungentrified until seized on in a moment of frantic rebuilding to great height and density in the early 21st century. Rebuilding Footscray has thus meant the construction of apartment blocks to varying heights (with one iteration of height limits revoked by the recent planning minister) rather than the house-by-house renovation implied by gentrification. Announcing a new urban renewal project in 2012, the then Planning Minister, Matthew Guy, lauded what he expected to become a '... complete change in the way central Footscray is used ... starting to place Footscray as one of the key inner-city growth areas' (Millar, August 2012).

In Footscray urban renewal is accelerated through state investment in a new rail by-pass, an upgraded Footscray station and work for a new metropolitan underground rail line. As this renewal process got underway, several developments completely turned their backs on the Footscray central activities district so as to emphasise views over water and to the city skyline. In this they are marketed as 'city edge', disconnected from the wider western suburbs (Maribyrnong City Council, 2014). Different apartment blocks, catering to students, have been constructed within the central business district of Footscray. A high rise office tower (State Trustee Offices at McNab Avenue) sits between the railway station and the commercial centre. This is a Victorian state government office building rather than a residential tower. Public-sector investment in large-scale building complexes is typically used to encourage private investment. In Footscray this been applied cautiously and strategically, reflecting the weaknesses in 1980s schemes to stimulate urban renewal along the Maribyrnong River waterfront. In Footscray, as a result, urban renewal increasingly takes the form of residential high-rise between the Footscray commercial district and the eastern border of the Maribyrnong municipality, the Maribyrnong River. The most completely gentrified precincts in Footscray in contrast are sited to the west of the commercial district.

GENTRIFYING THE HOUSES OF FOOTSCRAY

Housing problems in Footscray were highlighted following the deaths of rough sleepers in the former Kinnear's Ropeworks, Ballarat Rd, Footscray in 2017 (ABC News, 2017, February 3). Less than two years earlier a Coronial inquest investigated deaths in a house fire. Following this inquiry, finalised only in 2014, into the deaths of three international students in Footscray, Lucy Adams, lawyer from Justice Connect, pointed out that 'the students had no options other than to accept dangerous and overcrowded housing … these students were essentially homeless … their deaths were a tragic illustration of the chronic lack of affordable, adequate and safe housing' (Byrne, 2014). These events, the most tragic in a long line of disasters inflicted upon the rough sleepers and those in inadequate housing in Footscray, could easily be linked to gentrification. Footscray, remarked one writer responding to the deaths at Kinnear's, was "once an 'affordable' suburb, (but) became snared in the hipster and developer gentrification process" (James, 2017).

But the relationship is not that straightforward. When gentrifiers buy houses they do sometimes take dwellings out of the lowest rungs of the rental market, the places to which marginal renters, those 'effectively homeless', are forced to resort. Gentrifiers might buy rooming houses. More commonly gentrifiers purchase from deceased estates, from older immigrants, or from retired or rentrenched industrial workers. This can be seen as an inter-generational exchange by which older low-income residents can make a once-in-a-lifetime windfall gain. At the same time, across the suburb, rising prices paid by gentrifiers force up rates, land values and thus rents, driving some renters on low incomes out of the suburb, down to the rooming house sector, and even to homelessness. The City of Maribyrnong had more than 150 rooming houses in 2009 (City of Maribyrnong, 2011) but only 40 boarding houses were listed in the City of Maribyrnong in 2014 (Dalton, Huske, & Paw, 2015). In contrast, rooming houses in Melbourne as a whole have actually increased in number in the 21st century with the fastest rise in availability of boarding house accommodation in the outer south-eastern suburbs rather than in traditional low rent locales such as Footscray (Dalton, Huske, & Paw, 2015).

The connection between gentrification and availability of affordable, secure and comfortable single room accommodation is not straightforward. Any dramatic decline locally and increase elsewhere across the metropolis reflects wider investment and purchase patterns. For example, houses subdivided into sub-let rooms and abutting the central commercial district were the most vulnerable to change. This was because of retail and professional service expansion rather than restoration by gentrifiers. Restoration and rising land values in neighbouring properties force up costs and make resale and conversion to single-family dwellings attractive to rooming house operators. But a combination of forces can drive up citywide land values and state regulation can force boarding house operators into new-build structures away from Footscray (The Melbourne Homeless Crisis Help Network, 2017; Capone, 2014). If the worst that can be said of gentrifiers is that they buy and rehabilitate deathtrap buildings such as that in which the three international students died, then their impact on those 'effectively homeless' is not entirely negative.

When John Rex, Bill Logan and others wrote of housing and gentrification in the late 1980s, they insisted that the housing market was not a unified continuum. Developers, investors, owner-occupiers and several classes of tenants wanted different housing tenure types and structures. Importantly, Rex deliberately chose class to differentiate between groups vying for housing. These housing classes are structured around a market and compete for the capitalised goods of material production in housing. In Footscray the gentrifiers are found within a broader class of single dwelling owner-occupiers. Rough sleepers are connected to a formal housing market through rooming houses, and renters are divided between those in the apartment market and others in detached dwellings, who are often renting from short-term landlords whose interest in property amounts to finalising a will or awaiting capital gains rather than in any stable tenant-landlord relationship. Over the course of several years the City of Maribyrnong has sought to maintain an opportunity for social housing outside these relationships. Sometimes these efforts are frustrated by gentrifying home renovators (Millar, 2017). However looking at Footscray as a whole, although this is a significant issue for social justice and fairness, such gentrifier exclusivity remains a minor aspect of the transition of the suburb.

Nor in general is high rise apartment building directly connected to the problems of the least powerful housing classes. Certainly, as the river frontages are taken up by apartments and derelict factory sites are demolished, spaces used by rough sleepers vanish and there is stricter policing of rough sleepers and others in public spaces (Pennay, 2012). Yet this is not the end of the story. Urban renewal does not take dwelling units out of the lowest segments of the rental market (Bell, 1977; Rex, 1971). In fact by rapidly adding rentable space it has the potential to slow the increase in rents. At the same time the design of these units, combined with the selection and surveillance policies of rental agencies, can work to reduce access for particular groups: single parent households with several children, those with no consistent employment record or the kinship networks of recently arrived immigrants.

Gentrification and urban renewal can then have contradictory impacts on housing supply and tenure structure. With massive increases in apartment construction planned, urban renewal of Footscray will have an uncertain but potentially reductive impact on housing costs, and thus on the relation of distinct housing classes to the housing market. Footscray has certainly become more expensive for would-be purchasers and renters (at the 2016 Census more than half of Footscray's residents were renting). It still lags behind the suburbs with the most rapid increase in house and unit prices. In the context of low interest rates, the expanding population of Melbourne and state government policies of densification, all of Melbourne has experienced rapid price growth in land and housing. In Footscray, even if gentrification has contributed to price rises and accelerating rents, the scale of unit construction easily outweighs any influence from gentrifiers. Fifteen thousand new residential units will be added to Footscray by 2041, almost all of them in high rise apartment complexes. This is in effect an entirely new city (City of Maribyrnong, 2016; Real Estate Investor, 2016). Unit prices in Footscray had begun to fall by the end of 2016. We could expect then that high rise construction will reduce median housing costs in the suburb in relative rather than absolute terms. How much this aids those at the bottom of the housing class structure is uncertain. But a stagnant high-rise market with new units being added in significant numbers must have a deflating effect. At the very least these urban renewal projects will lessen the incentives for owners of older walk-up unit blocks to renovate and raise rents.

How this is being experienced by residents is complex and diverse. People interviewed for this study articulated the complexity of urban renewal and gentrification. The displacement of the marginalised was linked by some to failures by council to manage processes of change. Others were concerned that gentrification was meaning that 'local people on low incomes are being driven out, (by) extreme gentrification where newbies outnumber oldies' (participant 6). This would eventually lead to "further decline of the services from council, and lack of interest from council". Respondents were aware that change meant that less influential networks would be destroyed and groups 'pushed out' even though they felt that they themselves might be able to survive in Footscray. "People shouldn't be pushed out by rising costs, some businesses will be pushed out", said one participant, whilst noting that many businesses in the commercial centre only had short-term leases and could easily be forced out (participant 25). One Spanish-speaking respondent (participant 2) said that the least powerful "will get pushed out as more demanding white people move in, the migrants don't complain, (or) go on rallies".

GENTRIFICATION AND THE COMMERCIAL HUB

When the hipster cafes in Footscray were vandalised, the vandals managed to re-ignite commentary on the role of hipsters, and gentrifiers more generally, in the commercial centre of Footscray. While the discussion of housing in Footscray focuses on its legacy as an industrial working-class locality, the discussion of changes to the commercial centre of Footscray tends to be framed in terms of ethnicity, the fears that multiculturalism and diversity will disappear and that it will become an exclusionary commercial and cultural precinct or, as one of our research participants put it, a 'white bread suburb'. 'Hipster' may not have the same connotations as 'gentrifiers', but in discussion of the commercial district it tended to be used in much the same way, albeit framed in opposition to multiculturalism, not to working-class. The fear here was that multicultural diversity would be replaced with an exclusionary commercial and cultural precinct. That this might suggest a discourse that it is only anglos that can be hip points also to the complex ways ethnicity and class do need to be unpacked in considering the urban futures of ethnically diverse and working class suburbs. Likewise the processes of 'succession' in suburbs such as Footscray need to be carefully considered.

The physical and cultural geography of the Footscray CBD is an uncommon lay-out for shopping precincts in suburban Melbourne, both since it is a grid of streets rather than a single strip, and because the number of different countries from which migrants have arrived and then developed significant commercial hubs is high for a suburb in Melbourne. The combination of these two factors has meant that both physical and cultural place making has occurred, in large part, in separate zones of the suburb (Oke, Sonn, & McConville, 2016). Vietnamese shops dominate near the railway station and the main through traffic artery along Hopkins Street. The southern end of Nicholson Street is essentially African. Medical and welfare agencies line the western sector of Paisley Street. Chain stores and a major supermarket sit in the centre of the precinct. Along the western end of Hopkins/Barkly Street are remnants of commercial retail that have survived from an older Footscray retail centre, with shops selling computer equipment, specialist footwear or sporting goods. There are a few Italian cafes, and some African restaurants. A string of new cafes and bars are sited in and around a renovated former hotel building. In these, food styles, decor and clientele are those classed as 'hipster'. These, though, still remain a small minority in the commercial centre.

In thinking about gentrification and displacement, the experience is not universal across the suburb. While there are hipsters moving in, the growth of African businesses is part of the suburb too. In a documentary by Africa Media Australia about African businesses in Footscray, the businesses represented had been established fairly recently and were all quite positive about their experience. One owner of a small shop said that it was "… a very good place for business", but also for socialising and cutting hair (2012). Some of the Asian and African restaurants are adapting to a changing clientele and taking on some of the style typically associated with the hipster scene. But as some adapt others are unable to compete. One of our interviewees (participant 25) noted that many retail businesses in the commercial centre only had short-term leases and could easily be displaced. Shopkeepers were seen to be "afraid they don't have long term leases. When new building go up (they) will be pushed out" by gentrification. One interviewee (participant 12) reflected that:

> Diversity is 'about the mix'. I am happy to see the mix (which included the newcomers). Some businesses won't be able to compete, but not a bad thing either. Something has to change and you have to move with that change. I don't see any threat. [More expensive accommodation] will probably push a little bit the kind of diversity we have now. It will be good eventually, will take away some of the stereotypes. I am including the Anglo population as part of different cultures in terms of being vibrant and accepting. There is a history/tradition of accepting. I would like to see that tradition to continue and it will.

The physical landscape is part of the cultural identity of a place and many people we interviewed were concerned about the scale of the changes. The increased heights and densities and the large number of sites slated for redevelopment meant that the process was beyond local control and that their interest in community, diversity and tolerance would be seen as marginal.

If changes in other strip shopping centres in inner Melbourne provide any guide, the hipster outlets are unlikely to dominate the extensive precinct. Melbourne has a history of ethnic shopping strips that survive and indeed flourish long after the ethnic community which supported them has moved away. Little Bourke Street saw its first Cantonese shops in the 1850s. It has grown into an expanding Chinese and broader Asian shopping hub. Lygon Street, Carlton, where Italian cafes opened for business between the wars, remains firmly Italian in character. In these commercial precincts, shopkeepers from a range of ethnic backgrounds adjust to the style and demands of their own community and at the same time diversify stock and presentation to draw in new residents, hipsters included. The crucial issue for Footscray's retail character, as several of our interviewees were aware, remains the nature of commercial leases and building ownership. Vietnamese traders appear to have taken advantage of historic depressed prices in Footscray (1979–1985) and bought shops outright. Later arrivals, African shopkeepers for example, seem more likely to be renting premises and often on short-term leases.

Certainly the hipster cafes indicate that change is underway. How far this vague and probably short-lived cultural style can remake the CBD is uncertain, though the linked process of gentrification will likely be more ongoing. In late 2017, upmarket Melbourne restaurant conglomerates announced plans for new outlets in Footscray. Hart's Hotel was to be reinvented and renamed the Victoria and an older pizza shop in Footscray was to be converted and renovated by one of Melbourne's most fashionable restaurant groups (The Age, October 2017). But other processes are ongoing too, such as the increase in African businesses in the suburb. Likewise, the Vietnamese shop owners, and increasingly the African shopowners too, are politically and socially organised and are able to respond creatively to any change in planning controls. The major brand-name trading corporations, the supermarket chains and others, seem unlikely to relinquish prime sites in Footscray. Welfare and medical agencies generally have long-term leases and a stable clientele from across the western suburbs. Large scale change is some way off.

FOOTSCRAY: DISPLACEMENT, CULTURE AND GENTRIFICATION

When the Little Saigon Market burned down, just before Christmas 2016, the fire was widely seen as marking a turning point in the suburb's multicultural history. And yet this site was slated for redevelopment long before the fire. Around the market, older commercial complexes are making way for a range of multi-unit accommodation. Likewise the Ropeworks fire is understood as a signifier of the changing class composition in the suburb. How will new housing and some change in commercial outlets affect the cultural character of Footscray? In the words of the observer quoted earlier in this chapter, is it inevitable that 'the area as we know it (will) disappear'? Amongst our interviewees there was some recognition that the newcomers would appreciate and build on the strengths of Footscray rather than simply occupy an apartment for convenience. "Hopefully people move in here because they recognise these things (diversity and sense of community) about the place", thought one respondent. Many interviewees believed that the cultural strengths of Footscray, in particular its multicultural diversity, could survive the change in built form. The concern for residents and others in the suburb, then, is not only about displacement, about who is being pushed out of the suburb. It is also about the changing cultural politics in the suburb itself. Will the 'old Footscray's' working class networks and the ethnic business associations and cultural organisations survive? Our interviewees tended to welcome people who would contribute to the community, valued their enthusiasms, while being wary that others were 'turning their back' on the suburb. They were well aware that Footscray's character – what made the place and allowed their own networks to flourish – was itself a product of its social instability. In that vein they were prepared to 'wait and see' when it came to new residents.

The scale of the changes planned is so immense that there must be some cultural consequences. If votes for Green candidates at local government elections are seen as a proxy for gentrified politics, then gentrification has already made a political mark on Footscray. One Green councillor however was not a gentrifier and had grown up in Footscray. One of the independents re-elected was a member of a long-standing Footscray family (Millar, 29 October 2016). At state and federal elections Green and left independent candidates have made very few inroads into ALP votes, drawn from older industrial workers and recent immigrant networks. If political success is not a clear indicator of the cultural authority of gentrifiers then the significance of cultural festivals may be. In council supported events there is more emphasis on cutting-edge arts productions than in the past. Yet these are never far removed from the suburb's multicultural art networks (Maribyrnong City Council, 2014).

But the gentrifing networks do not dominate the politics and culture of Footscray. In terms of business networks, not only are there multiple Asian (but mainly Vietnamese) business associations, such as the Footscray Asian Business Association, and emerging African organisations, such as the African Asian Small Business Association, but these groups have joined forces to host events. Connections too were illustrated in the documentary from Africa Media Australia, cited above, where an African small business owner referred to the experience of the Vietnamese community as showing African businesses the path in their business endeavours. Newer gentrifying businesses need to engage with these networks, not 'go it alone'. The Dragon Boat Festivals are a key example of the ways in which the new businesses are locating themselves within the existing cultures and networks. To understand the power of the gentrifiers as overwhelming the existing networks is also to negate that – at least for the new residents we interviewed – the experience of ethnic diversity was key to their engagement with the suburb, and many were open in their concerns about the way they felt their residency and businesses were part of cultural change in the suburb (Oke, Sonn, & McConville, 2016).

From our interviews a distinct set of responses was made to questions on the impact of change. Initially these were expressed through criticism of planning processes and in particular the failures of local government. A number of respondents saw opportunities in the urban renewal of Footscray. But in responses from others a sense of powerlessness was evident. Secondly, there were concerns about the commercial transitions which change would bring. Thirdly, there was a feeling of disruption and loss of the sense of local identity linked to place. Fourthly, fears of displacement were balanced by a hope that Footscray's identity was sufficiently strong to accommodate the changes. Finally, there was an aesthetic reaction against the particular form of new buildings. One respondent who hated the new 'terrible' buildings insisted that they were only for 'white' people, that Africans, Chinese and others would be pushed out. Footscray would lose its multiculturalism entirely as the new developments went up. What is interesting, however, is the number of respondents who saw opportunities in the urban renewal of Footscray. The people we interviewed were all deeply attached to the place and value it, sometimes for its physical appearance but more often for its social diversity, its open and strong cultural networks, its tolerance and easy-going character and for the functions it provided in cheap food as well as social and health services. For these reasons they were rightly apprehensive about impending change.

CONCLUSION

So commonplace has become the use of the term gentrification that it is worthwhile returning in detail to the first formulation of the process. Ruth Glass, in introducing a collection of papers on London in 1964, wrote that:

> One by one, many of the working class quarters of London have been invaded by the middle classes – upper and lower. Shabby, modest mews and cottages – two rooms up and two down – have been taken over, when their leases have expired, and have become elegant, expensive residences. Larger Victorian houses, downgraded in an earlier or recent period – which were used as lodging houses or were otherwise in multiple occupation – have been upgraded once again … once this process of 'gentrification' starts in a district, it goes on rapidly until all or most of the original working class occupiers are displaced, and the whole social character of the district is changed. (Glass, 1964)

In this way it harks back to an older normalising process of urban analysis commenced by the Chicago theorists and summarised in the three stage transitions of invasion, succession, dominance (Cressey, 1938; Knox, 2015). Gentrification in Footscray fits within the first stages of this model. Whether or not it proceeds to complete cultural dominance is another matter. Glass's emphasis on working-class displacement and the housing types and tenure forms she identifies, may not find parallels, entirely, in today's processes of social change. In the remainder of her brief survey she noted the post-colonial character of the city, she questioned issues of whiteness, migration and suburban exodus, as well as a cultural homogeneity produced by consumerism. She identified the rise of new industries and deterioration of older staples of London employment (Glass, 1964). In the end she considered these separately to the displacements caused by gentrification (Combs, 2015; Freeman, Cassola, & Cai, 2015). But to try to understand its impacts and the political economic circumstances in which it evolves it is worthwhile returning to Glass' formula and treating more recent high density redevelopment as urban renewal, differentiating its impacts from gentrification. Events in Footscray point to their increased significance in driving urban change, at the expense of the gentrifying class.

In Footscray gentrification is circumscribed by far more potent political and economic influences than is urban renewal. The housing impacts of gentrifiers at a local level are not to be discounted but urban renewal's displacement effects are less significant in Footscray, where only a few isolated precincts are fully capable of housing restoration. Local level impacts are not sufficiently powerful to counter those of rapid metropolitan population increase and state policies for densification and reuse of derelict industrial sites. These policies in turn depend directly on transformations, deliberately intended, by neoliberal urban ideas. The destruction of Footscray's industrial base, the financialisation of the economy and the consequent inflation of assets like inner-city land, as well as the withdrawal of state agencies from home construction, all shape the realignment of classes in Melbourne's housing market.

Footscray's CBD will change, as it has always done. In this chapter we have referred to the stimulatory role of public-sector investment and the distinct trajectories of single-dwelling investment and high-density urban renewal. Further investigation could point to the increased role for localised consortia building medium-density housing and individual investors or small local partnerships renovating walk-up 1960s unit blocks. There are also signs of investment in the retail centre by both hospitality groups and local investors. Together these are changing central Footscray. As many people we interviewed pointed out, some ethnic groups, some housing tenure classes, businesses with short leases and marginal returns, and those who depended on the public space of Footscray would, in the phrase commonly used, be 'pushed out', though one man didn't fear this and pointed to the fact that as the development in Footscray proceeded African cafes were opening in Sunshine, the next major commercial centre to the west. But then in Footscray's commercial district retail outlets directed at gentrifiers are still few. Certainly they will increase in number but more significantly ethnic retailers are able to diversify their products and change the aesthetic of their stores so as to appeal to gentrifiers. Perhaps more importantly the new shops opening today belong not only to the hipsters, as the growth of African business attests. There is little sign that it will lose its multicultural identity though the nature of that multiculturalism may change. The class structure of the housing market will change too. Those with least power will suffer loss of some access to housing. Gentrifiers and older residents exchange property in a manner with little direct effect on the overall housing market. The massive expansion of available units in high rise blocks can actually minimise the effects associated with gentrification, the renovation of older 'walk-up' apartment blocks and speculative, superficial renovation of houses in the rental market for sale to home-owners. None of the positive aspects of change can come into effect so long as change in Footscray is defined as a struggle between a multicultural, welcoming suburb and gentrifying, exclusionary interlopers.

REFERENCES

ABC News. (2017, February 3). *Suspicious fire in Footscray*. Retrieved from http://www.abc.net.au/news/2017-03-02/three-dead-in-abandoned-footscray-factory-fire/8317256D

ABC Radio Breakfast. (2017, May 5). Is Footscray the next suburb in the gentrification firing line? *ABC 774 Breakfast with Red Symons*. Retrieved from http://www.abc.net.au/radio/melbourne/programs/breakfast/footscray-gentrification/8499326

Africa Media Australia. (2012). The positive story about African-Australians in Footscray [video]. Retrieved from http://www.africamediaaustralia.com/the-positive-story-about-african-australians-in-footscray-melbourne/

Bell, C. (1977). On housing classes. *The Australian and New Zealand Journal of Sociology, 13*(1), 36–40.

Blasius, J., Friedrichs, J., & Rühl, H. (2016). Pioneers and gentrifiers in the process of gentrification. *International Journal of Housing Policy, 16*(1), 50–69. doi:10.1080/14616718.2015.1071029

Byrne, B. (2014, September 9). Footscray house fire in 2008 prompts call from Coroner for all rental properties to be fitted with hard wired smoke alarms. *Maribyrnong Leader*. Retrieved from http://www.heraldsun.com.au/leader/news/footscray-house-fire-in-2008-prompts-calls-from-coroner-for-all-rental-properties-to-be-fitted-with-hard-wired-smoke-alarms/news-story/d15d5605287e71e76675a890538471b9

Cafarella, G. (2016, July 29). Bank's reaction is typical of our attitude to homeless. *Sydney Morning Herald*. Retrieved from http://www.smh.com.au/comment/banks-reaction-is-typical-of-our-attitude-to-homeless-20160728-gqgaco.html

Capone, A. (2014, August 26). Unregistered rooming houses prevalent in Melbourne's West. *Brimbank Leader*. Retrieved from http://www.heraldsun.com.au/leader/news/unregistered-rooming-houses-prevalent-in-melbournes-west/news-story/41b53a11072485748c7bf65d1cb2eabd

Choi, N. (2016). Metro Manila through the gentrification lens: Disparities in urban planning and displacement risks. *Urban Studies, 53*(3), 577–592. doi:10.1177/0042098014543032

City of Maribyrnong. (2011, December). *Maribyrnong housing strategy 2011*. Retrieved from https://www.maribyrnong.vic.gov.au/Building-planning/Future-planning/Current-strategic-planning-projects/Maribyrnong-Housing-Strategy

City of Maribyrnong. (n.d.). *City of Maribyrnong community plan: Footscray population and dwellings*. Retrieved from http://profile.id.com.au/maribyrnong/population?WebID=110

City of Melbourne. (n.d.). *Homelessness 2016*. Retrieved from http://www.melbourne.vic.gov.au/community/health-support-services/social-support/Pages/homelessness.aspx

Combs, J. L. (2015). Using Jane Jacobs and Henry George to tame gentrification. *American Journal of Economics and Sociology, 74*(3), 600–630. doi:10.1111/ajes.12105

Cooper, T., & Lanza, S. (2015, July). *Truck movements in the inner West of Melbourne: Understanding the issues*. In Australian Institute of Traffic Planning and Management (AITPM) National Conference, Brisbane, Queensland, Australia.

Council to Homeless Persons Rooming House Project. (2017, June). *The Melbourne homeless crisis help network listed only two registered boarding houses in Footscray*. Retrieved from http://www.melbourne.homeless.org.au/boarding-houses.htmlin

Cressey, P. (1938). Population succession in Chicago: 1898–1930. *American Journal of Sociology, 44*(1), 59–69. doi:10.1086/217916

Dalton, A., Hukse, K., & Pawson, H. (2015, August). *Rooming house futures: Governing for growth, transparency and fairness* (Discussion Paper No. 245). Melbourne: Australian Housing and Urban Research Institute. Retrieved from https://www.ahuri.edu.au/research/final-reports/245

Footscray Suburb Profile. (n.d.). *The age, domain section.* Retrieved from https://www.domain.com.au/suburb-profile/footscray-vic-3011

Freeman, L., Cassola, A., & Cai, T. (2015). Displacement and gentrification in England and Wales: A quasi-experimental approach. *Urban Studies, 53*(13), 2797–2814. doi:10.1177/0042098015598120

Gans, H. (2007). Remembering the urban villagers and its location in intellectual time: A response to Zukin. *City and Community, 6*(3), 231–236. doi:10.1111/j.1540-6040.2007.00215_1.x

Glass, R. (1964). Aspects of change. In Centre for Urban Studies (Ed.), *London: Aspects of change* (pp. xviii–xix). London: MacGibbon & Kee.

Graeme Butler & Associates. (1991). *City of Footscray conservation study.* Alphington: Graeme Butler & Associates.

Grodach, C., Foster, N., & Murdoch, J. (2016). Gentrification, displacement and the arts: Untangling the relationship between arts industries and place change. *Urban Studies, 55*(4), 807–825.

James, N. (2017, March 10). Homeless pay the price for landlord capitalism. *Green Left Weekly.* Retrieved from https://www.greenleft.org.au/content/homeless-pay-price-landlord-capitalism

Kleinhans, R. (2004). Social implications of housing diversification in urban renewal: A review of recent literature. *Journal of Housing and the Built Environment, 19*(4), 367–390.

Knox, P. (2015). Spatial transformation of metropolitan cities. *Environment and Planning A, 47*(1), 50–68.

Lack, J. (1991). *A history of Footscray.* North Melbourne: Hargreen.

Logan, W. S. (1985). *The gentrification of inner Melbourne: A political geography of inner-city housing.* St Lucia: University of Queensland Press.

Maribyrnong City Council. (2014). *City edge master plan.* Retrieved from https://www.maribyrnong.vic.gov.au/Building-planning/Current-and-future-planning/Public-space-projects/Maribyrnong-River-Edge-Footscray

Maribyrnong City Council. (n.d.). *Events.* Retrieved from https://www.maribyrnong.vic.gov.au/Events

Millar, B. (2012, August 28). Matthew Guy on the future of Footscray. *Maribyrnong and Hobsons Bay Star Weekly.* Retrieved from http://www.maribyrnong.starweekly.com.au/story/283457/matthew-guy-on-the-future-of-footscray/

Millar, B. (2016, October 29). Four new councillors in Maribyrnong shake-up. *Star Weekly.* Retrieved from http://www.starweekly.com.au/news/four-new-councillors-in-maribyrnong-shake-up/

Millar, B. (2017, February 8). Residents air concerns on housing the homeless. *Star Weekly.* Retrieved from http://www.starweekly.com.au/news/residents-air-concerns-on-housing-the-homeless/

Murdie, R., & Teixeira, C. (2011). The impact of gentrification on ethnic neighbourhoods in Toronto: A case study of Little Portugal. *Urban Studies, 48*(1), 61–83.

Newman, K., & Wyly, E. K. (2006). The right to stay put, revisited: Gentrification and resistance to displacement in New York City. *Urban Studies, 43*(1), 23–57.

Oke, N., Sonn, C. C., & McConville, C. (2016). Making a place in Footscray: Everyday multiculturalism, ethnic hubs and segmented geography. *Identities: Global Studies in Culture and Power*, 1–19.

Otuoğlu-Cook, Ö. (2006). Beyond the glitter: Belly dance and neoliberal gentrification in Istanbul. *Cultural Anthropology, 21*(4), 633–660.

Pearsall, H. (2013). Superfund me: A study of resistance to gentrification in New York City. *Urban Studies, 50*(11), 2293–2310.

Pennay, A. E. (2012). 'Wicked problems': The social conundrum presented by public drinking laws. *Drugs: Education, Prevention and Policy, 19*(3), 185–191.

Real Estate Investar. (n.d.). Retrieved from http://www.realestateinvestar.com.au/Property/footscrayMore than half residents rent

Rex, J. (1971). The concept of housing class and the sociology of race relations. *Race, 12*(3), 293–301.

Rex, J. (2013). *Race, colonialism and the city.* London: Routledge & Kegan Paul.

Robinson, T. (1995). Gentrification and grassroots resistance in San Francisco's Tenderloin. *Urban Affairs Quarterly, 30*(4), 483–513.

Shaw, K. (2004). Local limits to gentrification. In R. Atkinson & G. Bridge (Eds.), *Gentrification in a global context* (pp. 168–184). London: Routledge.

Shaw, K., & Hagemans, I. W. (2015). Gentrification without displacement and the consequent loss of place: The effects of class transition on low-income residents of secure housing in gentrifying areas. *International Journal of Urban and Regional Research, 39*(2), 323–341.

Slater, T. (2006). The eviction of critical perspectives from gentrification research. *International Journal of Urban and Regional Research, 30*(4), 737–757.

Smith, N. (2002). New globalism, new urbanism: Gentrification as global urban strategy. *Antipode, 34*(3), 427–450.

Spark, C. (2017, January 5). Footscray's "hipster" attacks are fault lines in a new class war. *Sydney Morning Herald*. Retrieved from http://www.smh.com.au/comment/footscrays-hipster-attacks-are-fault-lines-in-the-new-class-war-20170104-gtlmpo.html

The Age. (2017, October 10). The rising of Footscray. *Age Good Food*, p. 2.

Van Criekingen, M., & Decroly, J.-M. (2003). Revisiting the diversity of gentrification: Neighbourhood renewal processes in Brussels and Montreal. *Urban Studies, 40*(12), 2451–2468.

Chris McConville
Victoria University
Australia

Nicole Oke
Victoria University
Australia

TONY BIRCH

9. 'WE'VE SEEN THE END OF THE WORLD AND WE DON'T ACCEPT IT'

Protection of Indigenous Country and Climate Justice

INTRODUCTION

In a study of the relationship between racism, colonialism and climate change Razmig Keucheyan writes of the urgency to 'demolish the idea that humanity suffers the consequences of the ecological crisis in a uniform way'. He contends that the wealthy and powerful 'North', overwhelmingly responsible for global carbon emissions, owes a compensatory 'ecological debt' to the less prosperous and more environmentally vulnerable 'South' (Keucheyan, 2016, p. 8). Keucheyan is not the first to make such a claim on wealthy 'first world' nations or to direct our attention to the inequalities that the combination of capitalism and colonialism has produced and then reinforced. Rob Nixon's seminal *Slow Violence and the Environmentalism of the Poor* (2011) documents in detail the scale of inequity suffered by Indigenous and poorer communities as a result of western industrial development and the structural connections between colonisation and industrial expansion. The recent Anthropocene thesis argues for a new epoch, the Anthropocene, whose commencement is variously dated to 1610 or 'around' 1780, the birthdate of the Industrial Revolution, or 1945, the start of the nuclear age. Whichever date is accepted, the link between this 'new epoch' and the history of global colonial expansion, industrialisation and the increased reliance of fossil fuels is unambiguous.[1] While wealthier nations and wealthier communities within nations will be shielded from the more severe impacts of climate change in the short to medium term, it is evident that vulnerable nations and communities are faced with the immediate and permanent destruction of life and place as a consequence of environmental and ecological damage that brings with it loss of human and non-human life and the inevitability of forced physical, social and spiritual dislocation. Such communities suffer from what Henry Shue in his *Climate Justice: Vulnerability and Protection* refers to as 'compound injustice', which occurs when an initial injustice paves the way for further injustices (Shue, 2014, p. 4).

Within Australia climate change poses a direct threat to Indigenous country and this is in line with what we witness within colonial societies globally. The impact of a changing climate and the related extreme and erratic weather events is linked to histories of dispossession and the appropriation of Indigenous land to service agricultural and industrial expansion. Five hundred years of global colonial violence have contributed directly to the environmental crisis that many Indigenous communities face today. For Indigenous nations and communities the loss and destruction of country and the consequent climate injustice is not only a contemporary manifestation. For Indigenous people there is nothing new in a cultural, spiritual and physical sense about the 'man-made epoch' that has created our current crisis. A reading of the voluminous Anthropocene debate often leaves Indigenous scholars and activists bemused. As Kyle Powys Whyte states, 'climate injustice for Indigenous peoples is less about the spectre of a new future and more like the experience of déjà vu' (Powys Whyte, 2016, p. 88). Within the Australian context climate injustice is a two-hundred-year (and counting) project, shaped by 'the British Empire's exploitative, extractive project, with the concomitant effects of obscuring or effacing Indigenous peoples' autonomy, their connection to "country", their knowledges, and their agency and presence' (Davis, 2016, p. 184).

For climate change to be tackled seriously climate justice, predicated on a recognition of the destructive legacies of colonialism, must be a priority. In the Australian context recognition, rather than carrying little more than symbolic and reductive weight, must also include responsibility for the overt attempts by colonial authorities to devalue Indigenous country not only through direct violence but also through a fabricated narrative of Indigenous savagery and civil absence, a narrative that legitimated theft of land and destruction of people:

> The forces of British imperialism had the power to construct and determine who was 'truly' primitive and the universal horizon beyond which all humanity would become assimilated. Universal notions of civility justified the demonisation of our 'nativeness' and were used to destroy our relationships to land and our sovereign Indigenous being. (Watson, 2009, p. 2)

For genuine social and political change to occur in Australia, change that will value and protect country, innovative relationships need to be forged between Indigenous and non-Indigenous communities. Such relationships must privilege genuinely restorative measures that compensate for past acts of dispossession. They must also alleviate the suffering experienced by country itself. As long as government responsibility (at a commonwealth and state level) for the unfinished business of colonial violence committed against people and country remains elusive, climate justice will also remain a tenuous goal. And yet it is an outcome we must strive for. At the core of the collective challenge that we face in relation to climate change is an acceptance of ownership by white Australia for the colonial policies and practices that created the agricultural, mining and manufacturing industries. These industries have not only brought about the degradation of local ecologies but have also assisted the global expansion of industrialisation dependent on increased burning of fossil fuels.

THE LEGACIES OF COLONIALISM

The colonial practice of constructing a narrative of savagery around Indigenous peoples in Australia acted as a device that necessitated violent dispossession and legitimated the extraction of wealth from country. The appropriation of land for wide-acre single crop agricultural practice alongside the farming of sheep and cattle led to rapid destruction of local ecologies and a wasteful use of precious natural resources such as water and soil (Muir, 2016). But before land could be farmed unhindered by opposition from Indigenous owners of country, people were killed, forcibly removed or, at a minimum, pacified with the aid of repressive legislative measures. Jon Altman asserts that 'the brutal colonisation and political marginalisation of Indigenous Australians can be understood as a conflict over land and resource rights' (Altman, 2012, p. 7). Colonisation was, and to some extent remains, a conflict dependent on violence for its success. Deborah Bird Rose, amongst others, has correctly defined this ideology and practice as 'a dual war: a war against Nature and a war against the natives [that] includes both genocide and ecocide' (Bird Rose, 2004, pp. 33–34).

In his discussion of the disastrous failures of colonial agricultural practice in Australia Cameron Muir concludes that the forms of land usage underpinning imperialist expansion 'sought to remake the continent's interior as a paddock for England' by utilising 'brutality, massacres, corruption, animal cruelty and environmental waste on a scale that threatened to derail the entire settler project' (Muir, 2014, p. 2). As in Australia so on a global scale the 'settler project' often failed miserably, leaving behind extensive environmental damage and the destruction of human and non-human life, and producing the 'erosion of environmental justice' that we face today (Nixon, 2011, p. 8). In the absence of responsibility for the genocidal and ecocidal practices of global colonial expansion which contributed to climate change, narratives of the triumphant colonial settler struggling against country remain vital to the contemporary colonial psyche. My discussion below on coal is a recent example of these narratives. Additionally, in an attempt to obliterate the reality of Indigenous sovereignty and ownership of country, the blank slate of *terra nullius* is repeatedly called upon to assist the privileging, production and (re)performance of the colonial 'primal scene' of immaculate foundation, producing a fiction of the pure and innocent occupation of virgin land. While it may appear counter-intuitive, the colonial-foundational pantomime will occasionally 'acknowledge an original Indigenous presence but obscure the historical fact of violent dispossession, thereby enabling a nostalgic and idealised commemoration of the colonial past' (Bignall, Rigney, & Hattam, 2015, p. 4).

In Australia this foundation stone of settler history requires constant underpinning to legitimate itself, with flag-waving Australia Days reinforcing the barely disguised anxieties that undermine 'the [seeming] might of sovereign power' (Bignall, Rigney, & Hattam, 2015, p. 7). This tradition of colonial pageantry is also part of a global tradition, enacted to mask the realities of land theft and deny responsibility for environmental vandalism. As Rob Nixon had also noted:

> Something similar applies to so-called post-conflict societies whose leaders may annually commemorate, as marked on the calendar, the official cessation of hostilities, while ongoing intergenerational slow violence ... may continue hostilities by other means. (Nixon, 2011, p. 8)

'Celebration of the nation' mantras additionally inhibit the potential for a mature collective discussion that may begin the process of accepting responsibility for the extensive damage done to land, air and waterways as a result of unabated colonial expansion. In the absence of reflection the country lingers in a state of delusion, an act of blind or feigned faith in the fantasy of the continued prosperity of the national farm or mining industry. The fantasy at times calls upon a sanitised past of the heroic pioneer, while in contemporary Australia rather than heed scientific warnings about the dangers of fossil fuel burning and its impact on climate change, the commonwealth government itself continues to invest in a narrative of hagiography surrounding fossil fuels, and in particular the little black rock, coal (discussed below). Material wealth for some at the expense of others, which others include ecological systems as well as human and nonhuman species, relies on a story that resists interrogation. Decolonised ways of thinking and acting are vitally necessary if country is to be valued not as a saleable commodity or an exploited symbol of national pride but as an autonomous entity that each of us is connected to but does not own. 'Land Rights' is not simply a political catch-cry or the basis of a legitimate and important political struggle. In relation to acting on climate change we must engage with the idea of the inherent rights of land, including the right to reciprocity, recompense for past damages and a future of healing as a vital tenet of climate justice:

> Turning toward place [land] necessitates acknowledgement and reparations based on these histories: of settler colonialism, capitalism ... separations of mind from body, body from land. As humans make our planet increasingly toxic, unlivable, and at the same time increasingly inequitable, at what point might these cleavages be sewn back together, might we account for our pasts and to future generations? (Tuck & McKenzie, 2015, p. 4)

In order to appreciate the connection between colonialism and ecocide, we must produce a more vigorous critique of the relationship and co-dependence between colonialism and capitalism. In his essay, *Extinction: A Radical History*, Ashley Dawson writes that neither colonialism nor extinction can 'be understood in isolation from a critique of capitalism and imperialism'. Capitalism, argues Dawson, 'requires people to be [not only] destructive of the environment' (Dawson, 2015, p. 41), but of nations and communities standing in the way of unhindered expansion. Historically those who have been the most forceful barrier to an exploitative capitalist extraction mentality have been Indigenous nations, who, as a consequence of their acts of sovereignty and self-determination, have suffered levels of violence and dispossession beyond that experienced by other vulnerable and exploited communities.

142

In his analysis of colonial global expansion and its relevance to Australia's colonial history, Patrick Wolfe notes that the Industrial Revolution 'required colonial land and labour to produce its raw materials just as centrally as it required metropolitan factories and an industrial proletariat to work in them' (Wolfe, 2006, p. 394). The invasion of, and theft of, Indigenous country was supported by the sleight-of-hand, *terra nullius,* at a socio-political level, thus legitimating a systemic practice of colonial violence that Wolfe refers to as 'the logic of elimination', articulated in Wolfe's (oft-quoted) conclusion that 'invasion is a structure not an event'. The structure of 'frontier homicide' was an institutional requirement in a society underpinned by the compulsion to 'destroy to replace' (Wolfe, 2006, pp. 387–388). People were destroyed, as was land, producing the destruction of balanced ecologies which contributes to the situation we find ourselves in today, confronted by an unpredictable and damaging climate.

Global imperial expansion did not discriminate. Its violence was panoptical. Colonial rule, 'rather than replacing one owner with another', simply 'replace[d] an entire system of ownership with another' (Wolfe, 2016, p. 34). It could not countenance existing sovereign structures at either a legal or cultural/spiritual level. In Australia over the course of the nineteenth century (flowing into the twentieth century), in addition to direct frontier violence, structural models supporting conquest became increasingly dependent on a bureaucratic regime within which Indigenous people were catalogued, counted and legislated against in order to perversely reinforce a status of nonexistence – non-people in an 'empty land' (empty of Indigenous people, that is) – which in turn refused the vitality of Indigenous ecological knowledge, particularly as it applied to local country. Not surprisingly, having extracted economic value from country, colonial authorities targeted Indigenous family and kinship structures via interventionist dispersal and 'caste' legislation, undermining people's direct connection to land and subsequent attempts to legally claim country. As has been noted elsewhere in relation to global colonial expansion, 'to get to the land, they had to remove the women and children' (Simpson, 2016, p. 3). The exploitation of country, ecological damage and attempts to destroy Indigenous family and community life are inextricably linked. Institutional strategies enacted to eliminate Indigenous life in order that land could be fully exploited were pervasive in approach:

> the continuing operations of the logic of elimination can include officially encouraging miscegenation, the breaking-down of Native title into alienable individual freeholds, Native citizenship, child abduction, religious conversion, resocialisation in total institutions such as missions and boarding schools, and a whole range of cognate biological cultural assimilations. All these strategies, including frontier homicide, are modalities of settler colonialism. All of them come back to the issue of land. (Wolfe, 2016, pp. 33–34)

The consequences from the devaluation of, the failure to see, the deliberate erasure of Indigenous knowledge of country are now being recognised. In Bruce Pascoe's groundbreaking work, *Dark Emu – Black Seeds: agriculture or accident,* he discusses the first sightings and documentation of Indigenous people by European explorers and squatters. Pascoe notes that the new arrivals, often to their own surprise, did not find an 'untamed and primitive' land, as a literal interpretation of *terra nullius* would demand. In reality it was 'common [to find] in the first colonial records' detailed evidence and descriptions of Indigenous agricultural practices based on a deep knowledge of country. While land could be poetically described in explorer's journals as resembling 'a gentleman's park' in England, Pascoe notes that the optimistic tone of language masked a darker intention. 'Few were here to marvel at a new civilisation', he writes. 'They were here to replace it' (Pascoe, 2016, pp. 15, 33–35).

The narratives produced by eighteenth and early nineteenth travelers to Indigenous country continued a global imperial tradition that eulogised and coveted the sovereign lands of those the would-be colonist sought to conquer. The desire for exploitable land, reliant on conquest and obliteration for its 'success', had begun centuries before the British ventured to the southern hemisphere. Ashley Dawson notes that Christopher Columbus, writing about North America in the late fifteenth century, described the land as 'so beautiful and rich for planting and sowing, and rearing cattle of all kinds, and for building towns and villages'. The power of imperial writing would have far reaching consequences. The Columbus narrative 'set the tone for the European imperial expansion in the subsequent five centuries', with the 'greed and lust for power drip[ping] from Columbus's pen', as Dawson describes it (2015, p. 39), eventuating in not only the genocide of millions of Indigenous people but the transformation of land into regimented agricultural holdings to meet capitalist global demands.

The first wide-scale agricultural practice to exploit and transform Indigenous country in what would become Australia was the wool industry. In particular the farming of merino sheep provided the raw material for textile mills located predominantly in the north of England. The rapid expansion of wool farming and the need for an agricultural labour force had an immediate and devastating impact on Indigenous people and country:

> It took the discovery and development of a key export commodity, Australian merino wool, to provide the impetus for the frontier expansion and accompanying large-scale immigration that culminated in the settler takeover of the continent. (Wolfe, 2015, p. 40)

On a global scale European agricultural practices willfully ignored the particularities of the Indigenous ecological knowledge systems, labelled by imperialists as the 'new world'; a telling and sad irony, considering that Indigenous land management was informed by traditions and practices reaching back many thousands of years (Chambers & Gillespie, 2000, p. 228). The European practices were driven by an extraction mentality whereby cash crops, drawing valuable nutriment from soils and over-harvesting fresh water, were 'grown for export to the imperial metropole'. The impact was devastating:

In addition to displacing and killing many millions of people, the monocultures of the plantation economy quickly exhausted land in the colonies, destroying soil fertility, and increasing vulnerability to pests. (Dawson, 2015, p. 47)

In Australia, additional strain was put on Indigenous nations with the arrival of a frenetic gold-mining industry from around 1850 onwards. In the colony of Victoria alone the discovery of gold drastically reduced the documented population of Indigenous people to around ten percent of pre-invasion numbers by the 1880s (Wolfe, 2016, p. 44). The desire for gold proceeded across Indigenous country uninhibited, absent of any legal or moral obligation to either sovereign Indigenous nations or the manner in which Indigenous nations engaged with and maintained country. It was not necessary to test the legal strength of a concept such as *terra nullius* to acquire a mining lease. The appropriation of Indigenous country was predicated on an acceptance 'that such peoples as did exist had no sovereign rights or proprietary interests' (Bignall, Rigney, & Hattam, 2016, p. 5).

The glaring hypocrisy of colonialism is that the coloniser, be he explorer, squatter or mining prospector, was repeatedly confronted by another reality, an alternative universe, through constant meetings with and observation of people who articulated a sovereign engagement with country which did incorporate legal and cultural systems of ownership. In the historical records there are many instances of colonial officials documenting such encounters and colonial visitors recognising a deep knowledge of country conveyed by Indigenous people. (Pascoe, 2016 on Indigenous agricultural practice; the dairies of the explorer and government official, Sir Thomas Mitchell, as one of many such records.) And yet the same diarists, many of them government officials with legal status, refused to accept the lawful existence and rights of the very people living with country of which the coloniser had only had the briefest experience. These early encounters offered 'another way' of seeing and acting towards Indigenous nations. The legacy of failure to act in accordance with the rights of people and land is being experienced today. Climate change has a history, one that too few have grasped. We have learned little from it and continue to repeat its failures, as evidenced in the continued extraction of fossil fuels, often at the cost of Indigenous nations and their attempts to protect country.

THIS LITTLE BLACK ROCK

On a summer afternoon in 2017, the Commonwealth Treasurer, Scott Morrison, provided the lower house of the Australian federal parliament with a bizarre piece of theatre, assisted by a lump of coal about the size of a house-brick. Morrison presented himself as a business-suited gladiator displaying a trophy of war, pre-empting victory in a battle against those campaigning against the Adani mega-coalmine proposed for central Queensland. If the mine proceeds it will be located on country belonging to the Wangan and Jagalingou traditional owners. They are opposed to the mine because of the threat it poses to the ecological and spiritual health of country (Lyons et al., 2017, for a detailed summary of the issue). Lest any member of the House, or media viewers, may have been unsure of the object that Morrison held aloft he went on to heighten the sense of melodrama. 'This is coal – don't be afraid, don't be scared', he announced. 'It's coal. It was dug up by men and women who live and work in the electorates of those who sit opposite' (Butler, 2017). Morrison then grinned across the chamber toward the Labor Opposition benches before the piece of coal was passed around the Coalition benches, shared between senior government ministers, including the energy minister, Josh Frydenberg, and the deputy prime minister, Barnaby Joyce.

From mid 2015 onwards Frydenberg has been repeatedly stating that Australia's energy future necessitates the continuation of coal mining. The Adani mine has also been justified partly on moral grounds. According to Frydenberg's position, first articulated in 2015 (Kelly, 2015), in India, the country to which the Adani coal would be exported, 'two billion people today are using wood and dung for their cooking, due to the impoverished conditions suffered by many millions of people'. The attempt by Frydenberg to tug at the guilt of first-world heartstrings has been subsequently undermined by India's own national energy minister, Piyush Goyal, who stated as recently as June 2017 that 'thanks to the increased productivity of domestic mines, cheaper renewables and lower than expected energy demand', imported coal on the scale projected by the Adani company would not benefit the Indian economy (Safi, 2017). The Australian government's seemingly unconditional support of the Adani company has been questioned further following the Australian Broadcasting Commission's *4 Corners* investigation (Australian Broadcasting Commission, 2017), highlighting issues of financial corruption, worker and community exploitation and environmental vandalism involving the Adani company within India.

If there is an imperative guiding the Australian government's support for the Adani mine, moral or otherwise, it is one driven by a tradition of settler-colonialism's fixation with extraction as a nation-building project. Scott Morrison's 'booster' parliamentary soliloquy on the virtues of coal exemplifies this tradition. The beatification of mining, the enshrined notion that colonial societies must extract 'value' from land, in whatever form and at whatever cost, is vital to white Australia's sense of identity and sovereign legitimacy. Consequently the mining industry has been a major beneficiary of government policy and legislation framed to ensure that the exploitation of land proceeds unhindered, with companies taking advantage of privileges ranging from generous tax subsidies to the granting of mining leases that disqualify Indigenous peoples' ability to access country.

The Adani coalmine would require the compulsory acquisition of 2,750 hectares of Wangan and Jagalingou land. The mine would also result in a vital commodity, water, which is currently harvested for both domestic and farming use, being reallocated to the mine. Six massive open-cut pits would be constructed along with several underground mines. The mine would have a lifespan of approximately fifty years; five decades into an environmental future that cannot afford further fossil fuel poisoning. The coal would need to be transported 400 kilometres across country, much of it already in an ecologically fragile condition, on a yet to be constructed rail-line (for which the Adani company has applied for a one billion dollar loan from the state government) to the Abbots Point terminal located on the edge of the Great Barrier Reef (Lyons et al., 2017). The Barrier Reef is the world's largest coral reef system, composed of 2,900 individual reefs and 900 islands across an area of approximately 344,400 square kilometres. In recent years, large areas of the reef have suffered extensive coral bleaching as a result of an increase in water temperature. A rise in air temperature linked to climate change is partly responsible for the water temperature rise. A second contributing factor to reef degradation is the run-off into the ocean of water containing chemicals produced by the agricultural, mining and development industries. It is feared that the transportation of the coal would add further stress to the reef as a result of increased run-off.[2]

While the Commonwealth's environmental minister made claims for domestic coal as the saviour of 'third world' poverty, within Australia the project would continue a colonial tradition of disenfranchising Indigenous owners of country and culture in favour of mining. To restate the comment of Patrick Wolfe, a colonial 'event' occurs within time, whereas a 'structure', more powerful and pervasive, exists *across* time. These events are embedded within this continuum and linked to the structural forces of dispossession of the nineteenth and twentieth centuries, which also included the appropriation, supported by favourable legislation, of Indigenous land for agriculture and mining ventures.

Despite the threat to global ecologies posed by climate change and the increasing demands for climate justice being articulated by Indigenous nations and communities, the Australian government support for the proposed Adani mine refuses Indigenous sovereign rights and threatens the environmental health of the planet. As global citizens, we are currently faced with a clear choice between an urgently required shift towards a philosophy and lifestyle that privileges country rather than colonial power or continuing to maintain a destructive relationship with country dependent on exploitation and extraction at the cost of both Indigenous rights and ecological maintenance.

Coal is a major contributing factor to the destabilisation of global atmospheric conditions and the increase in temperatures which underpins climate change (Malm, 2016). Within Australia coal mining has caused extensive environmental damage and has been responsible for the most unnatural of disasters, including the destructive and extensive fires of February 2014 that devastated communities and country in Victoria's Latrobe Valley.[3] Along with other forms of mining coal has failed to deliver claimed economic and social benefits to Indigenous nations, who have witnessed the destruction of vital ecologies while being legally excluded from country they are culturally bound to protect.[4]

While the Adani group has been provided with vocal support by the state and Commonwealth governments, in recent years it and other coal mining conglomerates have been losing the public relations war. In response the Minerals Council of Australia (MCA), the peak body representing mining interests in Australia, initiated the advertising campaign, *Coal – It's an amazing thing,* distributed through the mass media and in particular on social media platforms. The advertisement begins with an image of seams of coal. The mineral appears to contain talismanic qualities. The coal glistens, it sparkles as if alive. Coal is transformed from a major atmospheric polluter into a black diamond. Its beauty is highlighted in the closing image of a lump of coal (perhaps the same one that Scott Morrison displayed in the parliament) rotating slowly for our wonderment. The image is accompanied by a seductive story, delivered in hushed, erotic tones. We are told that coal 'can provide endless possibilities. It can provide light and jobs … delivering six billion dollars in wages for Australians … injecting forty billion dollars each year … isn't it amazing what this little black rock can do' (Australian Mining Corporation, 2015).

It is vital that we fully consider what 'this little black rock can do'. From the commencement of the Industrial Revolution it has done quite a lot in contributing to climate change. In order that the Adani mine might proceed, the Australian government, with the full support of the Labor Opposition, rushed an amendment to the Native Title Act through parliament to the disadvantage of the traditional owners (Merhab, 2017). The use of parliamentary legislation to disempower Indigenous people is nothing new to the Wangan and Jagalingou nation. From the mid nineteenth century onward they have fought to overcome barriers imposed by colonial authorities, including being subject to living 'under the Act', the Queensland government legislation framed to dispossess Indigenous people of country. As discussed above, Protection Acts were designed to steal not only land but family, children, livelihood and human dignity. Within Queensland as a result of being governed by the Act:

> first and foremost, you lost almost every right for yourself and your family, rights which are, for the rest of us so basic as to defy listing … families were destroyed and women and children were kidnapped as sex objects, and it was common practice to capture adults and children and 'break them in' as servants. (Kidd)

The connection between the Protection Acts and the situation Indigenous communities confront today is direct and unambiguous. Murrawah Johnson, a young Indigenous woman, is a key spokesperson in the Wangan and Jagalingou battle against Adani. Johnson attributes her own fight to protect and sustain country to the political influence of her grandfather, Bowman Johnson. In 1954, fed up with the restrictive and demeaning regulations of the Act, Johnson moved his family off a government mission to the Wondai rubbish tip on the edge of a Queensland country town after being ordered by government officials to move his family to the Woorabinda mission. Instead he chose freedom for his family in the full knowledge that he would pay an immediate material cost, in that the family could no longer rely on government support (McGuire, 2017). Such practices, attempting to coerce or force Indigenous communities into submission by way of bureaucratically sanctioned poverty, have been historically utilised by governments. They also provide a grossly inequitable bargaining tool for mining companies who are able to subsequently 'negotiate' the right to mine land with people so impoverished that they struggle to feed their own families.

To fully appreciate the situation the Wangan and Jagalingou people face we must come to terms with the ramifications of this history. We must also remind ourselves that they are not a materially wealthy community. The proposed mining royalty deal being offered by Adani might appear attractive, yet they have refused money. They are more concerned with the protection of sacred country. Power is a relative concept. Murrawah Johnson articulated a sense of true power in late 2016, when she announced she would refuse to become 'the broken link in the chain' and witness the loss of country to a coalmine. Johnson, on behalf of the Wangan and Jagalingou, has chosen a self-determining and sovereign pathway to the future. 'We've seen the end of the world', she has told us, 'and we've decided not to accept it' (Johnson, 2016).

CONCLUSION: A STORY OF PLACE

Adrian Burragubba is a senior Wangan and Jagalingou elder leading the campaign against the Adani mine. He has taken his nation's struggle to the streets of Australia's major cities, to multinational bankers based in New York City and back home to country. He has made it clear that action to stop the mine from proceeding must be led by the traditional owners of country. He also understands that his people cannot succeed without the help of others:

I'm going to convince all of our people to stand together as one people, one voice. And then we're going to ask all Australian people and people from all over the world to stand with us, unite with us to fight this fight. (Burragubba, 2015)

Burragubba's statement should not be mistaken as a plea. It is an offering to the Australian nation and people the world over to engage in new relationships that are genuinely equitable, that recognise Indigenous rights and claims to justice and that also have the potential to deliver ecological justice to the planet. Murrawah Johnson recently stated that 'the most forward-thinking people' involved in the Adani fight 'are the ones who are the most disenfranchised and have the least resources', and yet 'we're doing it' (Johnson, 2016). The writer and activist, Naomi Klein, believes settler-societies 'have been colonized by the logic of capitalism, and that has left us uniquely ill-equipped to deal with this particular crisis [climate change]' (Klein, 2013, p. 12). Through the expression of their opposition to the Adani mine and through their fight to protect country, Burragubba and Johnson are inviting non-Indigenous people to re-assess their place in this country, and their views 'on country', by raising a series of profound questions that we need to answer urgently. Does the Australian nation possess the level of maturity required to recognise the sovereign authority and leadership of the Wangan and Jagalingou to protect country? Is non-Indigenous Australia capable of realising that country is an autonomous entity with inherent rights rather than a resource to be endless plundered? Is the Australian nation mature enough to accept an invitation to stand with Indigenous people to protect country and, in doing so, break the shackles of the destructive logic of colonialism?

Klein (2014), along with a range of activists and thinkers, believes that it is within Indigenous communities that a pathway forward exists for dealing with environmental instability and ecological maintenance.[5] In moving forward we will also need to address how knowledge of country and ecology can best be transmitted and shared amongst the non-Indigenous communities without that knowledge being corrupted, commodified or culturally 'stolen'. Zoe Todd has written extensively about this issue and how it impacts on Indigenous/non-Indigenous negotiations and relationships. She has drawn attention to the relationship between Indigenous knowledge systems, climate change and climate justice. Todd is critical of forms of western knowledge that 'quickly erase arctic Indigenous peoples and their laws and philosophies from their discourses' (Todd, 2016, p. 6). While engagement with Indigenous ecological knowledge by outsiders is increasing, Todd remains cautious. 'Indigenous thought', she writes, 'is not just about social relations and philosophical anecdotes, as many in ethnography would suggest', but something more complex, underpinned by Indigenous people increasingly 'fighting for recognition – fighting to assert their laws, philosophies and stories on their own terms' (Todd, 2016 p. 18). Indigenous thought is not simply a body of knowledge that can be opportunistically attached to an environmental cause, nor can it be reduced to the status of quaint folklore or myth. While Indigenous knowledge is sometimes disseminated as 'story', the narrative exists in 'a framework within which more detailed empirically derived knowledge about relationships can be placed and evaluated' (Todd, 2016, p. 12).

The history of colonialism in Australia cannot be understood without a critical engagement with the competing forces of Indigenous ownership and protection of country and a colonial mentality driven by an insatiable attachment for extraction – extraction of minerals, energy, nutriment and people opposed to the exploitation of country. For colonialism to unravel and climate justice and protection of country to become a reality vital and, at times, difficult conversations must take place. While the work will be hard, the potential benefits are clear. Facing a future of climate uncertainty and the potential for disastrous knock-on effects, we will require both patience and radical thinking. Joseph Roe, speaking of his relationship with Goolarabooloo Country in northwestern Australia, once stated, 'I don't have to be an environmental activist. If I do my job and look after country, protection for the environment will flow from our law and culture' (Muecke, 2016, p. 252). This is the shift in thinking we require. It involves the recognition of Indigenous sovereignty, law and culture, which will not only reflect an acceptance of Indigenous knowledge by non-Indigenous society but also prepare the ground for a genuine exchange of knowledge based on reciprocity and trust.

NOTES

[1] See Birch (2016) for an analysis of the Anthropocene thesis in relation to colonisation and climate change.
[2] For a history of the Great Barrier Reef, including the various environmental threats it has faced see McCalman (2014).
[3] See Doig (2015) for a post mortem of the 2014 fire at the Hazelwood coal-powered station in the Latrobe Valley.

4 For a summary of the relationship between mining companies and Indigenous communities see Altman (2012).
5 See Klein (2014) for a detailed commentary on Indigenous Rights and leadership with regard to climate change.

REFERENCES

Altman, J. C. (2012). People on country as alternate development. In J. C. Altman & S. Kerins (Eds.), *People on country: Vital landscapes indigenous futures* (pp. 1–22). Sydney: The Federation Press.

Australian Broadcasting Commission. (2017, October 3). Digging into Adani. *Four Corners.*

Australian Mining Corporation. (2015). *This little Black rock.* Retrieved from https://youtu.be/IKp8W1jBuHw

Bignall, S., Rigney, D., & Hattam, R. (2015). *Colonial letters patent and excolonialism: Forgetting, counter-memory and mnemonic potentiality.* Retrieved from http://www.borderlands.net.au

Birch, T. (2016). The lifting of the sky: Outside the anthropocene. In J. Adamson & M. Davis (Eds.), *Humanities for the environment: Integrating knowledge, forging new constellations of practice* (pp. 195–209). New York, NY: Routledge Environmental Humanities Series.

Bird Rose, D. (2004). *Reports from a wild country: Ethics for decolonisation.* Sydney: University of New South Wales Press.

Burragubba, A. (2015). *Stop Adani destroying our land and culture.* Retrieved from https://www.youtube.com/watch?v=ZB2JC6yKy_E

Butler, J. (2017). Scott Morrison brought a lump of coal and waved it around in parliament. *Huffington Post.* Retrieved from http://www.huffingtonpost.com.au/2017/02/08/scott-morrison-brought-a-lump-of-coal-and-waved-it-around-in-par_a_21710206/

Chambers, D. W., & Gillespie, R. (2000). Locality in the history of science: Colonial science, technoscience, and indigenous knowledge. *Osiris, 15,* 221–240.

Clark, N. (2016). Shock and awe: Trauma as the new colonial frontier. *Humanities, 5*(14), 1–22. doi:10.3390/h5010014

Clarke, P. A. (2016). The use and abuse of Aboriginal ecological knowledge. In I. D. Clark & F. Cahir (Eds.), *The Aboriginal story of Burke and Wills: Forgotten narratives* (pp. 61–79). Melbourne: CSIRO Publishing.

Davis, M. (2017). Walking together into knowledge: Aboriginal/European collaborative environmental encounters in Australia's north-east. In J. Adamson & M. Davis (Eds.), *Humanities for the environment: Integrating knowledge, forging new constellations of practice* (pp. 181–194). New York, NY: Routledge Environmental Humanities Series.

Dawson, A. (2015). *Extinction: A radical history.* New York, NY: Or Books.

Doig, T. (2015). *The coal face.* Melbourne: Penguin Books.

Donaldson, M. (1996). The end of time? Aboriginal temporality and the British invasion of Australia. *Time and Society, 5*(2), 187–207.

Dundas, A. (2016). *Towards climate justice: Decolonising adaptation to climate change.* Sydney: Environment Institute, University of Sydney.

Hage, G. (2016). Etat de siege: A dying domesticating colonialism? *Open Anthropology: A Public Journal of the American Anthropological Association, 43*(1), 38–49. doi:10.1111/amet.12261

Holthaus, E. (2006, March 7). Northern hemisphere temperature breaches a terrifying milestone. *New Scientist.* Retrieved from http://www.newscientist.com/article/2079775

Johnson, M. (2016). *Wangan Jagalingou traditional owners: We will not surrender.* Retrieved from https://www.youtube.com/watch?v=xIN8b1MAwvs

Kastner, J., & Najafi, S. (2002/2003). The wall and the eye: An Interview with Eyal Weizman. *Cabinet Magazine.* Retrieved from http://www.cabinetmagazine.org

Kelly, J. (2015, October 18). Strong moral case for Adani's coal mine: Josh Frydenberg. *The Australian.* Retrieved from http://www.theaustralian.com.au/business/strong-moral-case-for-adanis-carmichael-coal-mine-josh-frydenberg/

Keucheyan, R. (2016). *Nature is a battlefield: Towards a political ecology.* Cambridge: Polity Press.

Kidd, R. (n.d.). *Aboriginal protection in Queensland*. Retrieved from http://www.linksdisc.com/roskidd/tpages/13htm

Klein, N. (2013, March 5). Dancing the world into being: A conversation with idle no more's Leanne Simpson. *Yes! Magazine*. Retrieved from http://www.yesmagazine.org

Klein, N. (2014). You and what army? Indigenous rights and the power of keeping our word. In N. Klein (Ed.), *This changes everything: Capitalism vs. the climate* (pp. 367–387). London: Penguin Books.

Lyons, K., Brigg, M., & Quiggin, J. (2017). *Unfinished business: Adani, the state and the indigenous rights struggle of the Wangan and Jagalingou traditional owners council*. Brisbane: The University of Queensland.

Malm, A. (2016). *Fossil capital: The rise of steam power and the roots of global warming*. London: Verso Books.

McCalman, I. (2014). *The reef: A passionate history*. Melbourne: Penguin Books.

McGuire, A. (2017, June 3–9). Murrahwah Johnson and the indigenous fight against Adani. *The Saturday Paper*. Retrieved from https://www.thesaturdaypaper.com.au/news/indigenous-affairs/2017/06/03/murrawah-johnson-and-the-indigenous-fight-against-adani

Merhab, B. (2017, June 14). Native title changes pass parliament. *News.com.au*. Retrieved from http://www.news.com.au/national/breaking-news/native-title-changes-pass-the-senate/

Mitchell, M. T. (2007). *Three expeditions into the interior of Eastern Australia; With descriptions of the recently explored region of Australia Felix and the present colony of New South Wales* (2nd ed., Vol. 2). London: T. & W. Boone, Project Gutenberg Australia. Retrieved from http://gutenberg.net.au

Muecke, S. (2016). Indigenous-green knowledge collaborations and the James Price point dispute. In E. Vincent & T. Neale (Eds.), *Unstable relations: Indigenous people and environmentalism in contemporary Australia* (pp. 252–272). Perth: UWA Publishing.

Muir, C. (2014). *The broken promise of agricultural progress: An environmental history*. New York, NY: Routledge.

Nixon, R. (2011). *Slow violence and the environmentalism of the poor*. Cambridge, MA: Harvard University Press.

Pascoe, B. (2016). *Dark emu Black seeds: Agriculture or accident?* Broome: Magabala Books.

Powys Whyte, K. (2017). Is it colonial déjà vu? Indigenous peoples and climate injustice. In J. Adamson & M. Davis (Eds.), *Humanities for the environment: Integrating knowledge, forging new constellations of practice* (pp. 88–105). New York, NY: Routledge Environmental Humanities Series.

Pravinchandra, S. (2016). One species, same difference? Postcolonial critique and concept of life. *New Literary History, 47*(1), 27–48. doi:10.1353/nlh.2016.0002

Prochnik, G. (2015, October 18). George Prochnik interviews Eyal Weizman: The desert threshold. *Los Angeles Review of Books*. Retrieved from https://lareviewofbooks.org/article/the-desert-threshold/

Robertson, J. (2016, March 10). Dangerous global warming will happen sooner than thought – study. *The Guardian*. Retrieved from http://www.theguardian.com/environment/2016/mar/10

Safi, M. (2017, June 13). India has enough coal without Adani mine, yet must keep importing, minister says. *The Guardian*. Retrieved from https://www.theguardian.com/environment/2017/jun/13/

Shue, H. (2014). *Climate justice: Vulnerability and protection*. Oxford: Oxford University Press.

Todd, Z. (2016). An indigenous feminist's take on the ontological turn: 'Ontology' is just another word for colonialism. *Journal of Historical Sociology, 29*(1), 4–22. doi:10.1111/johs.12124

Tuck, E., & McKenzie, M. (2015). Relational validity and the "where" of inquiry: Place and land in qualitative research. *Qualitative Inquiry, 21*(7), 633–638. doi:10.1177/1077800414563809

Watson, I. (2009). Aboriginality and the violence of colonialism. *Borderlands E-Journal, 8*(1), 1–8. Retrieved from http://www.borderlands.net.au

Wolfe, P. (2006). Settler colonialism and the elimination of the native. *Journal of Genocidal Research, 8*(4), 387–409.

Wolfe, P. (2016). *Traces of history: Elementary structures of race*. London: Verso Books.

Tony Birch
Victoria University
Australia

PART 3

PLACE, PRIVILEGE AND SOCIAL SETTINGS

YON HSU

10. EATING CHINESE IN WHITE SUBURBIA

Palatable Exoticism for Home and Belonging

INTRODUCTION

White American suburbs are places of privilege structured by and for the white upper-middle class. These communities are mythically regarded as a utopia for their superior living standard, higher social status, economic prosperity and better amenities. Critiques run equally deep and attribute a dystopian counterpart to white suburbia since the unearned advantage is built upon racial exclusion, social injustice, excessive consumption, environmental waste and lack of diversity. Despite the opposing views, white suburbs weigh on the American imagination of home and belonging.

Be it utopian or dystopian, I consider the intertwinement of mythic placemaking and everyday consumption in white suburbs as an important research field where we can better understand exclusion and belonging in places of privilege. What are the answers if this process happens in a Chinese restaurant? How do the contrasts between the White and the non-White, between the privileged and the under-privileged, and between conformity and difference give us a different access to white suburbs? Finally, how do the ethnic puts down roots through a white community?

This chapter examines the cultural strategies of a Chinese American restaurant established and run by the same family for over 55 years in an affluent Bostonian suburb. The discussion on exclusion mainly refers to the lived experiences of Chinese restaurateurs and workers, as the cultural strategies, in the mythic placemaking of home and belonging, cater to white suburbanites' specific demands for palatable exoticism. These clients seek exotic adventure within the safety net of conformed values and tastes. Paradoxically, white suburbanites feel at home in the ethnic restaurant through everyday sociability and accumulative memories, where the ethnic also creates a niche between the palatable and the exotic and develops a time-bound sense of belonging in the hope of the American dream to come.

This chapter starts with a literature review on white suburbs as a way to tease out the intertwining of mythic placemaking of privilege and the American dream for home and belonging. It then turns to methodology and a brief description of the research field. Palatable exoticism between the two benchmarks of Chineseness and Americanness will then be explained for a complex understanding of exclusion and possibilities for belonging in a place of privilege.

© KONINKLIJKE BRILL NV, LEIDEN, 2018 | DOI:10.1163/9789004381407_010

WHITE SUBURBS AS PLACES OF PRIVILEGE

Recent suburban scholarship has challenged the simplified dichotomy between the rich and the poor, the white and the black, the suburban and the urban, and the upper-middle class and the working class. For instance, Wei Li (2012) conjures the term "ethnoburb" to distinguish the cultural, linguistic, and racial demands of Chinese Americans in the San Gabriel Valley near Los Angeles. Llana Barber (2017) explores the transformation of Lawrence, Massachusetts from an iconic textile centre to the first Latino-majority community in the Boston region. Andrew Wiese claims that "historians have done a better job of excluding African Americans from the suburbs than even white suburbanites" (Wiese, 2005, p. 5). Dianne Harris and her colleagues revisit the mixed nature of blue collar and upper middle class in Levittown, Pennsylvania, the quintessential case of white suburbia. Some researchers thus urge us to discard the suburbs-city dichotomy because "differences between the cities and the suburbs as a whole were quite minor and were dwarfed by variations within the city and among the suburbs" (Harris & Lewis, 2001, p. 284). However, I caution against overriding the power dynamics of privilege that white suburbs exercise.

The Boston metropolitan region, for instance, has the most racially concentrated areas of affluence (77 in total) in the United States. 43.5% of its white people live in neighbourhoods of more than 90% Caucasian population (Goetz et al., 2015). As rightly pointed out by Matthew D. Lassiter and Christopher Niedt, "... the literature still resolves around the tropes of 'white flight', the urban-suburban divide, and the hegemonic middle-class cultural ideal" (Lassiter & Niedt, 2013, p. 3). They then call for breaking the myth by revealing the truth. I agree that demystification is necessary, if it challenges stigmas and stereotypes. Nonetheless, myths themselves are informative about the hopes and fears, hype and secrecy, aspirations and apathy underlying social norms and cultural values. These emotional qualities are no less important in placemaking than rational decisions, financial restraints or urban planning.

Dianne Harris (2011) discusses the utopian version of white suburbs in shaping immigrants' aspiration for the American dream. Achieving upward mobility or being recognised as a successful American involves leaving the cramped inner city, owning a spacious suburban house, enjoying the serendipity of the natural settings and participating in conspicuous consumption. White suburbs house an immigrant's imagination of what being American is about, or at least what the standard American lifestyle looks like. The white suburban community might not necessarily be the actual place where the American dream is realised, but the myth shows how its socio-spatial relations inscribe the importance of individual achievement, private space, the economic reward through consumption and the dominance of bourgeois tastes and aesthetics. White suburbs are endowed with privilege precisely because the power dynamics spill out of their own spatial confines. Whiteness simultaneously defines the quality of being American with which the White and the non-White grapple.

For Alasdair MacIntyre (1970), myths are not about true or false, but about living or extinct. The dismissal of the false or the persistence in revealing inconsequentiality would miss examining how myths come alive and become decisive and divisive values and norms in placemaking. "[T]he myth of the white suburb serves both those seeking to defend cities and those seeking to flee them" (McDonough, 2006, p. 478). Subjecting suburban myths to the question of truth or falsehood would also miss considering the emotional gravity in the utopian or dystopian version of placemaking for home and belonging.

How myths play out in a place of privilege involves the power dynamics in discourses about desired end results, what Roland Barthes (1972) calls a "euphoric clarity". Expressed in common sense and everyday discourses, myths aim at disambiguation. When myths and placemaking are in sync, confusion and paradoxes can seemingly be resolved by simple imagination or by assigning a specific set of banal conditions to distinguish one place from another. The banality of these conditions is then lifted into something extraordinary, and a moral geography is mapped out through spatial and social transcendence. When white suburbs are utopian for the American dream, white privilege is simultaneously neutralised into the unquestionable status quo. White suburbanites might feel entitled and then emphasise their unearned advantage as the result of individual work ethic and achievements more than structural and systemic positions they enjoy. Nonetheless white privilege becomes universal or dominant only when it is entrenched, recognised and taken for granted as Americanness by the non-White. It is thus a paradoxical process through which privilege comes alive and magical while being transformed from a specific set of cultural values and social norms into ordinary living aspirations beyond the White. The power dynamics as such, in the mythmaking of white suburbs, tap into the American dream about individual freedom and material success.

In contrast when white suburbs are the place of the American nightmare, fear is invoked from losing equality as another pillar of the American dream. White suburbia becomes a bad place for its racial inequality, stagnated social mobility, rigid gender roles and moral conformity. While physical isolation prevails, democracy is menaced by self-interest and private consumption trumps the public good. The mapping of white suburban dystopia is also perforated by alienation and personal discontent. This bleak imagery of white suburbia is an aversion from the American ideal of home and belonging.

Whether utopian or dystopian, the myths about white suburbs require both discursive manners and everyday practices to keep them alive. Tangible materiality too is a place for mythic placemaking. From choices in décor, furniture style, to the balance between storage and display, the power of white suburban values and lifestyles are grafted onto ordinary American houses (Harris, 2011). When "little white houses" are neutralised as the average American property, the myth comes alive and the specific construction becomes the American standard. Be it present, absent, enticing or threatening, the tangible materiality of suburban iconography as such becomes the ordinary and the powerful, besetting Americans' imagination of home and belonging.

If mythic placemaking is an endeavour to reach euphoric clarity from unresolvable ambiguities, examining them in discourses, everyday practices and materiality is the pathway to exploring how white privilege is put in place. We then can claim that white suburbs are not a homogenous or manicured entity, but the intertwining processes of spatial racialisation and racial spatialisation. For instance, both Dianne Harris (2011) and George Lipsitz (2011) recognise non-Whites' vital roles in propping up the privilege of these communities. The former considers the domestic sphere where Hispanic people occupy housekeeping, babysitting, gardening, renovation and construction jobs. Lipsitz further critiques that "[the White] seeks to avoid paying taxes that might contribute to the shelter, health, education or transportation needs of their [non-White] employees" (Lipsitz, 2011, p. 33).

Other than the private domestic sphere, what about semi-public spaces of consumption, such as bars and restaurants, that equally rely on low-wage ethnic workers? Consumption can be banal, passive and unproductive, but it also works as an instrument for generating difference, as well as for distinguishing the superior from the inferior. In addition, if consumption is central to the mythic identity of white suburbs, it nonetheless remains an uncharted terrain in the existing scholarship, as we have yet to understand how privilege is maintained, exercised and/or subverted through the banal acts of dining and drinking. How does the non-White imagine and sustain white privilege? Can the non-White claim belonging by creating its niche in the mythic placemaking of privilege? To answer the above questions, I turn to the following case study.

CHINA BLOSSOM IN NORTH ANDOVER: A CASE STUDY

North Andover, Massachusetts, is one of Boston's bedroom communities. About 90% of its residents are white. Almost 60% of those over 25 years old have earned a bachelor's degree or higher. The average travel time to work is 31 minutes daily. The median household income is slightly above 100,000 US Dollars, double the American average (United States Census Bureau, 2017). Contrary to the dystopian myth, the local government emphasises the importance of open town halls and prides itself on being a thriving community where residents can participate in a variety of social activities. This suburb also addresses public issues from environmental conservation and affordable housing to historical preservation (Town of North Andover, 2017). In short the public good and the communal spirit are integral to the quality of suburban life.

China Blossom's location is a prime spot in North Andover easily accessible by cars. Serving mostly white clients, this restaurant features a spacious parking lot, a fully licensed bar, an outdoor patio, a dining area, a party room and a lounge. With a seating capacity of more than 500 people, *China Blossom* runs a comedy club on the weekends, and it hosts organised or spontaneous social gatherings on a daily basis. Except for Thanksgiving, this restaurant is open daily between 11:30am and 9:30pm. On weekends it is open until midnight. This place is popular on special holidays, such as Mother's Day and Christmas. Like most Chinese American restaurants in New England, *China Blossom* is extremely busy, if not exceeding its capacity, on New Year's Eve. More than 75 workers are required, since eating Chinese food on that day is a New England tradition.

Among 45 regular employees, the majority is ethnic Chinese. Most of these workers live at least 40 minutes away in Chinatown, or in Quincy, a Chinese ethnoburb an hour away by car. Except for the owner's family and a handful of employees, the daily commute for these workers is between 90 and 120 minutes, more than double or even triple that of the clients. This type of suburban Chinese restaurant continues to exist and is distinctive in itself. The spatial scale cannot be matched by those in Chinatown. A fully-licensed bar serving Polynesian cocktails is unlikely to be seen in Chinese restaurants in the ethnoburbs. Their lavish decoration is unthinkable for those in strip malls or rural towns. The uniqueness of this research subject thus reflects the conditions and status of white suburbs as a place of privilege.

This chapter relies on discourse analysis of ethnic advertising and online public relations, ethnographic observation and qualitative interviews. First, the textual analysis examines advertising materials, including 25 menus since the 1960s, the restaurant's current website and Facebook posts since 2008. Customer reviews and the management's replies on *Yelp* and *Google* are categorised as discourses for public relations. The online material is exhaustive, but menus are limited to the ones preserved by the restaurant. The research material from the menu collection is far from complete, but it gives the textual mapping of emplacement and displacement. The comparison between earlier and recent ones gives insight into the socio-spatial relations between the privileged and the disadvantaged throughout half a century.

Between 2013 and 2015 I spent 4 months visiting the research field on several different occasions. Given that no place of privilege and its associated power dynamic exists in a vacuum, I visited and observed the neighbourhood, its surrounding regions, as well as the ethnic communities where the restaurant workers reside. Since this restaurant has provided the workers with a shuttle service, I also conducted ethnography on the so-called *China Blossom* bus. Under Concordia University's ethical research code, 55 qualitative interviews were conducted with the restaurateurs, workers and clients. The interviews were semi-structured and lasted from 25 minutes to 2 hours. All respondents have been assigned pseudonyms. Minimal editing has been done to assure confidentiality and discussion flow. If the interviews were in Chinese, I transcribed them and then translated them into English.

PALATABLE EXOTICISM

For white clients at *China Blossom*, they do not need to leave their suburban comfort for the excitement of the city: the bar is a short distance from home, parking is spacious and the food taste is both habitual and exotic. I consider these paradoxical demands as palatable exoticism. *China Blossom*'s cultural strategies straddle two sets of benchmarks: the palatable and the exotic. Analysing how the restaurant strives for both demonstrates the power dynamics of inclusion and exclusion in the mythic placemaking of privilege. If the palatable is the cultural strategy of placemaking by inching closer to the dominant American standard, the exotic creates and sells the difference imagined, anticipated and judged by white people. I will unpack this argument from the benchmark of exoticism.

Exoticism

Exoticism first relies on the imagination of primitivism. bell hooks argues that primitivism romanticises the Other who lives harmoniously without the modern conditions of alienation or displacement. In addition, primitivism is endowed with mythic qualities as it recharges the civilised with its bountiful Mother-Nature-potent restoring power and incommensurable pleasure. Embracing the exotic therefore is to fulfill "the longing for *the* pleasure that has led the white west to sustain a romantic fantasy of the 'primitive' and the concrete search for a real primitive paradise, whether that location be a country or a body, a dark continent or dark flesh, perceived as the perfect embodiment of that possibility" (hooks, 1991, p. 27). The exotic as the primitive is necessary as it creates a distance from whiteness in order to return to whiteness more fully. This temporary escape to the primitive paradise accentuates the mythic placemaking of tourism and consumption, as "the commodification of difference promotes paradigms of consumption wherein whatever difference the other inhabits is eradicated, *via exchange*, by a consumer cannibalism that not only displaces the Other but denies the significance of the Other's history through a process of decontextualization" (hooks, 1991, p. 31). In other words, to be exotic is to render the Other into consumption for redressing the White's discontent. Lisa Heldke (2003) in *Exotic Appetites* simply calls out eating the Other as food colonialism camouflaged as urban cosmopolitanism or everyday multiculturalism.

In light of the Tiki lounge the primitive as the exotic played a heavier role in *China Blossom*'s early establishment. Decorated with Polynesian wood carving, totem poles and primitive Hawaiian gods, the lounge was endowed with the mythic power of a Pan-Pacific tropical paradise. The experience was reinforced by sipping such drinks as *Mai Tai, Frog Cutter, Hula Hula,* and *Ko Ko Head*. The white invention of Polynesian-themed cocktails first appeared in California in the 1930s. Two competitive chains, *Contiki* and *Trader Vic's*, set the trends across the United States. They reached the height of popularity in the 1950s when Hawaii was confederated, and gradually faded after the 1970s (Teitelbaum, 2007). Although the Tiki lounge had nothing to do with China, suburban Chinese restaurants at the time quickly adopted Tiki culture. *China Blossom* was no exception. As one family member explained, "If you think about it, what do the Chinese drink? Back then, there was nothing we could serve from [the communist] China".

As pointed out by Geoffrey M. White in his review of the book of the exhibition, *Tiki Pop: America Imagines Its own Polynesian Paradise*, Tiki culture that has been "refashioned for Western consumption" fetishises the exotic aesthetic in a social, cultural and political disjuncture from "the communities that produce, or have produced, the objects and images that inspired Tiki culture" (White, 2015, p. 561). Tiki culture is far from an appreciation of multicultural diversity and is not an intercultural exchange with the actual Other. Tiki drinks, created by the White for the White, entice the fantasy about primitivism. This myth is alive in the material form of the drinks as well as in *China Blossom*'s menus where both textual illustration and sketches for each concoction emotionally evoked the mythic quality of a primitive paradise away from western civilisation. For instance, *Mai Tai* was a lucky drink because "[it] means the best in [Tahitian]. It is 8-year old Jamaican Rum that makes it so". *Blue Hawaii* was a "romantic blend of light rums, liqueurs, and juices". An artist was hired to draw the ways these drinks are served. Coconut and pineapple shells, Tiki bowls decorated with totem gods, and tropical flowers and umbrellas on carved Tiki mugs all allude to a paradise conceived by the white American middle class as an antidote to everyday routines or an ephemeral escape from alienation to copious passion and pleasure (see Figure 10.1).

Figure 10.1. Exotic drinks served at China Blossom in the 1960s

While Tiki gradually faded as a trend of popular culture, appropriating the Chinese culture keeps exoticism distinctive. The current reception area is decorated with Chinese lanterns, furniture, tiles, carpets and vases. The main dining hall is furnished with Chinese round tables, calligraphy, and watercolor paintings as if it is a visual drama of the difference, immediately recognisable by white clients. These objects actively create the myth about the exotic and they draw imperative boundaries between the Us and the Other *for* the privileged white clients.

China and Chineseness have been imagined as the opposite Other from the White. "China" is associated with an excessive amount of meanings, and it "has been used as a symbol, negative or positive, for that which the West was not" (Ang, 2001, p. 32). Or in Rey Chow's words, "what is Chinese is often imagined and argued as completely distinct from its counterparts in the West, even as such counterparts are presumed and accepted as model or criteria for comparison" (Chow, 2001, Kindle Location number 2029). The sense of foreignness – if not oddness – is actively played out in *China Blossom*'s menu description where Chinese words are commonly seen as a visual reminder of its exoticism. A white client cannot tell what *Moo Goo Guy Pan* (Sauté mushrooms and chicken over rice), and *Char Sue Ding* (Sauté diced roasted pork with mixed vegetable) are unless they speak Cantonese or read the English description. Some other dishes are described in a mixture of English and Chinese words. For instance, *Egg Foo Young* is "a lightly wok-fried Chinese style omelet made with eggs, bean sprouts, onions, and topped with Cantonese gravy"; *Lo Mein Noodles* are "a provider of harmonious dietary balance in Chinese culture, [and] *lo mein* refers to the tasty yellow Chinese egg & wheat noodles". Moreover places in China are also used in the (re)creation of dishes in *China Blossom*. For instance, *YoHsiang Eggplant* is "Grandma's Chang Taipei City recipe of wok-stirred eggplant in a homemade *Yu Hsiang* spicy sauce". In a red bracket, *Young Chow House Rice* is introduced as "[p]repared only on special occasions in Richard Yee's Taishan village, *China Blossom*'s popular house rice is based on an original recipe with pork, shrimp, ham, onions, scallions, and bean sprouts" (China Blossom Menu, 2014).

The above examples paradoxically emplace and displace the exotic. First, these usages emplace cultural authority. Chinese words in menus enact a sense of cultural authenticity and ethnic difference that serves as a constant reminder of entering into the space of the exotic. White suburbanites need to take some risk to pronounce these Chinese phrases with a foreign accent or with the wrong intonation. As a result the clients either ask the wait staff about the "correct" pronunciation or timidly point at the items on the menu. These moments ephemerally reverse the power dynamics between the White and the Other, or between the superior and the inferior.

If we argue with bell hooks that eating the Other "asserts power and privilege", this temporary subversion can easily take a turn toward racism (hooks, 1991, p. 36). This assertion is rooted in racial stigmatisation that firmly fixes what the Other should be. An American-born, second-generation Chinese interviewee recounted the following: "Once a client asked me about Chinese characters in a painting. I said, 'I don't know. I don't read Chinese'. The client replied: 'How can you not know? You are Chinese!' I was thinking to myself that 'can't you tell that I am as American as you are since I speak perfect English?'" This anecdote shows a stagnation of riveting biological heredity to Chineseness or cultural otherness. Even if language is inseparable from culture in marking one's collective participation in a common identity and societal values, perfect or standard English alone is insufficient to admit the non-White into full American membership.

As much as stigmatisation emplaces and displaces home and belonging for both the White and the non-White, myths equally play an important role in this cultural strategy. We particularly consider the invocation of a homeland elsewhere by *China Blossom*'s second generation. "Grandma Cheng's secret recipe from Taipei", and "Richard Yee's special treat from his hometown" become an important cultural strategy for those who were born and raised in America. The validity of these claims is irrelevant as the textual emplacement of Chinese immigrants' hometowns serves two functions. First, it satisfies the privileged White's craving for a temporary escape from everyday routine and domestic chores. Second, the mythic placemaking of home and homestyle food reveals the exasperating nature of being second-generation Chinese Americans. On the one hand they do not receive full recognition in America and are perpetually regarded as the Exotic or the Other. On the other hand their values, mannerism, habits and language set them apart from those in Taiwan or China. The second generation thus can draw special power from the imaginary Chinese homeland, but their belonging to the so-called motherland remains symbolic without an actual place to return home.

The Palatable

Here it makes you feel right at home. They take good care of you. This place is spotless, and that's one of the first [things that] attracts me. Even the ladies' room is clean, the food, the good service. It's always been a pleasure. I don't think I have ever come here and heard anybody say I wasn't happy with what I had. I have been eating [here] for more than 40 years.

This is our spot for 20 something years ... We feel very comfortable. Absolutely comfortable and feel at home. Typically we have *Zombie* ... They have the best pork strips and buffet ... We are very impressed with the prime ribs ... I would say it's a Chinese restaurant, but several steps above the Chinese restaurants we are familiar with ... We like the quality of the food, the amount of the food, the service, the cleanness, and the open kitchen.

These messages from two different clients inform us that rooting an ethnic business in a white neighbourhood for 57 years is subject to white suburbanites feeling right at home. A Chinese restaurant does not gain recognition from its upper-middle class white clients unless it is "several steps above [other] Chinese restaurants ...". *China Blossom* has to conform to American standards such as the spotless ladies' room, the open kitchen and the impressive prime ribs. Furthermore, this sense of belonging also involves personal care and special treatment in the case of serving *Zombie*. This concoction is not even listed in recent menus. Being palatable thus means conforming to the values of comfort, pleasure and individual needs esteemed by the white privileged.

To argue along with Shun Lu and Gary Alan Fine, "ethnic restaurateurs desire to meet the needs of distinct customer groups and therefore market to these groups ... By their organisational arrangements, Chinese restaurants have adjusted to conflicts of aesthetic preference, economic status and activity schedules, gradually establishing their own market niches" (Lu & Fine, 1995, p. 548). Even cultural strategies for marketing are something important to be reckoned with. I plan to argue beyond that by taking a critical racial approach toward the exclusion and inclusion inherent in this strategy. This approach helps steer us away from the majority of the literature which focuses on the validity of historical origins and cultural authenticity in Chinese American foodways. Although there are a few exceptions in recent research (Cho, 2010), more critical reflection is needed to address what Timothy K. August (2016) calls "a telling disconnect from a rigorous theorisation that can juxtapose historical accounts, lived experience and structural issues in race and ethnicity".

First, *Mai Tai*, the most popular drink at *China Blossom*, gives us an idea of what the palatable means. Its popularity not only relies on imaginative exoticism as discussed earlier but also depends on a palatable taste that white American clients enjoy. To quote an employee, "All the drinks and food here are the same: they satisfy sweet and sour taste buds. That's what white people like". In addition, salt cravings also indicate this particular palate for stronger flavours. The top three appetizers at *China Blossom* are crab rangoon, chicken fingers and spring rolls. Crab rangoon are wonton filled with cream cheese and artificial crab meat. Chicken fingers are breaded chicken breast strips and spring rolls are rolls of mixed vegetables with or without ground pork. All are deep fried and served with a generous portion of duck sauce, a potent sweet and sour mixture.

To make Chinese food palatable thus is to conform to white clients' habitual tastes. One of the most common practices among white clients is to add soy sauce onto a bowl of bland, steamed rice. If fermented food depends on an acquired taste and is indicative of cosmopolitan capacities, soy sauce and cream cheese in crab rangoon win the hearts and stomachs of white suburbanites. In contrast, although an ordinary home food in the Chinese coastal regions and a common condiment for *China Blossom*'s kitchen staff, fermented fish of a pungent flavour never appears in the menu. What is palatable for white suburbanites is deep fried and industrialised strips of chicken breast rather than stewed chicken feet or smoked duck tongues of irregular shapes. While Chinese immigrant workers might reminisce about these delicacies for their gelatinous and sinuous texture, these less esteemed parts can be grotesque for white people, since they are either a reminder of filthiness or of animal morbidity. Spitting out fiddly tiny bones is against the etiquette of the white upper-middle class. Likewise deep-fried spring rolls have long been served in *China Blossom* instead of shumai, the popular snack in the southern Chinese region. The steamed item was briefly on the menu in the 1980s. While shumai have remained common for more than 30 years in Chinatown and in the ethnoburbs, introducing shumai to white suburbanites recently was doomed to fail.

Second, to be palatable means to hit the benchmark of Americanness. If the food conforms to white suburbanites' habitual tastes, so will other aspects of the dining experience, from menus, décor, spatial arrangement, to the serving manners. Once again, mythic placemaking involves transcending and neutralising a specific set of spatial and social conditions in discourses, in the banality of everyday life, as well as in tangible materiality. Whiteness, in this case, is lifted into the imperative of Americanness. To argue with Chow, "the white coloniser, his language, and his culture stand as the model against which the colonised is judged" (Chow, 2001, Location Number 1764).

In *China Blossom*'s menus, especially the earlier ones, we see the endless efforts to mimic American whiteness and measure its performance against the standard of American fine dining. Within a decade of its establishment, its menu cover and restaurant logo evolved from the obvious ethnic theme to a sleek design of modern minimalism. The restaurant gradually abandoned the chop-suey font, the definitive stereotype of Chinese exoticness and inferiority, with the replacement of an old English calligraphy (see Figure 10.2). A family member mentioned that *China Blossom*, since its inception, has strived to be a place of fine dining instead of a hole in the wall. Traces of relentless editing and proofreading in English from one version to another are evident in the earlier menus.

Figure 10.2. China Blossom's menu design in the 1960s

To strive for the standard of American fine dining also required spatial transformation. Similar to the menus, the earlier décor was outright exotic, but in a makeover the restaurant stripped out the dragon fountain and made the dining areas more suitable for family gatherings. Nowadays the bar at *China Blossom* looks like any American sports bar where seasonal games and news are broadcast. The Chinese pagoda that served as *China Blossom*'s signboard in the 1960s is long demolished (China Blossom Website, 2017). Furthermore, when *China Blossom* was ordered to shut down in 2009 the restaurant went as far as to re-design an open kitchen to comply with American hygiene standards. This is to make the point that an ethnic restaurant can be "spotless" just like an American one, although whether American restaurants live up to this myth is another question. A family member thinks that the decision on the open kitchen idea was the outcome of a racist inspection.

It's unfair. The inspectors had a tendency to be hair splitting with the Chinese. Last time when we participated in an outdoor charity event, the inspector pointed fingers at us because we put plastic containers where we stored meat on the ground! Well, if you looked at the neighbouring stall run by an Italian restaurant, they did exactly the same. Why didn't they get a warning?

This anecdote echoes Chow's argument that no matter how hard the non-White tries to be American, a full membership with the right attributes will never be granted. "For the ideal American, ethnicity is something to be overcome and left in the past" (Chow, 2001, Kindle Location 615). However, "[i]mitation will forever remain unsatisfactory. The colonised, her language, and her culture are thus relegated to the position of the inferior, improper copy" (Chow, 2001, Kindle Location 1782).

The sense of impossibility or incompleteness is particularly acute for the second generation as they are raised and educated to be American without "a full membership". In response to the question about their identities, none from the second generation simply described themselves as American. The reliance on the hyphenated identity between Chinese and American (Chinese-American) further indicates that they will never arrive home in either benchmark of Chineseness or Americanness. We have considered how this inbetweenness manifests itself in exoticism via mapping the imaginative Chinese homeland. The attempt to be palatable and to conform to Americanness continues to be a generational effort even after half a century, though the specific challenges and cultural capacities vary. The second generation has less concern about correct English in menus or advertising. Nor did they contrive to incorporate white suburban tastes and preferences in remodelling the restaurant. Nonetheless, inching closer to Americanness reflects the politics of identity as impossibility, incompleteness and inbetweenness for the non-White that in claiming a sense of belonging requires no less effort than for the previous generation.

To claim belonging in North Andover and to gain recognition from white suburbanites, *China Blossom*'s second generation draws cultural resources from its rich past and constructs the historical narrative about this restaurant in two distinctive ways. First, its Americanness is closely woven into the American dream:

> *China Blossom's* founder Richard Yee was born in China and immigrated to the United States in 1951 to pursue the American Dream ... He knew he wanted to be a restaurateur from an early age and worked every job from dishwasher to maître d' to learn every aspect of the business ... That's the great thing about America ... You can have a dream and it can come true, as long as you are willing to work hard. (China Blossom Website, 2017)

The above description of the founder's early immigration story facilitates the living myth of the American dream while normalising the cultural values of the white middle class. Individual hard work and determination are the reasons behind the success in turning the restaurant into a local institution. Meanwhile, the structural limits in the intersection of racial discrimination and social immobility are undermined. When I asked a family member about the founding of *China Blossom*, the reply was: "No choice! Richard came here as an immigrant, and he needed to survive. What else was there? Laundromat?" This remark shows the invisibility of the indentured experience and structural racism as part and parcel of the American dream.

The second distinctive way of ensuring *China Blossom*'s Americanness is to claim to be part of the American Us. Richard was drafted to the U.S. Army during the Korean War, and "he learned lessons in discipline and work ethic, which he credits in helping him achieve his version of the American Dream ..." (China Blossom Website, 2017). While the American dream and the myth of individualism and Protestant ethics continue to be emphasised, what is equally intriguing is how *China Blossom* constructs the palatable values. There is no better way to claim belonging than devoting oneself to American patriotism. This cultural/marketing strategy works well for ethnic advertising and public relations. American patriotism is reinforced by showcasing photos of Richard during his military service. He first stood beside the Governor of Alaska, and then with Jayne Mansfield, the Hollywood star who visited his military base. Over the years, these photos, along with a picture of the American flag, were posted online as *China Blossom*'s celebration for Veteran's Day and Independence Day. Its white clients grant recognition by giving the social media currency of "Like" clicks. In response to the photo of Richard and William A. Egan, Alaska's first Governor, Pez Power commented: "Damn [!] I didn't know he was a fellow 11b. That's a hard man there". Jack Roy replied, "I like your restaurant even more" (China Blossom Facebook Timeline Post, 2013). The emotional affection goes beyond the dining experience, as the affinity comes from the shared moral qualities these white clients value as the centrality of Americanness.

POSSIBILITIES FOR BELONGING

I have discussed how the cultural strategies of palatable exoticism create and maintain the place of privilege for white suburbanites while excluding Chinese workers and restaurateurs. Palatable exoticism through everyday consumption and mythic placemaking also creates possibilities of belonging for both white suburbanites and those who work in the restaurant.

The earlier quotes have shown how white suburbanites feel at home at *China Blossom*. In addition to the palatable exoticism tailored for their paradoxical demands of conformity and difference, feeling at home in a Chinese restaurant has a social dimension as well. A restaurant is a semi-public sphere where white suburbanites socialise and extend their domestic habitat. A client who frequents *China Blossom* stated,

We got invited to everything ... you get to know other customers. It's a social hub ... This is the family like we can get in a restaurant. People aren't just customers here ... Home is where we feel comfortable, very comfortable here. It's part of the family. When you are at home, your mom gives you food ... You can be in the finest restaurant, but you don't have the same feeling. When Andy hands me the food, it's like at home. It's like your cousin, uncle ... We are not the only one [who feels this way] ... It's like a second home.

The sentiments of intimacy and hominess are reproduced away from the private home; domesticity is adapted by a place of consumption with a great success. The effects and affects of belonging are as important as palatable exotic food, clean washrooms, an open kitchen and fine-dining ambiance. A good place has to be a human place of emotional connections. The servers are not only a substitute for a mother or cousins, as they can expand white suburbanites' relations and networks beyond their private homes. *China Blossom* becomes a local institution because it is a community centre where clients learn more about each other. In resonance with Catherine Jurca's analysis of a fictional restaurant in a white suburb, these lived experiences highlight both domestic comfort and conviviality. "People want to eat in places that remind them of home and to indulge in the experience of home, but the restaurant is sweeter for making that experience available some place besides where they live" (Jurca, 2001, p. 93).

In addition to everyday sociability, white suburbanites claim another sense of belonging through their common and personal memories at *China Blossom*. In a Facebook post, *China Blossom* asked its followers their best memories of the restaurant. Susan Farr Williams replied, "[we] used to go to *China Blossom* with our family. As a small child I can remember my parents ordering a poo poo platter ... I giggled every time!!! Living in Florida now and sure do miss your food!" Nancy Oakes Finn responded, "My favourite memory of *China Blossom* is every weekend since I was 18 (yes, that was the drinking age) through my college years, going there with my friends playing *PacMan* & eating popcorn with all the other townies. The place was always packed" (China Blossom Facebook, 2014). Whether walking down memory lane or cracking a light-hearted joke about the popular *pu pu* platter (an ensemble of popular appetizers), these clients show how they belong to an ethnic place between Americanness and Chineseness.

It is precisely in the space of inbetweenness where the Other also claims belonging. *China Blossom* has successfully rooted itself in North Andover for more than half a century. It subverts the power dynamics and turns palatable exoticism into the reason why North Andover is a place of privilege. In one of the latest menus *Mai Tai* has become the *Original Mai Tai*: "*China Blossom*'s original recipe that made North Andover famous 50 years ago, an ancient Chinese secret full of rums, hints of the tropics, tasty liqueurs, and sweet syrup" (see Figure 10.3). If we are fixated on the questions of originality or demystification, we would miss the confidence in mythic placemaking. This claim unsettles the White-Other relations through the most banal act of consumption. The fame of this white suburb is not about its living quality or its prestigious boarding school but the fun and pleasure its Chinese restaurant provides for all the other white suburbanites from the region. *China Blossom* has become a local institution and turns the spatial relations around as it draws clients who are willing to drive 40 or 50 minutes for its food, drinks and the homey ambiance between Americanness and Chineseness. Feeling at home, in short, is a privilege in itself.

A second-generation family member pointed out the irony of feeling at home in a restaurant as a privilege, "[i]t's a family restaurant for customers because there's lots

Figure 10.3. The description of original Mai Tai

of family gatherings. It's an anti-family restaurant because the hours are ridiculous ... It serves for the conventional family's schedule and time". When the hours are long and irregular, and when the restaurant closes only one day per year, the workers spend limited time with their own families. It is not uncommon to learn that they have a hard time at home because of cultural, linguistic and generational gaps with their children. For instance, one of the kitchen staff explained, "[my children] never want to eat here ... I speak my home language, but they speak English. I understand some [English] ... They don't want to speak my language". While emotional estrangement and communication impasse might run deep at home, the restaurant is not the place to claim belonging. In contrast to the regular clients' positive responses, none of the employees claimed to be at home in the restaurant.

Where are these workers at home then? China, or where they were "originally" from? The answer was ambiguous or uncertain when I asked this question. Leaving the home country usually indicates one's non-belonging for any number of reasons, but nostalgia or habitual practices from the home country usually give a false impression that these immigrants belong to elsewhere in the past. I, however, argue with Alison Blunt that "a nostalgic desire for home, and its enactment in practice, is oriented towards the present and the future as well as the past" (Blunt, 2005, p. 14). As a temporal signifier, "productive nostalgia" moves away from the unrealistic imagination of home as a place of origin or authenticity that no longer exists. This temporal home is not fixated on a sense of loss or the inability to accept the here and now. Blunt focuses on the political mobilisation of the past for the present and future, whereas I am interested in a persistent centripetal force countering the centrifugal diasporic experiences that Chinese ethnic restaurant workers have gone through. This centring force provides a stable condition in which they feel secure enough to express a sense of home and subjectivity.

The case of one of my interviewees helps to illustrate this point. She practiced medicine before moving to the United States three years prior to the interview. When I visited her in a seedy housing project, she was working in *China Blossom* as a temporary helper. She decorated her apartment with pictures of herself and her family from the past: practicing medicine in a white coat, attending parties in glamorous night gowns and vacationing in tropical destinations. As a single mother, this interviewee had uprooted herself for her sole child who wanted to study in America. She immigrated alone with the hope that her son's entry would follow. Even if only for a short period of time, working at the very bottom rung of an ethnic business added emotional heaviness to the longing for a home to come.

> I worked in a hospital for 19 years and I ran my own clinic for 10 years. You can say that those 10 years were my prime. But as a mother, I decided to come abroad to give my son a rich life. I haven't cried for a long time. When I first came, I really regretted it, but I chose to tough it out. My father was a high-ranked bureaucrat. I never had a tough time in life, so I wanted to give it a try. Three months after, I toughed it out … It's okay that people always look down on me, but I am better than that. Though my English isn't good, I work hard. Whatever people can do, I can do, too. My fingers are achy, but [it's fine] as long as I work happily.

Contrary to the positive attitude described above, this interviewee cried throughout the interview. The emotional sentiment gravitated more toward pain and sadness than nostalgia, since she could not afford to indulge herself with the past. No matter how privileged her life was in China, it was insufficient for an ideal home. The dream to come is in America and the centripetal force is the aspiration for her son's "rich life". This might be an extreme case given the dramatic downward social mobility. Nonetheless these sentiments and aspirations were widely expressed among other interviewees. Many workers also had tears in eyes or burst out crying, especially when they recounted their immigration histories.

The above narrative finally sheds light on the possibility of a time-bound home in the future. To be more precise, this home is the mythic utopia of the American dream. The past is not good enough, the present needs to be toughed out, but the best is always to come. It is the belief that current sacrifice can give the next generation success from higher education, social status and material accumulation. In other words, *China Blossom* can be as culturally distinctive as it is, but what matters the most for immigrants is to have a source of economic viability for their dreams to come. As a second-generation family member remarked, "it is livelihood for a lot of people … It's our commitment to demonstrate that we understand it provides for us".

This argument serves as a rejoinder to the earlier discussion about the intertwinement of white suburbia and the American dream. White suburbia has been considered as the *spatial* home of the powerful myth about American success with which both White and non-White wrestle. This intertwinement now entails a *temporal* significance of belonging, since its realisation for immigrants is yet to come. This time-bound home is not private – every immigrant can join – and it persists through generations, if we remember how the American dream is emphasised as the driving force behind *China Blossom*'s success over half a century. As an anchor as well as a propeller toward a desirable end result in the future, the American dream is kept alive through the mythic process of disambiguation: white privilege is inspirational, social and structural inequalities are discounted, and individual hardship is the key to one's success and belonging in America.

CONCLUSION

This chapter has demonstrated multiple sets of paradoxes between exclusion and belonging in the mythic placemaking of privilege. The case study showed that the intertwinement of myth and placemaking transcends the values and norms of Whiteness into that of Americanness. As white suburbs are the loci of Americanness, discourses, everyday practices and tangible materiality from these communities become the fabric of the American dream in the public imagination. To conform to the American standard, to be palatable according to the tastes of the privileged, and to cater to white suburbanites' aesthetic choice, *China Blossom* has strived to become an upscale place of fine dining. Although the efforts are endless from one generation to the next, Americanness can hardly be fully achieved. The case study also gave us insight into how exoticism recognisable by the White plays an equal role in and around the place of privilege. The exotic asserts the restaurant's Other identity. This effort is especially challenging for the second-generation restaurateurs, as the homestyle food symbolically involves the mythic placemaking of home in China without an actual place to claim belonging.

As palatable exoticism caters to white suburbanites' demands for difference in conformity, intimacy, memories and sociability do take place in the ethnic restaurant. Although palatable exoticism is also about the different conditions of exclusion that Chinese restaurant workers experience, the space of inbetweenness allows subversion between the privileged and the under-privileged. Finally, making the White feel at home in an ethnic restaurant creates the economic possibility of belonging and the time-bound home through which generations of Chinese immigrants centre their sense of belonging in the American dream to come. This possibility ironically perpetuates the mythic placemaking of white suburbia with the hopes that the second generation can make it and become like upper-middle class white Americans, although it involves the indentured experience of structural and everyday racism, as well as physical toil, emotional pain and relational estrangement.

ACKNOWLEDGEMENTS

I would like to thank the Community Identity Displacement Research Network and two anonymous reviewers for their constructive feedback. I would also like to thank Daria Gamliel for editing an earlier draft of this chapter.

Y. HSU

REFERENCES

Ang, I. (2001). *On not speaking Chinese: Living between Asia and the West.* New York, NY: Routledge.

August, T. K. (2016). What's eating Asian American studies? Authenticity, ethnicity, and cuisine. *American Quarterly, 68*(1), 193–203. doi:10.1353/aq.2016.0013

Barber, L. (2017). *Latino city: Immigration and urban crisis in Lawrence, Massachusetts, 1945–2000.* Chapel Hill, NC: University of North Carolina Press.

Barthe, L. (1972). *Mythologies.* New York, NY: Hill & Wang.

Blunt, A. (2005). *Domicile and diaspora: Anglo-Indian women and the spatial politics of home.* Malden, MA: Blackwell.

China Blossom Facebook Timeline Post. (2013). Retrieved from https://www.facebook.com/ChinaBlossom/photos/a.402303240162.180827.95263915162/10151501454855163/?type=3&theater

China Blossom Menu. (2014). *Food and drinks menu.* North Andover, MA: China Blossom.

China Blossom Website. (2017). Retrieved from http://www.chinablossom.com/

Cho, L. (2010). *Eating Chinese: Culture on the menu in small town Canada.* Toronto: University of Toronto Press.

Chow, R. (2001). *The protestant ethnic and the spirit of capitalism* (Kindle version). Retrieved from http://www.Amazon.com

Goetz, E., Damiano, T., & Hicks, J. (2015). *American urban inequality: Racially concentrated affluence.* Cambridge, MA: Lincoln Land Institute.

Harris, D. (2011). Introduction: A second suburb. In D. Harris (Ed.), *Second suburb: Levittown, Pennsylvania.* Pittsburgh, PA: University of Pittsburgh Press.

Harris, D. (2013). *Little White houses: How the postwar home constructed race in America.* Minneapolis, MN: University of Minnesota Press.

Harris, R., & Lewis, R. (2001). The geography of North American cities, 1900–1950: A reinterpretation. *Journal of Urban History, 27*(3), 262–292.

Heldke, L. (2003). *Exotic appetites: Ruminations of a food adventurer.* New York, NY: Routledge.

hooks, b. (1992). *Black looks: Race and representation.* Boston, MA: South End Press.

Jurca, C. (2001). *White diaspora: The suburb and the twentieth-century American novel.* Princeton, NJ: Princeton University Press.

Lassiter, M. D., & Niedt, C. (2013). Suburban diversity in postwar America. *Journal of Urban History, 39*(1), 3–14. doi:10.1177/0096144212463541

Li, W. (2012). *Ethnoburb: The new ethnic community in urban America.* Honolulu, HI: University of Hawaii Press.

Lipsitz, G. (2011). *How racism takes place.* Philadelphia, PA: Temple University Press.

Lu, S., & Fine, G. A. (1995). The presentation of ethnic authenticity: Chinese food as a social accomplishment. *The Sociological Quarterly, 36*(3), 535–553.

MacIntyre, A. (1970). *Sociological theory and philosophical analysis.* New York, NY: Macmillan.

McDonogh, G. (2006). Suburban place, mythic thinking, and the transformation of global cities. *Urban Anthropology and Studies of Cultural Systems and World Economic Development, 35*(4), 471–501.

Teitelbaum, J. (2007). *Tiki road trip: A guide to Tiki culture in North America.* Solana Beach, CA: Santa Monica Press.

Town of North Andover. (2017). *About our town.* Retrieved from https://www.northandoverma.gov/

United States Census Bureau. (2017). *Quick facts: North Andover, Essex County, Massachusetts.* Retrieved from https://www.census.gov/quickfacts/fact/table/northandovertownessexcountymassachusetts/PST045216

White, G. M. (2015). Book review of Tiki pop: America imagines its own Polynesian paradise. *The Contemporary Pacific, 27*(2), 560–565. doi:10.1353/cp2015.0033

Wiese, A. (2005). *Places of their own: African American suburbanization.* Chicago, IL: University of Chicago Press.

Yon Hsu
Concordia University
Canada

172

JOSEPHINE CORNELL, SHOSE KESSI AND KOPANO RATELE

11. DYNAMICS OF PRIVILEGE, IDENTITY AND RESISTANCE AT A HISTORICALLY WHITE UNIVERSITY

A Photovoice Study of Exclusionary Institutional Culture

INTRODUCTION

Higher education across the globe has been skewed in ways that have entrenched and reproduced the privilege of certain groups over others. This inequality is evident both in who is able to access and enter higher education and which students are privileged once they are enrolled *within* an institution. This chapter examines the dynamics of privilege, identity and resistance at a historically white South African university campus. Following post-apartheid transformation and the creation of policies aimed at redressing historical inequalities, black students in this institution are now in the majority, but the dominant institutional culture still materially and discursively excludes and marginalises students from certain categories of intersecting identities. The chapter draws on the findings from a participatory action research project which utilised photovoice methodology to examine how privilege is played out within this context, and how this shapes students' identities and sense of belonging on campus. Furthermore, it focuses on the resistances that emerge in response to oppressive institutional cultures and how this may offer the potential for new more hopeful student identities and solidarity between students across intersecting categories of identity.

PRIVILEGE AND INEQUALITY IN HIGHER EDUCATION

In many higher education institutions worldwide, structural inequalities persist despite widening participation from diverse groups of students (Burke, Crozier, & Misiaszek, 2017; Gale & Hodge, 2014; Gallacher & Parry, 2017; Leathwood & O'Connell, 2003). The education system "is an agency of differentiation and stratification" (Margolis, Soldatenko, Acker, & Gair, 2001, p. 18). In most neoliberal capitalist societies, higher education is characterised by economic and social exclusions to the continued benefit of the elite (Connell, 2016). As Gale and Hodge suggest, drawing on Connell's (2007) work in *Southern Theory*, higher education is "a social space colonised by and for the Global North" (Gale & Hodge, 2014, p. 698).

© KONINKLIJKE BRILL NV, LEIDEN, 2018 | DOI:10.1163/9789004381407_011

Inequality is particularly ingrained in the South African higher education landscape. Education in South Africa has a long history of inequality and exclusion, beginning in the early days of colonialism during which education was used to maintain white supremacy and to control indigenous people (Sehoole, 2006). During apartheid this was entrenched within the discriminatory higher education system further developed by the apartheid government. All higher education institutions subscribed to Western academic models in which indigenous knowledges were largely omitted and disregarded (le Grange, 2016). Like all aspects of life under apartheid, higher education institutions were segregated by race into "white only" and "black only" institutions, with disproportionate resources and funding allocated to the "white only" institutions. It was illegal for "white only" institutions to admit black students, to employ black academic staff, or to teach course content which the apartheid government considered "subversive" (Bunting, 2002; Kamsteeg, 2016). During the 1980s, the English-medium "white only" institutions attempted to enroll black students and raised some objections to the apartheid government's higher education policies. They had some success although the numbers of black students were low. This was not the case with the "white only" Afrikaans-medium universities, which fully supported the apartheid government's ideologies and rigorously implemented apartheid higher education racial policies (Bunting, 2002).

In 1994, after the dismantling of the apartheid regime and the first democratic elections, national policy focused on redressing the inequity and inaccessibility that characterised colonial and apartheid-era higher education. There were a number of transformation goals set by the democratic government. Most of these goals focused on numerical changes such as widening access to more diverse groups of students and addressing inequity in the allocation of resources to historically "white only" and "black only" institutions. Higher education institutions were now legally required to admit applicants from all racial groups (Cloete, 2002; Nomdo, 2017; Ramrathan, 2016). Through these policies there have been some gains in transforming the demographics of student bodies in many higher education institutions. However, as many theorists and student activists suggest, the higher education transformation processes have largely failed to address the entrenched colonial and apartheid legacies that still dominate higher education more than two decades into democracy (le Grange, 2016; Muswede, 2017; Ramrathan, 2016; Seabi, Seedat, Khoza-Shangase, & Sullivan, 2012). Transformation reform has proceeded sluggishly and historic patterns of inequality continue to be reproduced alongside transformation successes (Muswede, 2017). This has become particularly apparent since the beginning of 2015, as the deep dissatisfaction many students and staff feel with the entrenched lack of adequate transformation has spawned widespread student protests and the formation of a number of student movements focused on decolonising higher education (Badat, 2016; Murris, 2016; O'Halloran, 2016). The majority of higher education institutions are struggling to change their institutional cultures (Seabi et al., 2012), and it is critical to move beyond "the domain of counting numbers" (Ramrathan, 2016, p. 1) to focus on transforming the institutional cultures of universities. As Vincent (2016) suggests, the transformation of demographics and other changes at the level of policy have not corresponded with changes to the 'feel' of higher education institutions. Although there are other issues that require attention, dismantling and reconstituting institutional cultures is a vital part of the ongoing and much needed process of higher education transformation (Higgens, 2007; Suransky & van der Merwe, 2016).

Institutional Culture in Higher Education

Definitions of what constitutes institutional culture in higher education vary somewhat in the literature, and it can be a tenuous term to pin down (Higgens, 2007; Matthews & Tabensky, 2016). Theorists have suggested that it refers to a contested social reality. Suransky and van der Merwe (2016) propose that it is "multi-layered, mobile and a site of struggle which is manifested at many levels of institutional life" (p. 583). Following Higgens' (2007) argument that the focus should not be on pinning down this slippery term but rather on the character and terms of the contestation, Vincent (2016) proposes that, instead of settling on a precise definition of 'institutional culture', it can be understood at the level of the material and the discursive, and most importantly as the intra-action between these two.

In research and debate on higher education in South Africa, the use of the concept of institutional culture often focuses quite specifically on race. In particular, it is typically employed to refer to the whiteness of higher education institutions (Higgens, 2007). For example, in their study of the institutional culture of the University of Cape Town, Steyn and Van Zyl (2001) have concluded that the university has a culture of 'whiteness'. Our own studies have drawn similar conclusions (Cornell & Kessi, 2017; Cornell, Ratele, & Kessi, 2016). Whiteness is a normative shared social space and a position of structural advantage that grants privileges to those who occupy this space or position and denies them to those who do not (Frankenberg, 1993; McIntosh, 1990; Steyn, 2005). In South Africa during apartheid the privileges attached to whiteness were entrenched in law. In post-apartheid South Africa the "master narrative of whiteness" has taken a form which still influences relations within this country. Although whiteness no longer ensures political dominance, it still largely guarantees economic privilege, social capital and power, and Western white cultures are still held in high esteem and seen as essential for internationalism (Steyn, 2005, 2001). The whiteness of a university means not only that white students are privileged in ways which are denied to black students but also that whiteness is normative and dominant within the institution. This dominance and normativity is reflected, for example, in Euroamerican-centred curricula and the use of English as the exclusive language of instruction in an African university.

However, although race ideology and white normativity are undoubtedly important elements to examine in relation to institutional culture, it has become clear that concerns with institutional culture should be approached with an intersectional lens and go beyond a monistic concern with race. In addition to privileging

175

whiteness, institutional cultures of many South African higher education institutions (and institutions elsewhere) are heteropatriarchal, middle-class, cisgendered (Donaldson, 2015; Msibi, 2013; Walker, 2005) and inclined towards able-bodied persons (Engelbrecht & de Beer, 2014; Howell, 2006). Intersecting with race, many female, working-class and lesbian, gay, bisexual, intersex, asexual, and/or queer (LGBTIAQ+) students as well as those living with disability feel alienated and excluded, and question their belonging and identities.

RATIONALE AND RESEARCH AIMS AND QUESTIONS

There is a need to examine higher education in South Africa critically. Higher education institutions, and those of us who work within them, need to explore established processes of inclusion and exclusion, and the dynamics of power and privilege (Suransky & van der Merwe, 2016). If higher education institutions are left unscrutinised, successful and sustained change to oppressive institutional cultures is unlikely. In doing this, it is important that the voices of students, particularly those most excluded by the institutional cultures in their institution, are elevated and considered. Participatory methods are a useful means of ensuring this focus on student rather than institutional perspectives (Bowl, 2001).

In light of the considerations discussed above we aimed to examine how black students at a historically white university experienced transformation in this space. Specifically, we employed the following research questions:

• how do students experience the institutional culture in their university?
• how do students respond to these experiences?

METHODOLOGY

Study Setting: The University of Cape Town

This study was situated at the University of Cape Town (UCT), an English-medium university based in an affluent suburb in Cape Town in the Western Cape Province, South Africa. It is South Africa's oldest university and was founded in 1829. During apartheid, UCT was one of the designated "white only" universities. It was not until the 1980s that attempts were made by the university to admit students from the designated apartheid categories of "black African", "coloured" or "Indian", but the numbers of students from these groups was nevertheless low (Luescher, 2009). UCT responded to post-1994 calls for transformation by implementing an affirmative action or so-called 'race-based' admissions policy, which was in place until the end of 2015.[1] The admissions policy took into account the race of the applicants when selecting students. This was an attempt to redress past inequalities by using race as a proxy for disadvantage for acceptance into UCT. Thus the entrance requirements were different for students from different race categories. The five categories were: "black African", "Chinese", "coloured", "Indian" or "white"; with students in the "white" category needing the most points (calculated from their Matriculation scores) to be accepted; followed by the "Chinese" or "Indian" categories, then "coloured" and finally students in the "black African" category, who needed the lowest number of points (UCT, 2015). This has significantly changed the demographics of the student body at UCT, although the impact is much more evident in the undergraduate rather than postgraduate years. Black students at the university now form the majority of the student body. Despite this, since March 2015 UCT has been subject to ongoing protest from students and staff about the lack of adequate transformation post-1994. This will be discussed in more detail in the findings of the study.

Participants and Recruitment

The participants in this study were 30 black undergraduate and postgraduate students. The students were drawn from a range of faculties and disciplines. The only inclusion criteria was that the students were registered for fulltime study at their time of participation in the study. The term 'black' in this chapter is used to refer collectively to individuals classified under apartheid in the racial categories of 'black or African', 'Coloured' or 'Indian'. The use of socially constructed race categories in this chapter does not imply the acceptance of essentialised race groupings; however, it is important to acknowledge that these categories have very real material consequences in South Africa (Cooper, 2015; Morreira, 2015; Seabi, Seedat, Khoza-Shangase, & Sullivan, 2012). The participants were recruited through the UCT Psychology Department's Student Research Participation Programme (SRPP), by word of mouth and through some student organisations.

This study took place between 2013 and 2015, and during this time two distinct groups of students participated. The first group consisted of 17 students who took part in the study between 2013 and 2014. In the second stage of the study, which took place in 2015, 13 students participated. We make this distinction because the student movements that swept the South African higher education landscape in early 2015 occurred after the first phase of the project had concluded and before the second phase of the project commenced. This meant that there are some slight differences in the data drawn from the two groups and the specific questions that were asked of the two different groups in the focus groups. Both groups were asked about their experiences of higher education relating to transformation, but in the second phase of the project the context of widespread student protest around the decolonisation of higher education meant that the focus group discussions and participants' photographs sometimes explored events that had not occurred at the time of the first phase of the study.

Photovoice

The study drew on participatory action research (PAR) methods to explore participants' experiences. This was important given the focus on centring students' perspectives and voices in a setting in which they are frequently silenced. In particular, the visual research methodology of photovoice was employed. This methodology seeks to centre the experiences of those whose voices are often marginalised (Latz, 2017).

Photovoice was first developed by the critical public health researchers Wang and Burris (1997) as a tool for individuals to depict and develop their communities using a specific photographic process. This methodology is influenced by the Freirean notion of critical consciousness, by documentary photography and by feminist theory. Photovoice aims to allow individuals to document assets and weaknesses within their communities, to encourage dialogue around important issues and to reach policy makers and stakeholders through photographic exhibitions.

In the more than twenty years since its development photovoice has been used to document an extensive variety of issues and experiences. It has been employed successfully in previous research into higher education and students' perspectives (e.g. Jackson, 2013; Kamper & Steyn, 2011; Sahay, Thatcher, Núñez, & Lightfoot, 2016; Shefer, Strebel, Ngabaza, & Clowes, 2017). Minthorn and Marsh (2016), for example, used photovoice to explore how Native American students experience space in a North American university, and how discourses of colonialism and genocide influence higher educational spaces. In South Africa, Harris and Steyn (2014) utilized the methodology to examine black students' assets and barriers to success at a historically white university.

The photovoice process can vary but typically involves interviews or focus groups with participants around the subject of the study, photography training, workshops, and photographic exhibitions. In this study the photovoice process followed these steps: introductory focus groups with participants; short personal reflection essays written by participants; photography training and idea generating workshops; participants' production and development of their 'photo-stories' (i.e. photographs and captions); and finally photovoice exhibitions. The exhibitions have been a particularly important aspect of the photovoice process. They have enabled the participants' stories to reach a wide audience of fellow students, members of the public, academics and university management. The data analysed in this study includes the photo-stories, focus group transcripts and the 500 word personal reflection essays written by the participants. Due to space limitations, the data discussed in this particular chapter is drawn from 8 of the 30 participants. However discussions of the experiences and perspectives of the other participants can be found in other publications emerging from this broader study (see Cornell & Kessi, 2017; Cornell, Ratele, & Kessi, 2016; Kessi & Cornell, 2015).

PAR methodology was vital for this study as the first author is a white, middle-class, cisgendered postgraduate who thus experiences a great deal of privilege within this institution in comparision to many of the students in this study. The participatory nature of this research helps to an extent to moderate the power dynamics involved in a white, privileged student doing research around black students' experiences. For example, the participants played a pivotal role in the production of the exhibitions, which included making decisions around where and when to host the exhibition, who to invite, and how to set up the exhibition space. In fact one participant staged an exhibition of the photo-stories himself as part of an event he organised on campus that was separate to the research project and did not involve the researchers. What also helped to moderate these dynamics was that the second author, who supervised the first author, co-conducted the focus groups and ran the workshops with the students, occupies the position of a black activist-scholar heavily invested in transformation at UCT and has worked closely with students around transformation issues. Furthermore, the third author, a black man who has done extensive work on gender, race and sexualities, also supervised the first author during stages of the project. However, we are aware that negating one's role as a researcher positioned in particular ways in the research process is impossible. There are always limits to the extent to which research may be participatory. Each photograph was accompanied by an explanation written by the participants but the ultimate analysis of these photo-stories as presented in this chapter was conducted by the researchers.

Theoretical Framework and Analysis

Firstly the conceptualisation of institutional culture utilised in this chapter is based on Vincent's (2016) definition mentioned above which suggests that institutional culture should be understood as the intra-action between the material and the discursive. In this framing, Vincent draws on the theory of 'new materialism' and in particular the work of Karen Barad (2007). New materialism holds that the discursive and the material should not be compartmentalised but thought of together. Furthermore new materialism underscores the agency of material things and their role in the production of power relations. Vincent (2016) proposes that this "material-discursive" framing provides a more tangible way of understanding institutional culture. It elucidates how subjectivity and agency emerge in the intra-action between the discursive and the material, that is "in the spaces between bodies, chairs, floors, discourses and narratives that pervade an institutional setting" (p. 23). Institutional culture functions at this "nexus of intra-action (in)between discourse, subjectivity and materiality" (p. 23).

Secondly the idea of decolonising psychologies was used to frame the study and inform the analysis. Decolonising psychology is usually used interchangeably with 'postcolonial psychology'. In this study we have chosen to use the phrase 'decolonising psychologies' because the 'post-' implies that the colonial era has now passed and the postcolony can be neocolonised instead of decolonised. The findings of this study suggest that Euroamerican-centred coloniality of power, knowledge, truth and being (Quijano, 2007; Wynter, 2003) is still in operation. Decolonising psychologies seek to examine how present day power relations in psychology and beyond have their roots in colonial and apartheid history. The role of the mind in maintaining power relations between the coloniser and the colonised is of particular importance (Bhabha, 1994; Biko, 2004). The experiences of marginalised groups are centred and set against the hegemony of Western systems of knowledge. Attention is paid to the ideas and acts of domination and resistance that emerge when one group controls another (Hook, 2004; Macleod, Bhatia, & Kessi 2017). Thus, unlike many other psychological approaches to understanding oppression, decolonising psychologies acknowledge the complex and often hidden imbalances of power that are present. Furthermore this idea has explicit liberatory intentions. Processes of resistance and change are a key part of decolonising psychologies. In particular the concepts of double consciousness (du Bois, 1999) and black consciousness (Biko, 2004) were useful in the analysis of students' experiences.

FINDINGS AND DISCUSSION

The findings of the study are divided into three sections. The first section examines the dynamics of privilege within the exclusionary institutional culture of the university. The second section explores how these dynamics affect students' sense of belonging and identity. The final section considers students' possibilities for resistance, for constructing new identities for themselves and for building solidarities with other students.

Exclusionary Culture and Privilege

As discussed in the introduction, although the student body of this university is now relatively diverse, in the experiences of the participants the university's institutional culture, at both the discursive and material level, privileges certain students over others based on race, gender, sexuality and class. How students experience these variations in privilege depends on their particular identities. Below we discuss how three students of different intersecting identities, Kopano, Portia and Fiki, have experienced the ways that institutional culture privileges some students over others.[2]

Kopano

> In order to do well you need to be able to be eloquent, have that kind of confidence (…) it goes back to your background. If you are used to being in a family where (…) the medium of discussion is English already (…) you got used to communicating and then you get to a place where you speak in a 'foreign language' and you need to compete with people on that same level (…) you need to be very close with your facilitator (…) who is overseeing your research that year (…) your social background will influence that quite a lot. Things like going for coffee, having dinner [laughter from other participants in the focus group] for certain people that's a very foreign concept. Even just putting on that suit (…) sitting across the room from a white professor discussing your research project is going to be a very difficult thing as opposed to someone who does it with their dad on the weekend. (Kopano, FG1)

In this extract from Kopano, a black male student, the exclusionary institutional culture can be seen at both the material and discursive level, and in the intra-action between the two. Kopano describes how academic success in his department hinges on networking with and connecting to white (mostly male) academic supervisors. This networking is framed within the exclusionary institutional culture at the discursive level in that the language of both formal instruction and informal discussion is English. This is despite English being only one of 11 official languages and only the fourth most widely spoken language in South Africa (Stats SA, 2011). Students who do not speak English as their mother tongue are in the majority, but are denied the privilege of learning in the language that is most accessible for them. Additionally in South Africa the languages spoken are intimately interconnected to race and to class. Thus although this is a privilege based on language, it is also a privilege based on race and class. Furthermore it is a very particular type of English that is dominant, an academic middle-class English. This is because the dominant discourse of the academy typically mirrors middle- and upper-class, Westernised, white discourse patterns (White, 2011). White and Lowenthal (2011) suggest that there is "narrowness" in what is considered academic discourse, and an oppressive imbalance of power between those who can draw on these discourses and those who cannot. This type of academic literacy is not explicitly taught, and often students are expected to learn this through exposure. Higher education spaces are "discourse or speech communities" (White, 2011, p. 257) in which language usage is highly specialised. There are specific kinds of discourses and styles of communication that are promoted and expected within educational settings. Students who are not proficient in these discourses lack the "codes of power" with which to express themselves appropriately (White, 2011, p. 254). Similarly, Van Wyk (2008) describes how despite being granted physical access to higher education, many black students are denied "epistemological access" because they are unable to employ the accepted language (grammar, logic and rules).

The importance placed on networking with supervisors in English is deeply exclusionary at the discursive level, but is also intimately bound up with the material. The process of interacting with academic supervisors involves, for example, the physical activities of having coffee with or going for dinner with supervisors, sitting across from them in an office and wearing a suit. These activities privilege students both at the level of class and race. There is a degree of wealth required to afford dining at restaurants or purchasing suits that excludes many poor students. Additionally implicit in the dining practices in some restaurants are a set of rituals which may be unfamiliar and exclusionary to some black working-class students. As Kopano suggests, there is a level of physical and psychosocial comfort that comes more easily to white students in sitting across from a white professor in these situations.

This kind of implicit or "hidden curriculum" (see Margolis et al., 2001) evident in Kopano's experiences in his department privileges certain students over others, sends messages to students about who is considered a 'legitimate student', and attempts to socialise students in particular (white, middle class, heteropatriarchal) ways. This hidden curriculum is implicated in the structural production of inequality.

Portia

In her photo-story, Portia begins with an examination of her able-bodied privilege at the material level of institutional culture. This is a university campus built on a hill with a number of flights of stairs, such as these featured in the photograph. These stairs, which enjoy a prominent place on the university's Upper Campus, are a common thoroughfare and central gathering point for students. Portia draws attention to the inaccessibility of these stairs for some students and reflects on the privilege that she enjoys in being able to climb them easily. This is a campus which is difficult to navigate for differently-abled students (Dirk, 2016; Hendricks, 2016) to the point where students from a student organisation, UCT for Disability Justice, have recently reported the university to the South African Human Rights Commission (SAHRC) for allegedly violating the rights of differently-abled students (Konyana, 2017). Portia recognises the ease with which she is able to move through the physical campus space, unlike many other students. However, at the discursive level of institutional culture, or as she says "symbolically", she acknowledges the difficulties she has experienced as she has proceeded through her degree. These difficulties are based on other aspects of her identity and, although she does not explicitly state it in this photo-story, may relate to her race and gender as a black female student.

Figure 11.1. Getting into and staying at this university has been challenging.
The landscape has been fairly breezy for me to move through, but is definitely
difficult for those who do not have the able-body privilege that I do.
Symbolically, the institutional culture has been difficult to navigate and it still
feels like a privilege (even though I know that it isn't meant to be) that I have
even come this far (Portia photo-story)

Fiki

> A transformed UCT would be waking up at home, getting into a Jammie [the campus bus], getting off at Upper Campus, maybe going to the library, going to the toilet without anybody policing my genitals (…) the system has created such a structure that black people will assert violence on other black people. So, you have CPS [campus security] walking around, security, in coats policing each and every other body that doesn't fit the spectrum, and in such a way that, I get this question every day, "Are you male or female?" So, always in my mind I think, "What makes you think I'm female? What makes you think I'm male? So, in your head are you seriously trying to figure out what's happening between my legs?" (Fiki, FG4)

Within the dominant institutional culture of this university, gender is discursively positioned as occupying a fixed binary. As a transgender person, Fiki does not fit the rigid understandings of what it means to be 'male' or 'female' to which the university subscribes. These discursive constructions are materially manifest in the dominance of single gender bathrooms on campus and the assignment of students to residences based on the genders they were designated at birth rather than their own self-identification (a more in depth discussion of this can be found in an early publication from the study, Cornell, Ratele, & Kessi, 2016). When Fiki as a female to male transgender person performs everyday activities on campus, such as going to the toilet, he is challenged at both the discursive and material level because of the cisgendered dominance within the institutional culture,. Based on the dominant discursive positioning of gender, Fiki is physically stopped by campus security and denied access to certain bathrooms. Discursively he is scrutinised by security guards in their questioning and talk around his gender. This policing of transgender and gender non-binary students is common to university campuses across the world (Nicolazzo & Marine, 2015; Msibi, 2013). However in this extract when Fiki exposes the gendered and sexuality-inscribed nature of the institutional culture he also acknowledges the influence of race and class. The majority of university staff in service and administrative positions, such as security guards, cleaners and gardeners, are black and working-class, whereas the majority of academic staff and those in positions of leadership within the institution are white and middle-class. Black security guards, who likely experience similar marginalisation within this institutional culture, are used to assert the dominance of the institutional culture over fellow black bodies. This speaks to how institutional oppressions reproduce hierarchies and horizontal forms of violence that serve to maintain the status quo.

Identity and Belonging

For many black, female, working-class and LGBTIAQ+ students as well as students living with disability existing in an institutional culture that privileges able-bodied, middle-class whiteness and heteropatriarchy can have implications for students' identities and their sense of belonging within the institution. For some students this alienation creates a struggle between the desire to see themselves positively as legitimate UCT students, and the awareness of their so-called problematic bodies, blackness, queerness, and/or poverty in the eyes of the dominant campus culture. This section will discuss some of these struggles through the perspectives of two students, Mpho and Anele.

Mpho

Mpho discusses this ambivalence in his photo-story entitled, "I think my name is UCT?" when reflecting on his identity as a black student on this campus:

Figure 11.2. The crucible that is UCT left me trying to figure out my identity within the context of transformation, admission policies, societies and events held. The missing student card symbolises confusion and the loss of identity due to a muddle of suggestions on what it is meant to be a person of colour at UCT (Mpho, photo-story)

The concept of 'double consciousness' may be useful here for understanding this process of internal questioning that students may undergo. Double consciousness is du Bois' (1999) term for the contradictory experience of simultaneously viewing yourself through the eyes of a culture that stigmatises you and yet wanting to view yourself positively. As Mpho describes in this photo-story, the "muddle of suggestions on what it is meant to be a person of colour at UCT" or, in other words, the messages that the institutional culture sends out about blackness conflict with his own view of himself. This forces him into a difficult questioning of his own identity as a UCT student. There are many affective consequences that can accompany the process of double consciousness. In particular students may struggle to develop feelings of belonging within an institution.

Anele

The idea of blackness as a "problem" tied to the "double self" (du Bois, 1999, p. 9) can be seen in Anele's statement taken from the focus group discussion in which she reflects on what a transformed university would look like:

> I have this picture of me being able to stand up (...) Where I'll just feel like a normal human being (...) Where I will (...) know regardless of my colour (...) this is where I belong (...) the current feelings I think represent a direct opposite (...) it's a space where nothing is about you (...) where the emphasis is being a problem, not a person with a problem. (Anele, FG3)

In this extract, Anele draws attention to the deeply dehumanising experience of being a black student within an institutional culture that privileges whiteness. Instead of a sense of belonging Anele experiences a profound alienation. Given the exclusionary institutional culture that dominates most higher education institutions, the difficulty black (as well as working-class and LGBTIAQ+) students face in developing a sense of belonging in higher education is well documented (Hurtado & Carter, 1997; Johnson et al., 2007; Read et al., 2010; Steyn & Van Zyl, 2001; Woods; 2001; Yeager & Walton, 2011). In contrast white and middle-class students frequently hold "taken-for-granted" assumptions of participation in higher education and seldom doubt their right to belong within higher education spaces (Read et al., 2003).

Resistance and the Possibilities for New Identities and Solidarity

Although these participants experience marginalisation and exclusion, and at times question their belonging within this institution, they also frequently offer resistances and disruptions to the institutional culture they encounter. Instances of resistance were evident in the data from the first group of students that we collected in 2013 and 2014 (Cornell & Kessi, 2017 for a more detailed discussion of this). However, in early 2015 there was an example of student resistance on a far-reaching scale. As mentioned briefly above, 2015 saw the start of ongoing and widespread student protests and the formation of student movements focused on decolonising higher education in South Africa. This started with the RhodesMustFall movement which was triggered by a student, Chumani Maxwele, throwing human feces on the statue of the colonialist Cecil John Rhodes in the university's Upper Campus (Maxwele, 2016). The concept of 'black consciousness' was an important influence on the student movements, and it can be employed here to understand how new more hopeful student identities may be open to students, as well as the possibilities for solidarity between students.

185

Black consciousness holds that political freedom can only be achieved once black minds are psychologically and culturally liberated (Biko, 2004). Biko emphasises the need to overturn years of negative black self-image and instil in black people a sense of pride in themselves, their culture, their values, their religions and their worldviews. Black consciousness is essentially a form of solidarity and shared experience amongst black people, where people rally together and develop a sense of hope and community feeling. In doing so, individuals and groups can move towards self-determination and empowerment. An important aspect of black consciousness is the development of a critical consciousness (Biko, 2004; Hook, 2004; Manganyi, 1973). Consciousness is an intensified recognition of "oppressive political conditions of existence" (Hook, 2004, p. 105) and a "mutual knowledge" of black suffering under white domination (Manganyi, 1973, p. 19).

Mandisa

In her personal reflection essay Mandisa (see Figure 11.3) is rather pessimistic about pursuing an academic career in her chosen department given the lack of representation of black students at postgraduate level and black academics generally:

> An issue that I constantly struggle with (…) is the lack of representation in terms of lecturers and professors in the classroom. When I first came to UCT and made friends with a guy who was in his fourth year, he asked me what I was studying and what I wanted to do. I told that I was studying [name of discipline] and wanted to pursue that professionally, he frowned and mentioned that many of his friends (black) had applied for honours and not one of them had gotten in (…) So between that and lack of representation of lecturers, it has been very disheartening to pursue such a discipline. However, the most significant of the black experience at UCT was during the Rhodes Must Fall campaign. (Mandisa, personal reflection)

In this extract she describes the process of critical consciousness as she learns from a friend about the lack of representation and the exclusion black people face in this department. This initially demoralises and demotivates Mandisa about her future in academia. However at the end of this section of her reflection she raises the student protest movements as pivotal in her experience as a black person at university. Subsequently in the photo-story Mandisa creates she raises the same concerns about the current lack of representation of black and particularly black female academics at UCT.

However she also positions herself smiling and confident in front of the office door of a black female academic and contemplates her hope for the future and the potential of seeing herself as an academic in her department one day. She is able to consider a more optimistic student identity. This illustrates the role of consciousness in destabilising previous identities and generating the possibility for the reconstruction of new subjectivities (Vincent, 2016). At the time of her participation in this study,

*Figure 11.3. To answer the question: what does a transformed UCT look like to you?
I present this picture. A transformed UCT is a place where I am able to see more name
tags like this are found on office doors. This is to say I would like to see more names
which resemble my own. The name of Black women. And hopefully my very own
name in the [name of discipline] department (Mandisa, photo-story)*

Mandisa was an undergraduate student. She has since indeed pursued postgraduate studies within this discipline, although at another university.

In addition to developing a more hopeful identity, as black consciousness suggests, resistances also open up the opportunity for solidarity between students across intersecting identities within blackness. In the following extract from the focus group transcriptions, for example, Unathi describes how because of her middle-class background she initially did not relate to Chumani's act of resistance:

Unathi

My first reaction was like (…), "How could he be doing this!? This thing smells!?" and that for me, is because my experience of being black, I never had to smell shit outside my door (…). Umama [my mother] was from the lalies [rural areas] but (…) at the time where I could think, I've been living with white people, I learned to do this white dance so well that my immediate reaction is like, "Bhuti! [brother] Why would you do something like that!?" And (…) later when Chumani was like, "No, Unathi! Just come listen!" I was straight up like, you know what, let it smell, and let them smell it! (…) I had to take the smell and take the understanding, but it's definitely (…) related to class, because class has created these divides (…) you can pick being black, but then (…) I don't want to be that Black". (Unathi, FG3)

However once she had begun to engage with Chumani around his motivations she experienced feelings of solidarity with him. Integral to this experience of solidarity was Unathi's development of a critical consciousness of how her experience of blackness has been influenced by the internalisation of whiteness: "I learned to do this white dance so well".

It is clear that student resistance allowed for more hopeful identities and the possibility of solidarity between students. But what was also evident in the students' reflections was that even in spaces of belonging other oppressions and exclusions may exist. Nomsa described how in some student movement spaces she felt that her sexuality and gender were unacknowledged.

Nomsa

> I felt like I had finally found a place where I can just exist and finally be unapologetic about who I really am (…) it was a very liberating space but then I found (…) I started noticing (…) subtle (…) little things that crop up that show you (…) actually (…) even this space where I think I am safe with others (….) who have the same skin colour, who preach intersectionality and then I found (…) that actually (…) I'm only here close to this structure because of my (…) skin colour. What about my other intersecting identities? The fact that I was a woman, it didn't matter to most of them because they were heterosexist. The fact that I was (…) gay, it was also a problem (…) I cannot separate my gayness from my blackness, and that is what they are expecting me to do. (Nomsa, FG4)

For Nomsa, solidarity was possible on the basis of race but not in relation to her sexuality or gender. As Nomsa suggests, this illustrates that experiences of solidarity are varied by the intersection of students' identities.

CONCLUSION

This chapter has employed photovoice methodology to explore how black students experience the institutional culture of a historically white South African university at both the material and discursive level and in the intra-action between the two. The findings suggest that students' experience of privilege is bound up with their particular identities: Kopano's experience of the 'whiteness' of his department is also intimately connected to class; Portia acknowledges her material privilege as an able-bodied student but as a black woman she experiences an institutional culture that discursively positions her as inferior; the heteropatriarchy reflected in the scrutiny Fiki faces is supported by an institutional whiteness that employs working-class black men to enfore its rigid understandings of gender. For all of these students, their experiences of the 'whiteness' of the institutional culture of UCT are complicated, extended and intersected by their class, gender, ability and sexuality. These experiences illustrate how students may exist within a higher education system that in many ways questions their position and legitimacy as students and, to an extent, even their humanity. This can have deeply troubling affective consequences for students such as Mpho and Anele, who are forced to question their identity and belonging within their university. However students also have profound agentic potential and capacities for resistance as has been illustrated by the systematic and extensive student protests and resistance movements that have developed since early 2015. Through a process of critical consciousness these resistances can offer the potential for the formation of more hopeful student identities and solidarities between students across intersecting identities such as class, race, disability and sexuality. However, as with any higher education space, new forms of oppression and exclusion may occur simultaneously with experiences of belonging, even in spaces of resistance.

Ultimately, although students may successfully reshape and disrupt their institutional spaces, this should not solely be the responsibility of these students. The institution, staff and other students with more privileged identities should also work to dismantle exclusionary higher institutional cultures and ensure that higher education may be a space of belonging for all.

NOTES

[1] From 2016 onwards, the admissions policy considers a combination of applicants' Admissions Points Score (based on their school-leaving results); their scores on various university entrance examinations; and a Weighted Points Score (calculated using the 'disadvantage factor' applicable to each applicant) See UCT, 2017 for a more detailed description of this new admissions policy.

[2] All names used in this chapter are pseudonyms.

REFERENCES

Badat, S. (2016). Deciphering the meanings, and explaining the South African higher education student protests of 2015–2016. *Pax Academia: African Journal of Academic Freedom, 1–2,* 71–106.

Barad, K. (2007). *Meeting the universe halfway: Quantum physics and the entanglement of matter and meaning.* Durham, NC: Duke University Press.

Bhabha, H. K. (1994). *The location of culture.* London: Routledge.

Biko, S. (2004). *I write what I like.* Johannesburg: Picador Africa.

Bowl, M. (2001). Experiencing the barriers: Non-traditional students entering higher education. *Research Papers in Education, 16*(2), 141–160.

Bunting, I. (2002). The higher education landscape under apartheid. In N. Cloete, R. Fehnel, P. Maassen, T. Moja, H. Perold, & T. Gibbon (Eds.), *Transformation in higher education: Global pressures and local realities in South Africa* (pp. 35–52). Cape Town: Juta.

Burke, P. J., Crozier, G., & Misiaszek, L. I. (2017). *Changing pedagogical spaces in higher education: Diversity, inequalities and misrecognition.* Oxon: Taylor & Francis.

Cloete, N. (2002). Policy expectations. In N. Cloete, R. Fehnel, P. Maassen, T. Moja, H. Perold, & T. Gibbon (Eds.), *Transformation in higher education: Global pressures and local realities in South Africa* (pp. 87–108). Cape Town: Juta.

Connell, R. (2007). *Southern theory: The global dynamics of knowledge in social science.* Sydney: Allen & Unwin.

Connell, R. (2016). What are good universities? *Australian Universities Review, 58*(2), 67–73.

Cooper, D. (2015). Social justice and South African university student enrolment data by 'race', 1998–2012: From 'skewed revolution' to 'stalled revolution'. *Higher Education Quarterly, 69*(3), 237–262.

Cornell, J., & Kessi. S. (2017). Black students' experiences of transformation at a previously "White only" South African university: A photovoice study. *Ethnic and Racial Studies, 40*(11), 1882–1899.

Cornell, J., Ratele, K., & Kessi, S. (2016). Intersections of race, gender, and sexuality in student experiences of violence and resistances on a university campus. *Perspectives in Education, 34*(2), 97–119.

Dirk, N. (2016, January 27). UCT 'not friendly to the disabled'. *Independent Online*. Retrieved from http://www.iol.co.za/news/south-africa/western-cape/uct-not-friendly-to-the-disabled-1976221

Donaldson, N. (2015). What about the queers? Institutional culture of heteronormativity and its implications for queer staff and students. In P. Tabenksy & S. Matthews (Eds.), *Being at home: Race, institutional culture and transformation at South African higher education institutions* (pp. 130–146). Scottsville: University of KwaZulu-Natal Press.

du Bois, W. E. (1999). *The souls of black folk*. New York, NY: Norton.

Engelbrecht, L., & De Beer, J. J. (2014). Access constraints experienced by physically disabled students at a South African higher education institution. *Africa Education Review, 11*(4), 544–562.

Frankenberg, R. (1993). Growing up White: Feminism, racism and the social geography of childhood. *Feminist Review, 45*, 51–84.

Gale, T., & Hodge, S. (2014). Just imaginary: Delimiting social inclusion in higher education. *British Journal of Sociology of Education, 35*(5), 688–709.

Gallacher, J., & Parry, G. (2017). Student participation in the twenty-first century. In P. Scott, J. Gallacher, & G. Parry (Eds.), *New languages and landscapes of higher education* (pp. 65–83). Oxford: Oxford University Press.

Harris, T., & Steyn, M. (2014). Understanding students' perspectives as learners through photovoice. In D. J. Loveless, B. Griffith, M. E. Bérci, E. Ortlieb, & P. M. Sullivan (Eds.), *Academic knowledge construction and multimodal curriculum development* (pp. 357–375). Hershey, PA: IGI Global.

Hendricks, A. (2016, January 27). Disabled UCT students demand access. *GroundUp*. Retrieved from http://www.groundup.org.za/article/disabled-uct-students-demand-better-access/

Higgins, J. (2007). Institutional culture as keyword. In Council on Higher Education (Ed.), *Review of higher education in South Africa: Selected themes* (pp. 97–122). Pretoria: Centre for Higher Education in South Africa.

Hook, D. (2004). Frantz Fanon, Steve Biko, 'psychopolitics' and critical psychology. In D. Hook (Ed.), *Critical psychology* (pp. 84–113). Cape Town: UCT Press.

Hook, D. (2005). A critical psychology of the postcolonial. *Theory & Psychology, 15*(4), 475–503.

Howell, C. (2006). Disabled students and higher education in South Africa. In B. Watermeyer, L. Swartz, T. Lorenzo, M. Schneider, & M. Priestly (Eds.), *Disability and social change* (pp. 164–178). Cape Town: HSRC Press.

Hurtado, S., & Carter, D. F. (1997). Effects of college transition and perceptions of the campus racial climate on Latino college students' sense of belonging. *Sociology of Education, 70*(4), 324–345.

Jackson, D. L. (2013). A balancing act: Impacting and initiating the success of African American female community college transfer students in STEM into the HBCU environment. *The Journal of Negro Education, 82*(3), 255–271.

Johnson, D. R., Soldner, M., Leonard, J. B., Alvarez, P., Inkelas, K. K., Rowan-Kenyon, H. T., & Longerbeam, S. D. (2007). Examining sense of belonging among first-year undergraduates from different racial/ethnic groups. *Journal of College Student Development, 48*(5), 525–542.

Kamper, G. D., & Steyn, M. G. (2011). Black students' perspectives on learning assets at a former white university. *Journal of Asian and African Studies, 46*(3) 278–292.

Kamsteeg, F. (2016). Transformation and self-identity: Student narratives in post-apartheid South Africa. *Transformation in Higher Education, 1*(1), 1–10.

Kessi, S., & Cornell, J. (2015). Coming to UCT: Black students, transformation and discourses of race. *Journal of Student Affairs in Africa, 3*(2), 1–16.

Koyana, X. (2017, May 17). UCT addressing concerns of disabled students. *Eye Witness News*. Retrieved from http://ewn.co.za/2017/05/17/uct-addressing-concerns-of-disabled-students#

Latz, A. (2017). *Photovoice research in education and beyond: A practical guide from theory to exhibition*. New York, NY: Routledge.

Leathwood, C., & O'Connell, P. (2003). 'It's a struggle': The construction of the 'new student'in higher education. *Journal of Education Policy, 18*(6), 597–615.

le Grange, L. (2016). Decolonising the university curriculum. *South African Journal of Higher Education, 30*(2), 1–12.

Luescher, T. M. (2009). Racial desegreagation and the institutionalisation of 'race' in university governance: The case of the university of Cape Town. *Perspectives in Education, 27*(4), 415–425.

Macleod, C., Bhatia, S., & Kessi, S. (2017). Postcolonialism and psychology: Growing interest and promising potential. In W. Stainton-Rogers & C. Willig (Eds.), *The Sage handbook of qualitative research in psychology* (pp. 312–319). London: Sage Publications.

Manganyi, N. C. (1973). *Being Black in the world*. Johannesburg: Ravan Press.

Margolis, E., Soldatenko, M., Acker, S., & Gair, M. (2001). Peekaboo: Hiding and outing the curriculum. In E. Margolis (Ed.), *The hidden curriculum in higher education* (pp. 1–19). New York, NY: Routledge.

Matthews, S., & Tabensky, P. (2015). Introduction. In P. Tabenksy & S. Matthews (Eds.), *Being at home: Race, institutional culture and transformation at South African higher education institutions* (pp. 1–17). Scottsville: University of KwaZulu-Natal Press.

Maxwele, C. (2016, March 16). Black pain led me to throw Rhodes poo. *Business Day Live*. Retrieved from http://www.bdlive.co.za/opinion/2016/03/16/black-pain-led-me-to-throw-rhodes-poo

McIntosh, P. (1990). Unpacking the knapsack of White privilege. *Independent School, 49*(2), 31–36.

Minthorn, R. S., & Marsh, T. E. J. (2016). Centering indigenous college student voices and perspectives through photovoice and photo-elicitation. *Contemporary Educational Psychology, 47*, 4–10.

Morreira, S. (2015). Steps towards decolonial higher education in Southern Africa? Epistemic disobedience in the humanities. *Journal of Asian and African Studies, 52*(3), 287–301.

Msibi, T. (2013). Queering transformation in higher education. *Perspectives in Education, 31*(2), 65–73.

Murris, K. (2016). #Rhodes must fall: A posthumanist orientation to decolonising higher education institutions. *South African Journal of Higher Education, 30*(3), 274–294.

Muswede, T. (2017). Colonial legacies and the decolonisation discourse in post-apartheid South Africa: A reflective analysis of student activism in higher education. *African Journal of Public Affairs, 9*(5), 200–210.

Nicolazzo, Z., & Marine, S. B. (2015). "It will change if people keep talking": Trans* students in college and university housing. *The Journal of College and University Student Housing, 42*(1), 160–177.

Nomdo, G. (2017). 'When you write you are not expected to come from your home': Analysing 'fateful moments' as a reclaiming of 'self' in a historically white university. *South African Journal of Higher Education, 31*(2), 192–210.

O'Halloran, P. (2016). The African university as a site of protest: Decolonisation, praxis, and the Black student movement at the university currently known as Rhodes. *Interface, 8*(2), 184–210.

Quijano, A. (2007). Coloniality and modernity/rationality. *Cultural Studies, 21*(2–3), 168–178.

Ramrathan, L. (2016). Beyond counting the numbers: Shifting higher education transformation into curriculum spaces. *Transformation in Higher Education, 1*(1), 1–8.

Read, B., Archer, L., & Leathwood, C. (2003). Challenging cultures? Student conceptions of 'belonging' and 'isolation' at a post-1992 university. *Studies in Higher Education, 28*(3), 261–277.

Sahay, K. M., Thatcher, K., Núñez, C., & Lightfoot, A. (2016). "It's like we are legally, illegal": Latino/a youth emphasize barriers to higher education using photovoice. *The High School Journal, 100*(1), 45–65.

Seabi, J., Seedat, J., Khoza-Shangase, K., & Sullivan, L. (2012). Experiences of university students regarding transformation in South Africa. *International Journal of Educational Management, 28*(1), 66–81.

Sehoole, C. (2006). Internationalisation of higher education in South Africa: A historical review. *Perspectives in Education, 24*(4), 1–13.

Shefer, T., Strebel, A., Ngabaza, S., & Clowes, L. (2017). Student accounts of space and safety at a South African university: Implications for social identities and diversity. *South African Journal of Psychology, 48*(1), 61–72.

Statistics South Africa (Stats SA). (2011). *Census 2011: Census in brief* (Report No. 03-01-41). Retrieved from http://www.statssa.gov.za/census/census_2011/census_products/Census_2011_Census_in_brief.pdf

Steyn, M. E. (2001). *Whiteness just isn't what it used to be: White identity in a changing South Africa*. Albany, NY: SUNY Press.

Steyn, M. E. (2005). "White talk": White South Africans and the management of diasporic whiteness. In A. J. Lopez (Ed.), *Postcolonial whiteness: A critical reader on race and empire* (pp. 199–136). Albany, NY: SUNY Press.

Steyn, M. E., & van Zyl, M. (2001). *"Like that statue at Jammie stairs": Some student perceptions and experiences of institutional culture at the University of Cape Town in 1999* (Report). Cape Town: Institute for Intercultural and Diversity Studies of Southern Africa. Retrieved from https://open.uct.ac.za/bitstream/handle/11427/7569/Like+that+statue+at+Jammie+stairs.pdf?sequence=1

Suransky, C., & Van der Merwe, J. C. (2016). Transcending apartheid in higher education: Transforming an institutional culture. *Race Ethnicity and Education, 19*(3), 577–597.

University of Cape Town (UCT). (2015). *2015 undergraduate prospectus*. Retrieved from https://www.uct.ac.za/downloads/uct.ac.za/apply/prospectus/uctugprospectus2015.pdf

University of Cape Town (UCT). (2017). *2018 undergraduate prospectus*. Retrieved from http://www.students.uct.ac.za/sites/default/files/image_tool/images/434/prospective/ug_prospectus/ug_prospectus.pdf

Van Wyk, B. (2008). Learning and an African lifeworld in (higher) education. *Indilinga: African Journal of Indigenous Knowledge Systems, 7*(2), 171–181.

Vincent, L. (2016). "Tell us a new story": A proposal for the transformatory potential of collective memory projects. In P. Tabenksy & S. Matthews (Eds.), *Being at home: Race, institutional culture and transformation at South African higher education institutions* (pp. 21–44). Scottsville: University of KwaZulu-Natal Press.

Walker, M. (2005). Simply not good chaps: Unravelling gender equity in a South African university. In C. Marshall (Ed.), *Feminist critical policy analysis II* (pp. 38–55). London: Falmer Press.

Wang, C. C., & Burris, M. A. (1997). Photovoice: Concept, methodology, and use for participatory needs assessment. *Health Education & Behavior, 24*(3), 369–387.

White, J. W. (2011). Resistance to classroom participation: Minority students, academic discourse, cultural conflicts, and issues of representation in whole class discussions. *Journal of Language, Identity & Education, 10*(4), 250–265.

White, J. W., & Lowenthal, P. R. (2011). Minority college students and tacit "codes of power": Developing academic discourses and identities. *The Review of Higher Education, 34*(2), 283–318.

Woods, R. L. (2001). "Oh sorry, I'm a racist": Black student experiences at the University of Witwatersrand. In R. O. Mabokela, K. L. King, & R. F. Arnove (Eds.), *Apartheid no more: Case studies of South African universities in the process of transformation* (pp. 91–110). Westport, CT: Bergin & Garvey.

Wynter, S. (2003). Unsettling the coloniality of being/power/truth/freedom: Towards the human, after man, its overrepresentation – An argument. *CR: The new centennial review, 3*(3), 257–337.

Yeager, D. S., & Walton, G. M. (2011). Social-psychological interventions in education: They're not magic. *Review of Educational Research, 81*(2), 267–301.

Josephine Cornell
Institute for Social and Health Sciences
University of South Africa
and
South African Medical Research Council – University of South Africa Violence
Injury and Peace Research Unit
and
Department of Psychology
University of Cape Town
South Africa

Shose Kessi
Department of Psychology
University of Cape Town
South Africa

Kopano Ratele
Institute for Social and Health Sciences
University of South Africa
and
South African Medical Research Council – University of South Africa Violence
Injury and Peace Research Unit
South Africa

ALISON M. BAKER, AMY QUAYLE AND LUTFIYE ALI

12. REFLEXIVITIES OF DISCOMFORT

Unsettling Subjectivities in and through Research

INTRODUCTION

In this chapter we draw on our personal stories to explore particular experiences and feelings of discomfort in our research that show up the nexus between our positionalities and the dynamics of power, privilege and the normativity of whiteness in our everyday lives. With a disciplinary background in community psychology we have a shared research focus on issues of social justice that include power, identity, subjectivity and social relations across difference. Some of the insights and lessons we have learned by engaging with issues of injustice and the ways in which inequality affects people differentially have emerged through dialogue. We are part of a broader collective of interdisciplinary academics at Victoria University called the Community Identity Displacement Research Network (CIDRN). We have come together as part of this network and our friendship has developed through a shared commitment to social change and our struggles to face and understand privilege and oppression in our everyday lives. While in our own discipline of psychology such conversations are seemingly uncommon or concealed, we have sought to mobilise personal stories which are valued as legitimate knowledge and central to unpacking, but never completely transcending, our entanglements in privilege and oppression. We recognise that a bifurcated conception of privilege and oppression is misleading and we have sought to carefully work with and through the various forms of privilege and disadvantage that shape our identities, opportunities and relationships. In this way we are seeking to learn from encounters and entanglements – our social relations – which Nuttall (2009) described as "complicated, ensnaring, in a tangle, but which also implies a human foldedness. It works with difference and sameness but also with their limits, their predicaments, their moments of complication" (p. 1). This chapter is the product of ongoing intentional conversations between each other and with other colleagues about the challenges of working against and across difference and relations of power.

Everything we speak, write and understand is filtered through our own biographies, which are shaped by social relations of power in a broader historical context. We live and research in a colonial context with a history of denial around white privilege and racism. Thus our coming together is a symbolic disruption. While we are each positioned differently in relation to whiteness, we have sought to

© KONINKLIJKE BRILL NV, LEIDEN, 2018 | DOI:10.1163/9789004381407_012

create spaces and opportunities to show up the structures of oppression and privilege that exist in what Pratt (1991) has defined as the contact zone, "where cultures meet, clash, and grapple with each other, often in contexts of highly asymmetrical relations of power, such as colonialism, slavery, or their aftermaths as they are lived out in many parts of the world today" (p. 34). In our conversations we draw on our diverse experiences and positionalities, which give way to feelings of discomfort – inferiority, shame and guilt – arising from our biographies and our relationships with privilege, racism and sexism. Reflecting a concern that self-reflexivity can become a reductionist, comfortable exercise that brings the promise of release from "tension, voyeurism, ethnocentrism – a release from your discomfort with representation through a transcendent clarity" (p. 186), Wanda Pillow (2003) proposed the notion of reflexivities of discomfort, "a positioning of reflexivity not as clarity, honesty, or humility, but as practice of confounding disruptions" (p. 192). We use our personal stories to show the complexities of our relationships with and in communities, and of engaging in reflexivities of discomfort (Pillow, 2003). The landscape of our stories is one that has been formed through coloniality and the continued social, cultural and economic dominance of whiteness.

The Australian Context and Our Positionalities

Australia's colonial and migration history has and continues to be shaped by what hooks (1984) has called an 'Imperialist-white-supremacist-capitalist-patriarchy', and what Moreton-Robinson (2003) has called patriarchal white sovereignty. As a settler colonial nation, Australia's history is marked by the systematic dispossession of Aboriginal and Torres Strait Islander people from land, culture, language, community and family through frontier violence and assimilationist policies and practices (Moreton-Robinson, 2003; Walter, 2010). This colonial history is similar to the colonial experience in other parts of the world and especially other settler colonies, including New Zealand, Canada, and the United States of America, where the colonisers have not left, where they remain institutionally and culturally dominant and where the Indigenous population constitutes a numerical minority of the population. Importantly many have emphasised that colonisation is not a discrete event but is an ongoing experience. Moreton-Robinson has used the term 'post-colonising' "to signify the active, the current and the continuing nature of the colonising relationship" (p. 38).

Australia is also a multicultural society. Prior to the introduction of the official policy of Multiculturalism in 1972 by the Whitlam Labor government, Australia's history of migration encompassed policies and practices that privileged white migration under the Immigration Restriction Act of 1901 (i.e. the "The White Australia Policy"), which was in place until the late 1960s (van Krieken, 2012). This history contributed to the development of an emerging nationalism, which was centred on an Anglo-Celtic identity; a 'white Australia', which implemented a strong assimilationist approach to 'integrating' migrants into Australian society (Hage, 1998; van Krieken, 2012).

Despite an official policy of multiculturalism, which brought particular gains such as those related to the acknowledgement of diversity in Australia, this history of colonisation and migration has regulated and blocked opportunities to belong for those who are non-white. This has led to the Othering of different migrant groups. In recent years this has included the Muslim Other (post 9/11), and the incoming communities from Africa (e.g., Southern Sudanese). These different groups, like those preceding them, have experienced discrimination, racism, and uncivil attention, which must necessarily be understood in a historical and contemporaneous context of whiteness (Hage, 2000; Moreton-Robinson, 2003).

Each of us brings different life histories to this chapter and we recognise the importance of this, not only for our understandings but also our relationships with each other. Lutfiye was born and raised in Melbourne's West. Her parents migrated to Australia from Northern Cyprus and worked in Australia predominantly as labourers despite their qualifications. She grew up with the typical challenges associated with being an 'ethnic, Turkish Muslim women' in Australia, often internalising and resisting racism and sexism. Alison has become acutely aware of the unearned privileges afforded by whiteness through her experiences of migration as child and adult between Canada and Australia, but particularly through her time in the southern US and El Salvador. In each of these places the different racialised and colonial landscapes continue to shape the ways in which race and racialisation reproduce power and privilege. Amy grew up in country Victoria before moving to Melbourne for university and the opportunities that come with it. With predominantly Irish and English ancestry, she too carries the taken for granted power and privilege that comes with her social positioning as white in Australia. Amy grew up not having to think about race as the place she was from was predominantly white. This move, a displacement from periphery to centre (i.e., country to city), brought to the fore a set of experiences that had been closed off in the country where there was minimal connection with Aboriginal people, history or culture, or with other cultural groups. It provided a different vantage point for seeing. The encounters with difference required her to begin to think about racialised power relations and the casual racism that has always been part of the Australian cultural landscape. While each of us is positioned differently in relation to whiteness, it is important to acknowledge that we are all beneficiaries of Aboriginal dispossession, given our presence on stolen land.

Central to each of our stories are shifts in awareness that came from a dislocation of self across racialised geographies and identities. As we discuss in each of our stories, these histories and lenses play out in our everyday lives and relationships with each other.

Creating Micro-Spaces for Critical Reflexivity

In this chapter we seek to highlight the messiness of engaged, qualitative research by focusing on particular moments of disruption which prompted reflexivity within discomfort. These moments of disruption provide insight into the dynamics of power and privilege and the affective component of our work. This contribution is therefore part of an effort to place and unsettle our own subjectivities and the intersubjective relationships between us. We have written individual pieces capturing moments of discomfort in our research that we were working with and through. However these personal reflections were only made possible through the opening up of dialogic spaces, in which relationality, ethics and accountability are central. Our texts then are braided polyvocal compositions that reflect intentional conversations with each other and colleagues around us. In highlighting these moments of discomfort we seek to emphasise the complexity of subjectivities and to disrupt "numbing, disaffective, disembodied" ways of knowing within the social sciences, as we move towards inquiry that is both relational and emotive (Richardson, 1993, p. 705).

We can conceptualise this inquiry and writing as a polyvocal auto-ethnographic piece in which we each reflect on our personal histories and experiences, while analysing the dynamics of power, privilege, and processes of knowledge production as part of our efforts to engage in what Stevens et al. (2013) have described as transformative psychosocial praxis. Methodologically we draw on auto-ethnographic inquiry and writing, which "describes and analyzes personal experience as a way to understand cultural experiences. In so doing, [this method] demonstrates the numerous layers of consciousness as a way to connect the personal to the cultural" (Raab, 2005, p. 2). It is to look into the multicultural, post-colonising context of Australia and ask: What possibilities are there for solidarity and new futures? What kind of emotional, psychological and social spaces must we work through to carve out possibilities for these new futures?

We describe and journey through moments with the aim to 'show' rather than solely to 'tell', giving the reader the sense of 'being there' (Geertz, 1988, p. 6). Such accounts aim to link story with theory, creating a dialogue that connects self with the social, the cultural and the other (Reed-Danahay, 1997). This form of inquiry and writing can include personal essays, short stories, journals or poetry and it surfaces "action, dialogue, emotion, embodiment, spirituality, and a sense of self-consciousness" (Ellis & Bochner, 2000, p. 739). In drawing on feminist ways of writing Sanger (2003), emphasised that polyvocality is more than a textual strategy. Instead, she noted, "it is a perspective that guides praxis", which not only allows for the voices of many to be supported and heard, but also focuses on the ways in which "the text might serve to objectify (or not) the voices, lives and experiences of those involved in the research" (pp. 37–38). Importantly our process of engaging in reflexivity did not provide a way out of the challenges, but instead generated more questions about the struggles and uncertainty of working within and across borders of difference, shifting and ongoing.

TRAVELING BETWEEN WORLDS: LUTFIYE

In 2007 I 'found' myself enrolled in a PhD exploring the subjectivity of Muslim women at the intersecting ideological cornerstones of Islam, gender, sexuality, race and ethnicity. The research explored racism and Islamophobia, the role of patriarchy and the gendered nature of Muslim identity. In particular I wanted to disrupt and unsettle monolithic representations of the 'veiled' Muslim, which have resurfaced in colonial representations since the turn of the century. But as I went further along in my PhD journey it quickly became evident that the social and cultural dynamics within the community, particularly those relating to gender and sexuality, were not so easy to delve into. My resistance became apparent at a conference presentation in Portugal in the early stages of my PhD, when I found myself presenting the stories of Muslim women to show liberation and resistance in relation to colonial representations. Whilst I was comfortable deconstructing experiences of oppression arising from racism and Islamophobia, I was reluctant to turn the gaze and apply a critical lens to patriarchy in the lives of Muslim women. I came back to Melbourne and my thesis wondering if the audience noticed how defensive and one-sided my analysis was. I felt discomfort because I was not attending to the multiple sources of oppression and power that inform Muslim women's subjectivity.

This discomfort was critical. It became an important turning point and I was moving into a space of consciousness. Looking back I can see that I felt silenced. I was afraid of bringing to light patriarchal oppression experienced by Muslim women because I knew what was at stake. I felt I would be further reinforcing the racist colonial representations of Islam and Muslims in Australia and beyond by bringing these issues to light. I needed to take a step back as I realised I was getting ahead of myself. Before delving into the women's stories I needed to do a U-turn and go back to the worlds I have travelled, and continue to travel, to understand what bought me to this thesis topic and to find my voice. Lugones (2003) explains 'world traveling' as a way of navigating one's plural identities that are born out of the experiences of oppression and resistance to oppression, a way of life that is familiar to women of colour. In the journey to find my voice I had to travel in and out of different worlds, which was at times very confronting because I had to trace and face my experiences of oppression and how I negotiate and negotiated, resist and resisted power within and outside my community. Journeys through our identities are often rife with discomfort and uncertainty because they surface questions around belonging and non-belonging simultaneously – a sense of not being at 'ease' in the world (Lugones, 2003).

The World of Family and Community

I have very fond memories of my journey of being raised in the '80s in a relatively new migrant community. I remember our family gatherings at my grandparents' home, the coffee visits and BBQ's. I remember the stories and '*masal's*', the Turkish music, the dancing and singing and having fun with my cousins. Growing up, I could feel the gaze from our parents; it started at a young age. My parents would always reiterate '*hafiflik yapma*' and to be '*asker gibi*', which meant don't be playful, be serious like a soldier. I never felt restricted or bound to feminine and masculine behaviour but sexuality was heavily governed. I was expected to be a good daughter and a modest woman, particularly in behaviour and dress. In Mediterranean cultures, even if Islam is not the system of order, strict patriarchal discourses are evident (Koctürk, 1992).

From early on I learnt that being Cypriot Turkish and a Muslim woman was also about being different to Australians, particularly Australian women, who, unlike us, were constructed as '*serbes*', which, in its best translation, means 'Free'. Freedom was specifically related to notions of gender and sexuality. Understandings of honour and sexuality are often supported by referencing Islamic discourses but it is embedded in much more complex relations of power. Gender plays a pivotal role in ethnic identity making and the maintenance of culture. Women are often positioned as markers of difference where the sexuality of women is used to maintain 'moral' power, particularly among communities that have been racialised and marginalised (Espiritu, 2003). My sexuality and gendered body was also implicated in the status of my family within the community. I performed my daughterly duties. The fear of being shamed and compromising the status of my family in the community kept me in line. This shame was real. I remember one of our family friend's daughters being publicly shamed for having a boyfriend. I don't recall much about the event but I remember being at her parents' house with other families and people talking about her with her parents while she was in her bedroom. Her mum seemed upset and quiet. I remember feeling afraid of what was happening and 'learning' what happens to girls who don't listen to their parents. Drawing on Ahmed (2004b), "in order to avoid shame, (I entered) the 'contract' of the social bond, by seeking to approximate a social ideal" (p. 107) around myself.

I remember my dad encouraging us to memorise '*dua's*' – in fact we would be rewarded with money. I also recall going to '*din ders*' at the Cypriot Turkish mosque in Sunshine. My parents wanted us to learn about Islam and be good Muslims. Apparently, they didn't know Islam enough to teach; their understandings of Islam were not 'authentic'. Coming from a Cypriot Turkish family meant veiling was not an everyday practice although veiling was common at funerals or at the mosque on religious nights. Although fasting was very important, praying was not an everyday practice. Instead, being Muslim was about being a good person, not cheating, and not lying. A common saying among Cypriot Turks is '*insanın kalbi temiz olsun*' which, when translated, means 'To wish and think well of other people'. Being Muslim was about believing in '*Kısmet*', the will of the universe, believing in the existence of Allah and the words of the Prophet Muhammed, and reciting '*Kelime Şaadet*'. My understanding was that anyone could be a Muslim so long as they believed, not necessarily through being observant of practices. Following migration my parents also encountered new (read: proper) versions of Islam, which position Cypriot Turks as 'improper' relative to other migrant Muslim communities in Australia. 'Our' version of Islam was considered somewhat inauthentic to other Muslims from different ethnic backgrounds. During '*misafirlik*' at our family friends house, I recall hearing discussions around Islam and that our understandings of Islam were influenced by un-Islamic Western ideology and also by Greek culture. Over time practising Islam became more important than believing in Islam and feeling and being Muslim.

Traveling in Colonial Spaces

Now I travel into another space of discomfort, of belonging and non-belonging, beyond the borders of family and community. In these spaces, since I was little, I have been marked as the Other, as not being Australian because I was 'ethnic'. Not only did I not speak 'accent free' (Painter, 2008) English, but I also spoke another language. I also looked different. This gaze made me feel subordinate to 'Australians', and surfaced strong feelings of discomfort. In my world traveling following September 11, discourses of difference, which emphasised racial difference in terms of ethnicity, were being mapped onto Muslim identities. I was positioned as different on the basis of being Muslim and ethnic.

Difference arising from my Muslim identity was much more complex than ethnic difference which clearly positioned me as the Other. This complexity arises from the narrow representations of Muslim identity, which exclude many Muslim people in Australia. Muslims are constructed as a monolithic group. These narrow representations at times silenced my Muslim identity and I was often assumed to be a non-Muslim ethnic, predominantly Greek or Italian, and at other times I was interpellated into my Muslim identity. On one occasion a teacher from my children's primary school proudly informed me that he had purchased *helal* sausages for the upcoming school family night. Eating *helal* was not something that comes into my consciousness when making food choices. To me *helal* is merely about not eating pork products that are not necessarily *helal*.

Exclusionary representations were complex and not always oppressive. The inaccessibility of my Muslim identification protected me from hostility and discrimination, enabling me to access white privilege. And even though, at times, I am positioned as a 'non-proper Muslim', I certainly feel like an outsider as a result of everyday incivility. I identify with the marginalisation and negative representations of Muslims in Australia. The representations of the veiled Muslim woman's identity frustrated me. The discourses around the veil suddenly positioned me as 'one of the good ones', a 'moderate Muslim', 'not the religious ones', 'more like us', 'not like the ones that veil', and 'not a fundamentalist'. Most frustrating of all were comments such as 'you don't look like a Muslim' and 'you're not a proper Muslim'. Narrow representations constructing Muslim identities as veiled, which I did not reflect, were most evident in conversations about Islam, oppression, terrorism and threat, where people would position me as a non-Muslim. It appeared that heterogeneity among Muslims was being silenced by broader social discourses. I started to feel the weight of an authentic (archetype) Muslim woman.

Theorising from the Flesh

This process of looking inward to understand the dialectic relationship between subject, affect and the political as embodied theorising has been referred to as "theory in the flesh" (Moraga, 1981, p. 21). Anzaldúa (2007) further contends that the social and physical world is experienced through the body, therefore "only through the body, through the pulling of the flesh, can the human soul be transformed. And for images, words, stories to have this transformative power, they must arise from the human body ..." (p. 97). From a very young age, I was aware of the challenges faced by Muslim ethnic women, not only through my experiences but also through the stories shared among the older women in my family and among close friends in safe spaces. However, only by going back to explore and by putting words to the feelings that I embody could I move forward. I had to face my own internal journey of oppression, resistance, and my multiple and conflicting subjectivities that have been shaped by the worlds that I have travel/ed. I belong in the borderlands. The borderlands is where my consciousness has emerged through my multiple experiences and the contradiction of voices. My identity cannot be confined within boundaries because I, drawing on Anzaldúa (2007), "... continually walk out of one culture into another, because I am in all cultures at the same time ..." (p. 99).

I had to acknowledge my emotions, particularly the discomfort that I have grown so accustomed to navigating, suppressing, and denying. I drew on my anger to find courage to write and to overcome the fear enough to write – I no longer felt silenced. In saying this, when my thesis was published online, my feelings of discomfort reappeared. I thought, 'shit, what did I write'? I immediately embargoed my thesis. I felt like a traitor, betraying family and community. I wear the burden of knowing that the knowledge that I have produced can be co-opted to vilify Muslims and Islam. This was despite my careful attention to place issues of power related to gender and sexuality within broader patriarchal power circuits and to show up strategies of resistance to white Western hegemony, which defines difference as Otherness and inferiority.

TURNS IN AND OUT OF WHITENESS: AMY

Growing up in country Victoria, I never really thought about race. I never had to – I was 'just Australian'. My parents and grandparents were 'just Australian'. Most people I knew were 'just Australian'. While I did not know any actual Aboriginal people, the everyday casual racism, the disregard which Walter (2010) described as being threaded into the fabric of the nation's conversations, made it so I 'knew' from a young age that to be Aboriginal in this place was 'bad', that it was a denigrated identity. I came to 'know' about Muslims only in the post-September 11 world – a world that constructed them as an incompatible, dangerous and misogynistic 'Other' against a particular 'we', a group that I did not necessarily want to be part of (i.e., hyper-masculine/misogynistic males adorning themselves with the Australian flag and Southern Cross tattoos and drinking beer).

Turning into Whiteness

My interest in researching racism and later on whiteness/white privilege first began in my honours year. It was not long after the Cronulla Riots[1] of December 2005, which had made me feel ashamed to be Australian. The footage of the riots shocked me and pushed me to think about race/whiteness in Australia, the nation of the 'fair go'. I came to recognise everyday forms of racism and to place particular constructions of national identity and belonging and forms of Othering and exclusion against the longer history of white supremacy/Anglo-Celtic dominance in this country. My Masters research involved problematising the colour-blindness and wilful forgetting of history that characterises non-Indigenous Australians' explanations of barriers to Indigenous and non-Indigenous partnership and issues facing Indigenous communities more broadly. Through my engagement with critical race theory, whiteness studies, critical Indigenous studies and Aboriginal people's experiences and perspectives the idea of being 'just Australian' began to trouble me. I was a white settler Australian complicit in a shared history of dispossession, assimilation and racism. In my research I made a conscious turn "towards and away from those bodies who have been afforded agency and mobility" by white privilege (Ahmed, 2004a, para. 59), which so easily hides itself, particularly amongst those who are white. I was turning the gaze onto whiteness, focusing on the discourses that people have access to for making sense of self, other and the social world which both reflect and (re)produce racism at a structural and everyday level.

In many ways in this previous work I was distanced. The focus was on those other white people: the Cronulla rioters, the Andrew Bolt and Pauline Hanson supporters, the flag wavers, the ones with "fuck off we're full" stickers on their car, those who carry on about 'special treatment' and 'black armband views of history'. While this work involved recognising my own structural positioning as one of privilege, the focus was on the discourses 'out there', that I myself was in the privileged position of problematising and resisting. As a university student I had access to resources that enabled me to begin to forge an ethical white subjectivity (Sullivan, 2006) and the privilege to begin to disrupt common sense assumptions as part of a process of conscientisation. Moreover, as someone originally from the country now living in Melbourne, I was exposed to everyday multiculturalism. Encounters with difference, with the diversity of 'diversity', facilitated this academic process of disrupting discourses that dehumanise and Other and seek to construct a homogenous 'us' against a monolithic 'them'.

The focus on discourse enabled a way to approach whiteness that recognised that white people are not a homogenous group and that whiteness was not just about skin colour. There were possibilities for resistance, refusal and for change. While I carried recognition of my privileged positionality in terms of whiteness, and some shame and guilt of this history as a history of the present (Ahmed, 2004a), I also carried a sense of responsibility for change, for resistance and for refusal. I was not stuck in my guilt or shame as it quickly became clear that this has a tendency to invoke forms of paralysis and so it was not a productive response to the awareness of white privilege. Nicoll (2004) has emphasised the importance of resisting "a tendency to try to 'resolve' our discomfort at the recognition of whiteness into individual(ising) affects of shame and/or guilt" (p. 5). For her critical whiteness studies should be about unsettling white subjectivity rather than creating "opportunities for individual confession, catharsis and redemption" (p. 5). I was comfortable in unsettling my white subjectivity. It was appropriate for me, as an insider, to be interrogating whiteness as part of understanding and challenging racism and processes of social exclusion. I did not feel like I was crossing any lines. This was my work to do, my responsibility. The lines I was crossing as a white critic of whiteness (Probyn, 2004), I was happy to cross. I knew the importance of this kind of work, as the discourses that I was problematising/deconstructing were so familiar to me. I grew up surrounded by such 'common sense'.

The Discomfort of Turning towards Others

My PhD research saw me take a different path. I necessarily began to engage in more difficult questions, particularly those in relation to how I would engage in this work as an ally, in solidarity, to accompany, to work in ways that avoid (re)colonising. This required me to turn inwards in some ways, reflecting at a more personal level on who I am as a white settler Australian and what I can and should/should not be doing here. The tensions were around taking up or over space. At times I felt uncomfortable and vulnerable encroaching on a space where I did not belong and these are questions that I continue to grapple with.

This research focused on a community arts and cultural development project called Bush Babies, which involved Noongar Aboriginal people sharing stories of being born in the bush and/or of growing up in reserves, missions and on the fringes of towns at a time of strict control and segregation. Initially, the research was focused on the role of community arts for both Aboriginal and non-Aboriginal people. The stories shared in these spaces were conceptualised as symbolic resources with the capacity to shift people's (and in particular white Australians') understandings of Aboriginal people, history and contemporary social issues. The Bush Babies project was approached as an intervention into the cultural sphere of meaning-making with implications both within and beyond the Aboriginal community. I was comfortable with this task although I also had some hesitation borne out of my growing understanding of the history of oppression and colonialism and the complicity of the academy in this process.

I recall being concerned during the early stages of the research with having both Aboriginal and non-Aboriginal participants involved in the project. I felt I had more legitimacy working on/with/against whiteness as the problematic centre of racism (Frankenberg, 1993). I found myself preoccupied with wanting to show up the shifts that might happen for non-Aboriginal people in hearing these stories: I wanted to show possibilities for transformative action at the intercultural interface. I later came to question if my concern with exploring non-Aboriginal responses to and experiences of the project was in fact about feeling the need to redeem white people, and therefore myself, to show that there can be change, that there are good white people, by showing how they were moved by the stories (Sullivan, 2006). This preoccupation also reflected my anxieties over taking up or over space by focusing on the stories of Aboriginal people, stories that were not mine to tell. I was scared of the politics. I was scared of how I would be perceived – that I could be construed as a white saviour (Aveling, 2013) or as appropriating those stories for my own advancement. In a way there is no escape from this reality. Through this research I received my PhD qualification.

While working through the research and the tensions of representation and location, I had made decisions. These decisions were based in values about relationality, ethics and accountability. I had a research plan but I went off script. I needed to be flexible and responsive. I went to interviews asking about the participants' experience of the arts project and what it meant to them to be involved. However the Noongar Elders came to the interviews, often with documents, photographs and newspaper articles, wanting to share their life stories. Elders told me stories about being removed from their families and the legacy of this in the lives of their own children and grandchildren. The focus of the research was therefore redirected to a focus on the life stories of these Elders. I understood that what they were generously sharing were their stories, which they wanted to rekindle within the broader project. My task was to work beyond and through my various locations and assumptions to carve out a way of ethically and justly documenting these stories, to bear witness to and amplify their stories (Fine, 2006). As a white body in this space the explicit focus on the Elders' stories brought some discomfort. Yet these were the stories that they wanted to share with me as a researcher and a white settler Australian. They communicated the ongoing history of colonial dispossession, assimilation and racism, and they wanted me to listen responsibly (Dion & Dion, 2004; Shulman & Watkins, 2001).

My feelings of out of place-ness were brought to the fore on different occasions in the research and its reporting. During the data analysis phase I found myself stuck for an extended period of time, not knowing what to do with these stories and somewhat immobilsed by these incredibly moving, tragic stories, painful stories of loss and trauma, stories that are about the lives of Aboriginal people but through which I learn more about who I am in this place. At the CIDRN Place, Politics and Privilege conference in 2017 I presented one aspect of the research findings as part of an Indigenous panel where I was one of a few non-Indigenous people discussing work with Indigenous people in Australia. In one of the presentations preceding mine an Aboriginal Noongar woman delivered a very powerful presentation with the overriding message, "STOP TELLING OUR STORIES!" There I was about to get up and present on the Elders' stories, focusing on their stories of resistance, cultural continuity and survival. This was the first time I would present on this aspect of the research. Previously I had focused on stories of oppression, past and present, captured in the Bush Baby storytelling. I had felt reasonably comfortable in reporting on that aspect of the findings because the gaze was directed explicitly at the oppressive social conditions that are (re)produced by whiteness/coloniality as opposed to the cultural stories and the hidden transcripts of the oppressed (Scott, 1990). During this presentation I felt self-conscious and hyper-aware of my white body telling these stories. I had a very small momentary taste of feeling like the problematic 'Other': I was the problematic white person telling/appropriating/redeeming myself through their stories and the act of re-telling. I felt very uncomfortable and my anxiety and out of place-ness was evident. While I was arguing the need to recognise and document the resistance and survival of Aboriginal people in what Tuck (2009) has discussed as 'damaged centered research', I was still a white Australian researcher retelling these stories. Had I crossed a line? Was this action viewed as colonising, as appropriation, as condescending (as if Aboriginal people need a non-Aboriginal person to come along to highlight their cultural continuity, resistance, survival)? And is there a way out of this?

I was grappling with expressions of power in presenting on research concerned with showing up power, oppression and resistance. By engaging with stories of those from positions of alterity, I was attempting to take on what Chase (2005) has described as the supportive voice. The questions lingered: should I be here, and how should I be here? I felt out of my comfort zone and vulnerable, encroaching on a space where I did not belong. But what was the other option? Keeping silent? Being a bystander to injustice? It is important to name this discomfort, as naming this discomfort and the feelings that are brought to the surface is about acknowledging the histories we carry and their implications for subjectivities and relationships. It points to some of the challenges we as a nation face in healing from an ongoing history of dispossession. We cannot escape these dynamics. Rather it is necessary to learn to find a way to work within and against them.

STRADDLING SILENCE: ALISON

I began by collaborating with New Change, a program at that time run by the local council with young African–Australian (primarily South Sudanese) women aged 18–23 who were using an arts-for-social-change framework to challenge media misrepresentation and stereotyping of young people from their communities. The research project took a staged approach to involvement and methodology, initially starting with ethnographic fieldwork and then moving into arts-based action research. Over a 10 month period the group moved away from being a council run program and changed into an independent arts collective. One other facilitator and myself were part of this process. As part of the ongoing arts work the group has been developing a range of documentary and film pieces that use collective spoken word poetry on topics related to culture, identity and belonging, and more recently, mental health and relationships.

Do You Have Our Backs?

As a white woman of Canadian and Australian background, I gave serious consideration to my entrée into this setting. I have had experiences of being an outsider in other contexts, including El Salvador and Ghana, so I was also very conscious of the sort of privileges and seeming ease with which white people can enter and inhabit spaces. Sullivan (2006) has described ontological expansiveness as the tendency for white people to assume that "all cultural and social spaces are potentially available for one to inhabit" (p. 25). At the time the group was busy with writing, refining and performing their collective spoken word poem called 'Breaking News'. This poem challenged media misrepresentations of young South Sudanese Australians as gang members and violent criminals. I was conscious of not wanting to disrupt their work by asking questions or offering my opinion on the poem, much of which was making reference to structural racism and white privilege. My silence, I felt, was about understanding my position in Australia's racial formation and not wanting to recentre whiteness.

At the third session I attended the group had news delivered by one of the program leaders that those 'higher up' in council did not approve of a line in the poem implicating 'the white man[2] ' in racist media misrepresentation in Australia. The line, they said, was violating the diversity and inclusion policy by singling out one particular group in the community, arguably a community of people constituted by white men. The group was fully attuned to the irony of this censorship. A heated discussion ensued among group members and facilitators on how to handle the issue. I sat in silence, listening to the proposed responses to this assertion of reverse racism and to the deeper conversation about historical oppression and structural racism. One young woman, whose family had been recently affected by issues of racialised policing, was adamant that the poetic video clip would change nothing and the group should abandon the project. This was yet another instance of control and denial of the existence of systemic racism by white people. She asked, when the video made its way into the world and was met with backlash and white betrayal, who would step in? At that point she turned to me and said, 'Do you have our backs?" Shaken out of my silence, I responded, "Yes". The question was a literal one: it seemed to be both a challenge and an invitation. Yet it was more than that – it was a metaphorical question: was I going be the white man in this space? This provocation was a "revelatory moment" (Trigger, Forsey, & Meurk, 2012). It felt intense. Attention was focused on me as a white person in this space that had just censored them in speaking their truth.

The Place of Silence in the Contact Zone

The moment of that provocation stands out for a few reasons. One, because, for me, it raised serious questions about being silent and the trustworthiness of the white man. Second, because it makes palpable the coloniality of power, how whiteness continues to shape our daily lives, the possibilities for 'being' and intergroup relations. In this continual questioning about whiteness comes a focus on historicity, on how colonisation and subsequent acts of white supremacy such as the 'White Australia Policy' have brought us to where we are today and on the present ways in which white privilege is maintained. The question reflected a dual tension for me, how can one both 'be white', displaying the physical characteristics such as pale skin, and work against 'being whitely' which is "a deeply ingrained way of being in the world" that encompasses behaviors, habits and dispositions that are a result of white supremacy (Sullivan, 2006, p. 330). Put another way, if "… the self is infected with the state of the world", how might white people contribute to the creation of a different place? (Vice, 2010, p. 330).

One starting point could be the different theoretical and conceptual tools that allow for complexity, but also those which start to deconstruct power in these intercultural settings. To this end, the contact zone as developed by Mary Louise Pratt (1991) has been useful. These places of intercultural entanglement form a contact zone. New Change, as a collective, can be understood in this way, not only because of our different racial identities but also because of the ways in which each person's history and being becomes part of the relational web. Over the past ten months we have been sharing and unpacking stories about how race, class, culture, language, tribal affiliation, gender roles and socialisation, migration histories and developmental shifts become entangled and how we feel, react and process differently, alone and together. In the contact zone whiteness and all it stands for becomes visible; it is no longer an apolitical body that 'blends in' and stands by. The contact zone opens up the need to interrogate and question silence. I felt that staying silent was keeping the space open, a move away from the habits of ontological expansiveness Sullivan speaks of. Taylor (2004) describes this as an act of careful listening:

> Silence, on this reading, is the complement to the other's voice; it signals one's willingness to receive the other's struggle to find words both for his or her experiences and for the self that those experiences have conspired with the act of expression to create. Silence … is part of listening for a voice. (p. 239)

In the current political and social climate in Australia the stakes are high and uncivil attention is a daily-lived reality for many of these young women and their families. In the contact zone, especially one where the artwork is political and aims to create awareness about the experiences of marginalised groups, there isn't room for white people to completely retreat into silence and invisibility. White people have to be accountable and we have to know when to speak and on whose terms. While I knew there were ways for me to speak up and mobilise white privilege through acts of solidarity with the group, there is an ongoing struggle that obliges us to occupy alternative psychic spaces. It is in these spaces and in silence that we "hold our history in ways that can inform our present" and "nurture our capacities for grief and mourning, for truth and reconciliation" (Shulman & Watkins, 2001, p. 17).

Silence then is not something just occurring within the contact zone but it is also a result of being part of it. I would argue that the discomfort produced in this space could become a generative silence as a result of the 'clashes', the grappling and ongoing understanding of white, patriarchal and capitalistic histories that Vice (2010) posits has caused whites to be morally damaged selves. Vice, who writes from the vantage point of a white South African of English decent, suggested that whites must work on their damaged moral selves in humility and (a certain kind of) silence. While I had been grappling with what I could *do* to act and speak up, I have also been silent in not writing reflexively about the feelings of guilt, shame, anger and sadness, which are all too common examples of what we know to be white fragility (DiAngelo, 2011). My feeling was that words would not suffice and writing reflexively in traditional linear prose will be read as another example of ontological expansiveness or the reflexivity for redemption that Amy has already described. This silence through text can also be read as complicity and as a choosing to remain invisible and disconnected. There is no way of writing ourselves out of whiteness. In fact Taylor (2004) would argue that attempts to do so are whitely:

> ... claiming that there's nothing I can say on a matter that manifestly concerns me, if I claim this sincerely, is a way of denying my connection, and, at the same time, of refusing to examine myself closely enough to uncover and find words for the connection ... Participating in whiteness-as-invisibility means denying that one has a perspective on or stake in the racial terrain. It means rejecting, or ignoring, the burden of identifying – of conceptualizing, of seeing which words apply to – one's place in a system of social forces and relations ... And that is a paradigmatically whitely thing to do. (pp. 231–232)

Of course, this is the part where the reader asks: But you have written this reflection and in doing so aren't you overcoming your silence? It is the trap of reflexivity that lures us in to seek out this release. However, even as I finish this piece, I was asked by one of the young women to read aloud what I was writing about the group. Everything that we are involved in – presentations to schools or the public, writing for a magazine – must be discussed. I suddenly felt panicked by the question. How would each young woman feel when I 'psychologised' our relationships and focused on 'race' in this way? There were many responses from initial feelings of betrayal and surprise to acknowledgment of the tension for 'people like me' to 'walk the line'.

Breaking the 'codes of silence' that have been enforced and reinforced for generations requires living with the silence of discomfort and the discomfort of silence. Shulman and Watkins (2010) noted that it is a deep listening, which I believe needs to be with others and ourselves, "followed by care, an intention to understand and support, and by gestures of reparation" (p. 8). hooks (2003) contends that "to build new community requires vigilant awareness of the work we must continually do to undermine all the socialization that leads us to behave in ways that perpetuate domination" (p. 36).

DISCUSSION

This chapter is part of an ongoing dialogue in which we have been discussing and working with and through the web of our own positionalities and the broader power structure in our everyday lives. With a commitment to relational ethics and social change we have sought to create microspaces for engaging in what Pillow (2003) has described as reflexivities of discomfort in efforts towards disrupting, but never completely transcending, entanglements of power and privilege. We have found that this form of inquiry and writing in our discipline of psychology could potentially be "writing on the edge – and without a safety net" (Vickers, 2002, p. 608). We view such pieces as important because they connect the personal with the political and cultural, creating a dialogue that attempts to "lift the veil of public secrecy surrounding fieldwork" (Van Maanen, 1988, p. 91), and confront positivist notions of objectivity and expertise. As noted by Van Maanen (1988), through telling our stories we illuminate "'the unspeakable, private and too often hidden dimensions' of our work" that shape our personal and professional identities (p. 83).

One common thread in our reflections is the importance of vigilance in the contact zone and in world traveling. Lutfiye, though critical reflexive practice, unpacked her personal experiences of discomfort arising from the experience of "epistemic violence" (Spivak, 1988) reflected in competing hegemonic discourses constructing the Muslim woman and understandings of Islam and ethnic and Australian identity. These experiences, which were initially a 'hidden' dimension of the research, were pivotal in understanding the intersubjective nature of her research as well as the intersecting subjectivities of Muslim women. Lutfiye's reflection also highlights the ongoing discomfort associated with speaking to patriarchy and white hegemony. These struggles demonstrate Spivak's (1988) proposed question "Can the Subaltern speak?" This question raised another question about how we – two white women and one non-white woman – can write together in a way that does not reproduce racialised power dynamics. For Amy and Alison, the warnings from Pillow (2003) and Ahmed (2004a), who identify the ways in which self-reflexivity becomes another assertion of white power and supremacy and an attempt to garner the anti-racist title of ally, resonate. Declarations of privilege and whiteness, as Ahmed (2004a) has noted, end up becoming non-performances in which we make 'admissions' about mistakes and attempt to transcend them through our endless reflections about interpersonal interactions. The point of this reflection then is not to garner sympathy or to delve into white victimhood and fragility, although that may very well be what comes across. Rather it is a push to consider the uncomfortable emotional and psychic spaces that we choose to grapple with as part of engaging in the challenging work of transformative psychosocial praxis (Stevens et al., 2013). Our use of metaphors that convey movement and process is deliberate. The 'turns' 'crossing' and 'walking' of lines in and out of silence, across boundaries and worlds, speak to the complexities of intersubjective spaces and the ongoing struggle to carve out ways of being, together.

Importantly these processes of care extend to the writing process, which involves examining both language and form in attempts to decolonise our writing about positionality. Indeed the task of writing together has been challenging and we have necessarily had to negotiate dynamics of power in this process. The dialogic spaces we have created, whether understood as a contact zone, a third space or the quiet spaces of our own consciousness, become sites for 'working through'. The notion of 'working through' has been taken up in depth in liberation psychologies to counter the social and historical amnesia that has resulted in the perpetuation of racist and patriarchal systems (Watkins & Shulman, 2008). In these spaces discomfort with our own histories is shared through stories – with colleagues, community members and through internal dialogue. Shulman and Watkins (2001) have noted that when we begin to face the legacy of rigid dissociations between history, colonialism and our own biographies we experience "unheard feelings, symptoms and narratives" (p. 11). In our writings the processes of 'working through' have involved the psychological, emotional and relational spaces of discomfort that arise when we seek to disrupt the oppressive everyday habits, practices and structures we have been socialised into, accept and reproduce. As Sullivan (2006) noted, our own reflexivity should not lead to "'paralysis and inactivity' but a 'hyper- and pessimistic activism' or 'tragic meliorism' that attempts to change the world, knowing that many of those efforts will fail and that new dangers will be created in the place of the old" (p. 185). However, we remain steadfast in our commitment to the creation of microspaces in which discomfort is an inevitable part of our push for solidarity. We have sought to embody Moraga's (1981) assertion that "the real power, as you and I well know, is collective. I can't afford to be afraid of you, nor you of me. If it takes head-on collisions, let's do it: this polite timidity is killing us" (p. 34).

NOTES

[1] The Cronulla Riots were a series of riots that took place in Cronulla, Sydney in December 2005, stemming from tensions between 'Middle Eastern' and white members of the community, see: http://www.sbs.com.au/cronullariots/documentary
[2] The White man is used as a metaphor for structural racism.

REFERENCES

Ahmed, S. (2004a). Declarations of whiteness: The non-performativity of anti-racism. *Borderlands E-Journal, 3*(2), 1–12. Retrieved from http://www.borderlands.net.au/vol3no2_2004/ahmed_declarations
Ahmed, S. (2004b). *The cultural politics of emotion.* New York, NY: Routledge.
Anzaldúa, G. (2007). *Borderlands/La Frontera: The new mestiza* (3rd ed.). San Francisco, CA: Aunt Lute Books.
Aveling, N. (2013). Don't talk about what you don't know: On (not) conducting research with/in indigenous contexts. *Critical Studies in Education, 54*(2), 203–214. Retrieved from http://dx.doi.org/10.1080/17508487.2012.724021
Chase, S. (2005). Narrative inquiry: Multiple lenses, approaches, voices. In N. K. Denzin & Y. S. Lincoln (Eds.), *The Sage handbook of qualitative research* (3rd ed., pp. 651–680). Thousand Oaks, CA: Sage Publications.
DiAngelo, R. (2011). White fragility. *The International Journal of Critical Pedagogy, 3*(3), 54–70.
Dion, S. D., & Dion, M. (2004). The braiding histories stories. *Journal of the Canadian Association for Curriculum Studies, 2*(1), 77–100.
Ellis, C., & Bochner, A. P. (2000). Autoethnography, personal narrative, reflexivity. In N. K. Denzin & Y. S. Lincoln (Eds.), *Handbook of qualitative research* (2nd ed., pp. 733–761). Thousand Oaks, CA: Sage Publications.
Espiritu, Y. L. (2003). *Home bound: Filipino Americans lives across cultures, communities and countries.* Berkeley, CA: University of California Press.

Fine, M. (2006). Bearing witness: Methods for researching oppression and resistance: A textbook for critical research. *Social Justice Research, 19*(1), 83–108. doi:10.1007/s11211-006-0001-0

Frankenberg, R. (1993). *White women, race matters: The social construction of whiteness.* London: Routledge.

Geertz, C. (1988). *Works and lives: The anthropologist as author.* Stanford, CA: Stanford University Press.

Hage, G. (2000). *White nation: Fantasies of White supremacy in a multicultural society.* New York, NY: Routledge.

hooks, b. (1984). *Feminist theory from margin to center.* Boston, MA: South End Press.

Koctürk, T. (1992). *A matter of honour: Experiences of Turkish women immigrants.* London: Zed Books Limited.

Lugones, M. (2003). *Pilgrimages/Peregrinajes: Theorising coalition against multiple oppressions.* Oxford: Rowman & Littlefield Publishers.

Moraga, C. (1981). La Güera. In C. Moraga & G. Anzaldúa (Eds.), *This bridge called my back: Writings by radical women of color* (pp. 28–29). Watertown, MA: Persephone Press.

Moreton-Robinson, A. (2003). I still call Australia home: Indigenous belonging in a White society. In S. Ahmed, C. Castaneda, A. Fortier, & M. Sheller (Eds.), *Uprootings/regroundings: Questions of home and migration* (pp. 23–40). Oxford: Berg.

Nicoll, F. (2004). "Are you calling me a racist?": Teaching critical whiteness theory in indigenous sovereignty. *Borderlands E-Journal, 3*(2), 1–8. Retrieved from http://www.borderlands.net.au/vol3no2_2004/nicoll_teaching.htm

Nuttall, S. (2009). *Entanglement: Literary and cultural reflections on post-apartheid.* Johannesburg: Witwatersrand University Press.

Painter, D. W. (2008). The voice devoid of any accent: Language, subjectivity, & social psychology. *Subjectivity, 23*, 174–187.

Pillow, W. (2003). Confession, catharsis, or cure? Rethinking the uses of reflexivity as methodological power in qualitative research. *International Journal of Qualitative Studies in Education, 16*(2), 175–196.

Probyn, F. (2004). Playing chicken at the intersection: The White critic in/of critical whiteness studies. *Borderlands E-Journal, 3*(2), 1–42. Retrieved from http://www.borderlands.net.au/vol3no2_2004/probyn_playing.htm

Raab, D. (2013). Transpersonal approaches to autoethnographic research and writing. *The Qualitative Report, 18*(21), 1–18.

Reed-Danahay, D. (1997). *Auto/ethnography.* New York, NY: Berg.

Richardson, L. (1993). Poetics, dramatics, and transgressive validity: The case of the skipped line. *The Sociological Quarterly, 34*(4), 695–710.

Sanger, P. C. (2003). Living and writing feminist ethnographies. In R. P. Clair (Ed.), *Expressions of ethnography: Novel approaches to qualitative methods* (pp. 29–44). Albany, NY: State University of New York Press.

Scott, J. C. (1990). *Domination and the arts of resistance: Hidden transcripts.* New Haven, CT: Yale University Press.

Shulman, H. L., & Watkins, M. (2001). Silenced knowings, forgotten springs: Paths to healing in the wake of colonialism. *Radical Psychology, 2*(2), 1–19.

Spivak, G. C. (1988). Can the subaltern speak? In C. Nelson & L. Grossberg (Eds.), *Marxism & the interpretation of culture* (pp. 271–313). London: Macmillan.

Stevens, G., Duncan, N., & Hook, D. (Eds.). (2013). *Race, memory, and the apartheid archive: Towards a transformative psychosocial praxis.* New York, NY: Palgrave Macmillan.

Sullivan, S. (2006). Race, space, and place. In S. Sullivan (Ed.), *Revealing whiteness: The unconscious habits of white privilege* (pp. 143–166). Bloomington, IN: Indiana University Press.

Taylor, P. (2004). Silence and sympathy: Dewey's whiteness. In G. Yancy (Ed.), *What white looks like: African-American philosophers on the whiteness question* (pp. 227–242). New York, NY: Routledge.

Trigger, D., Forsey, M., & Meurk, C. (2012). Revelatory moments in fieldwork. *Qualitative Research, 12*(5), 513–527.

Tuck, E. (2009). Suspending damage: A letter to communities. *Harvard Educational Review, 79*(3), 409–428.

van Krieken, R. (2012). Between assimilation and multiculturalism: Models of integration in Australia. *Patterns of Prejudice, 46*(5), 500–517. doi:10.1080/0031322X.2012.718167

Van Maanen, J. (1988). *Tales of the field: On writing ethnography* (pp. 73–100). Chicago, IL: University of Chicago Press.

Vice, S. (2010). How do I live in this strange place? *Journal of Social Philosophy, 41*(3), 323–342.

Vickers, M. H. (2002). Researchers as storytellers: Writing on the edge — And without a safety net. *Qualitative Inquiry, 8*(5), 608–621.

Walter, M. (2010). Market forces and indigenous resistance paradigms. *Social Movement Studies: Journal of Social, Cultural and Political Protest, 9*(2), 121–137. doi:10.1080/14742831003603273

Alison M. Baker
Victoria University
Australia

Amy Quayle
Victoria University
Australia

Lutfiye Ali
RMIT University
Australia

NOTES ON CONTRIBUTORS

Lutfiye Ali, PhD, is the Health Promotion Policy coordinator at Women's Health West and an adjunct lecturer at Victoria University. Her areas of research interest include social identity, community making and belonging among racialised and ethnicised identities. These sit within the context of Australian multicultural social relations, informed by current and historical global relations of power. A major focus of her research explores the complexity and the diverse ways in which identity among Muslim women, migrant and second-generation Australians are negotiated at the intersections of gender, culture, religion and race. This research draws on Third World and postmodern feminist theories.

Alison M. Baker, PhD, is a Senior Lecturer in Social Pedagogy at Victoria University in Melbourne, on the land of the Wurundjeri of the Kulan nation. Her research focuses on the implications of structures that produce inequality in the lives of various disenfranchised groups as well as those in positions of privilege. One strand of Alison's research focuses on young people's experiences of racialisation and the implications for identity and belonging across contexts. She is interested in blending creative research methodologies and documentary techniques, particularly visual and sound modalities, to develop young people's sense of social justice and capacity for action.

Paola Bilbrough, PhD, is a documentary practitioner, widely published poet and early career researcher. Her critical media and cultural studies research is informed by many years of working in a community development context, and as an artist-teacher on anti-racism and advocacy projects. Both Paola's practice-based documentary research, and her theoretical research focus on questions of representational and relational ethics, identity and belonging.

Tony Birch, PhD, is the inaugural Bruce McGuinness Research Fellow in the Moondani Balluk Academic Centre at Victoria University. His research is concerned with Climate Justice, the Protection of Country and Aboriginal Knowledge Systems.

Sally Clark attained her PhD from Swinburne University where she also lectures across the Politics and Sociology departments. Her PhD titled 'Navigating Asylum: Journeys from Indonesia to Australia' charts the precarious nature of life in transit for Haraza asylum seekers undergoing the UNHCR refugee status determination process and explores the connection between conditions in transit and irregular migration. Her research interests include forced migration, human rights, political geography and the intersection of race, nationalism and colonialism.

Jora Broerse is a PhD student in the Institute of Sport, Exercise and Active Living at Victoria University, Melbourne, Australia. In 2017, she completed a two-year Research Master in Sociology at the University of Amsterdam, the Netherlands. In her master's thesis, she looked at intercultural encounters and lived multiculturalism in the context of sport. In her PhD project, she continues looking at similar topics and is further interested in space making practices in super-diverse neighbourhood sports settings. In her research, sport is seen as a critical environment for understanding broader issues such as migration, social cohesion, and feelings of belonging.

Josephine Cornell is a PhD candidate in the Department of Psychology at the University of Cape Town and a researcher at the South African Medical Research Council-University of South Africa Violence, Injury and Peace Research Unit and the Institute for Social and Health Sciences at the University of South Africa. Josephine's research interests include higher education transformation, identity and space.

Yon Hsu is a Research Fellow at the Concordia Centre for Broadcasting and Journalism Studies, Montreal, Canada. Trained as a critical theorist in Sociology and Communications Studies, she is interested in voices, narratives and everyday practices of the socially marginalized. Her current work focuses on untold immigrant stories about Chinese diaspora, racial injustice and the American dream.

Lou Iaquinto has taught at RMIT University in both the vocational and higher education divisions since 2007. His teaching has focused on leadership in human services, disability studies and community sector management. Prior to his time at RMIT University, his professional experience involved the management of direct services to clients in a broad range of human services in the government sector. Lou was also responsible for the management of the program for students with disabilities in Victorian state schools. His research interests include service user participation in the practice of community sector organisations. He recently submitted his PhD thesis for examination.

Karen Jackson is a Yorta Yorta woman and Director of the Moondani Balluk Indigenous Academic Unit at Victoria University. Karen is an advocate for culturally safe spaces that enable Aboriginal people to aspire to personal, family and community goals; land rights and the recognition of Sovereign Peoples; and the delivery of relevant educational programs by Aboriginal people for Aboriginal people. She has held membership in the Victorian Aboriginal Heritage Council, the Victorian Equal Opportunity and Human Rights Commission, the Indigenous Family Violence Regional Action Group, and is currently Chair of the Western Metropolitan Regional Aboriginal Justice Advisory Committee and the Indigenous Family Violence Regional Action Group.

Shose Kessi is senior lecturer in the Department of Psychology at the University of Cape Town (UCT). Her research centers on political psychology, community-based empowerment and social change, exploring issues of identity, such as race, class, and gender, and how these impact on people's participation in transformation efforts. A key focus is the development of Photovoice methodology as a participatory action research tool that can raise consciousness and mobilize community groups into social action.

Rebecca Lyons is a proud Wiradjuri woman who works at Victoria University Moondani Balluk Indigenous Academic Unit. She is currently undertaking an interdisciplinary PhD study exploring challenges to Aboriginal Identity formation with a focus on Australia's Stolen Generations Responses to Intergenerational Trauma.

Chris McConville has taught at several universities most recently at Victoria University. He has published widely on urban social and environmental issues. His most recent book is *Hanging Rock – A History* (2017).

Nicole Oke, PhD, is a senior lecturer in sociology at Victoria University, Melbourne. She works on issues about migration in Australia, particularly temporary migration as a form of precarious employment, as well as a project about precarious employment in transnational Australian companies. Recently she has published on migration and multiculturalism in Footscray, a multicultural and gentrifying suburb in Melbourne.

Amy Quayle holds a PhD in community psychology and her research interests are in the areas of race, racism and intergroup relations, and empowerment and social change through arts and cultural practice. Amy has co-authored numerous peer reviewed journal articles and book chapters in this area, and presented her research at conferences both nationally and internationally. In 2017, Amy was a recipient of an Australian Psychology Society Community Psychology conference award.

Alexandra Ramírez is a PhD candidate at Victoria University. Her thesis is a cross cultural migration study that focuses on the experiences of identity, belonging, and community for Nigerians, Colombians, and local residents in Melbourne and Trento (Italy). Originally from Colombia, her own experiences of dislocation informs her research questions. Alex graduated as a social worker at the University of Antioquia; and also pursued social studies at the University of Trento after she moved to Italy in 2003. She has collaborated on different projects and published some articles related to her collaborations.

Kopano Ratele is Professor at the Institute of Social & Health Sciences at the University of South Africa (UNISA) and a Researcher in the South African Medical Research Council-UNISA's Violence, Injury and Peace Research Unit. His research focuses on the areas of African psychology, violence, race, culture, sexuality, gender, and masculinity.

Christopher C. Sonn, PhD, is Associate Professor in Community Psychology at Victoria University, Melbourne, Australia on the land of the Wurundjeri of the Kulan nation. His research examines histories of colonialism and oppression and its continuities in various forms of structural violence and its effects on social identities, intergroup relations and belonging. He a was Mellon Distinguished Scholar (2010–2013) at the University of the Witwatersrand and a Senior Visiting Researcher at the Institute for Advanced Studies at the University of Bologna in 2012. Some books include *Psychology and Liberation* (2009 with M. Montero) and *Creating Inclusive Knowledges* (2018, with A. Baker).

Ramón Spaaij is a sociology professor in the Institute of Sport, Exercise and Active Living at Victoria University, Melbourne, Australia. He also holds a Special Chair of Sociology of Sport at the University of Amsterdam, the Netherlands. His research focuses on questions of social cohesion, conflict and social change. He has two established fields of research that address these questions: the sociology of sport and the sociology of terrorism. His recent books include *Sport and Social Exclusion in Global Society* (Routledge, 2014) and *The Age of Lone Wolf Terrorism* (Columbia University Press, 2017).

INDEX

D

Decolonisation
  emancipatory, 93
  of psychology, 92
Decolonised
  ways of thinking, 142
Decolonising
  approach to placemaking, 90
  methodologies, 90
  story-telling, 91
Diaspora
  formation, 113
  sense of belonging, 105
  sporting events, 110
Displacement
  as an outcome of colonialism, 90
  colonisation and, 88
  due to violence, 21
  gentrifications's effect, 123
  neoliberal urban management, 123
Doi Moi. *See also* socio-economic reform

E

Education. *See* cultural politics
Empowerment, 122
Empowerment, 31, 46, 83, 88, 93, 186
Ethnicity
  class and, 129
  intersectionality, 106, 124, 199
  othering based on, 119
  refugee background and, 56
Ethnographic
  auto-ethnography, 23
  cultural safety, 94
  observations, 95
  research method, 36

G

Gender
  binary, 183
  cisgender, 183
  heteropatriarchal, 176
  intersectionality, 106, 176

transgender, 183
Gentrification
  displacement, 124
  economic opportunism, 127
  Footscray, 125
  gentrifiers, 129
  housing affordability, 127
  politics of, 125
Global
  colonial violence, 140
  industrialisation, 139
  neoliberalism, 124
Global North. *See* Western

H

Healing
  as tenet of climate justice, 142
Human rights. *See* disability rights
    movement

I

Identity
  cultural identity of a place, 130
  Footscray's, 133
  hybrid, 113
  hyphenated, 166
  local, 133
  marginalising/intersecting categories
    of, 173
  national, 17, 105
  politics of, 166
  Somali, 111
  student's in higher education, 173
  Sudanese-Australian, 55
  white Australian, 53
Institutions. *See* cultural politics

K

Knowledge
  indigenous epistemologies, 90
  production, 90
  professional, 68
  traditional, 89